COMPUTERIZED
ACCOUNTING
with
BEDFORD

Peter H. Fuhrman

Gregory F. Buck

PRENTICE HALL, Englewood Cliffs, New Jersey 07632

Library of Congress Cataloging-in-Publication Data

FUHRMAN, PETER HARRY.
    Computerized accounting with Bedford / Peter H. Fuhrman, Gregory
  F. Buck.
      p.   cm.
    ISBN 0-13-168485-X
    1. Accounting—Data processing.   2. Accounting—Computer-assisted
  instruction.   3. Bedford accounting system (Computer program)
  I. Buck, Gregory F., 1951-   . II. Title.
  HF5679.F84 1989
  657'.028'5—dc20   89-37120
                                                            CIP

Bedford® is a registered trademark of Bedford Software Limited

Lotus® 1-2-3 is a registered trademark of Lotus Development Corporation

SuperCalc® is a registered trademark of Computer Associates International, Inc.

Production Editors: Dick Hemingway / Peter Buck / Maryrose O'Neill
Production Coordinator: Sandra Paige
Design and Text Formatting: Julian Luckham and Robert Wall — Desktop Publishers

©1989 Prentice-Hall, Inc.
A Division of Simon & Schuster
Englewood Cliffs, New Jersey 07632

Printed and bound in Canada by Webcom
10 9 8 7 6 5 4 3 2 1

ISBN 0-13-168485-X

Prentice Hall International (UK) Limited, *London*
Prentice Hall of Australia Pty. Limited, *Sydney*
Prentice Hall Canada Inc., *Toronto*
Prentice Hall Hispanoamericana, S.A., *Mexico City*
Prentice Hall of India Private Limited, *New Delhi*
Prentice Hall of Japan, Inc., *Tokyo*
Simon & Schuster Asia Pte. Ltd., *Singapore*
Editora Prentice Hall do Brasil Ltda., *Rio de Janeiro*

TABLE OF CONTENTS

INTRODUCTION

The Bedford Accounting System is easy to use. It is specifically written for smaller businesses, and for people who are not professional accountants or highly trained computer users. The Bedford program can therefore be used by almost any one in the business: the manager, the owner, a clerk or a person specifically hired for the job on a part time basis.

If you are new to Bedford this book provides a working knowledge of the program and basic accounting theory and procedures. After completing this tutorial you should be able to set up the books for the company and use the accounting program.

Use of the tutorial procedures in this book should be sufficient for you to understand how the Bedford Accounting System works. The exercises at the end of each chapter, beginning with Chapter 6, the General Ledger, are designed to give extensive experience in entering transactions into the program and proficiency in its use.

To help you become thoroughly familiar with the Bedford Accounting System a separate comprehensive practice set is also available; this allows you to set up a company and enter several months of transactions. To allow you to check your own work the practice set contains the printout of all journal entries as well as all reports and financial statements. A separate diskette is available containing the actual data files which can be used to gain some insight into how the transactions were entered or as a backup for your own data files should you have problems completing the business entries or if you make a mistake.

HOW TO USE THIS BOOK

This book is a step by step guide to operating the Bedford Accounting System. If you have some knowledge of accounting you should read Chapter 1, 3, and the latter part of Chapter 4, which provide specific information about the Bedford program. Chapters 5 to 11 take you through the various accounting modules of the program.

In Chapter 5 you set up the books for a service company, Fast Delivery Inc., a company that delivers parcels to various cities. In Chapter 6 we look closely at the Bedford SYSTEM module, where you enter the particulars about the company and tell the program about the hardware of your computer system. Also in Chapter 6 you will learn about the GENERAL ledger. This is followed by the accounts PAYABLE module in Chapter 7, the accounts RECEIVABLE module in Chapter 8, the PAYROLL module in Chapter 9, the INVENTORY module in Chapter 10, and finally, the JOBCOST module in Chapter 11.

A comprehensive set of exercises follows each of the chapters that discuss the various modules. If you choose to complete this series of exercises, you will set up a new company, Americana Decorating Sales & Service, Inc. At the end of Chapter 6, after learning about the Bedford SYSTEM module and GENERAL ledger, you will enter a comprehensive set of business transactions, which are based on an actual company. As you learn about each of the accounting modules of the Bedford Accounting System in the chapters following the GENERAL ledger, you can enter additional transactions designed to give you experience with a particular accounting module.

If you prefer, you can complete the tutorial part of the book first and then work through the practice exercises. In either case we are certain that by completing this series of exercises you will become proficient in using the Bedford Accounting System as well as in entering business transactions.

You should proceed to each of the above mentioned chapters in order. To help you understand the program each succeeding chapter builds on the previous one.

After completing the main chapters dealing with the Bedford Accounting System, chapters 5 to 11, you should read Chapter 12, which provides important information about closing the books at the end of various time periods. You will also learn how to setup a system of passwords for accessing the various accounting modules.

Finally, Chapter 13 provides information about add on programs available to enhance the preparation of reports and graphs of financial data from the Bedford program.

For those of you not familiar with computers, Chapter 4 provides some basic information about how to set up a computer system for use with Bedford. You should also become familiar with the operating manual that comes with your computer. Numerous books are available to help you understand computers and the various application programs available.

ACKNOWLEDGEMENTS

We are indebted to many individuals who have been actively involved in the preparation of this book. We would like to mention and thank the people at Prentice Hall in both Canada and the United States — Joe Heider, Executive Editor, Accounting and Taxation, Prentice Hall, Inc. New Jersey, for introducing us to this project and to Yolanda de Rooy, Senior Editor, College Division, Prentice Hall Canada, Inc. for taking on the preparation of the Canadian edition; and David Jolliffe, Peter Buck, and Dick Hemingway for their editing of the manuscript and help in expediting the production of the book.

We would also like to mention Julian Luckham and Robert Wall for their work in the layout and formatting of the book. Great appreciation also goes to Miles Mumford for his work in creating the extensive set of exercises. We would also like to thank the management of Bedford Software, especially Tom McKie, for providing us with information and resources in completing this project, and Bren Tedders at Bedford Software for her careful scrutiny of the manuscript and for pointing out problems and suggestions for changes. . Particular thanks goes to Mary Watson who has helped us to get much needed information, and who provided her time to help us in numerous other ways.

We appreciate the effort of those who have reviewed the manuscript and have worked through the various chapters and exercises. We would like to thank Jeannine Brooks, who reviewed the Canadian Edition; E. Miklis, Cuyahoga Community College, Warrensville, Ohio; Janet Cassagio, Nassau Community College, Garden City, N.Y.; and Letha Jeanpierre, CPA, DeAnza College, Cupertino, California, who reviewed the American Edition. The following people worked through the chapters and exercises step by step to ensure everything worked as it should — Beatrice Ruggles, Karen Reimer, Joginder Sidhu, Sharanjit Sunner, and Jeffrey Fuhrman.

Last, but not least, we must thank our families for their patience, understanding, encouragement and support while we were preparing the manuscript.

Peter H. Fuhrman   Gregory F. Buck

Chapter 1
COMPUTERIZED ACCOUNTING

Chapter 1
COMPUTERIZED ACCOUNTING

PREVIEW

This chapter explains what computerized accounting is, who should computerize, and the features of the Bedford Accounting System. You will get a brief overview of the general ledger and each accounting module that makes up this accounting system. In addition, some idea of the limitations as well as the ease of use of this system are discussed. Finally you will learn about the hardware required to run the Bedford Accounting System.

OBJECTIVES

After reading this chapter you should be able to explain:

1. The advantages of computerizing the accounting function;

2. The basic features of the Bedford Accounting System and the various modules that make up the total system;

3. The general program features and limitations, and the computer hardware required to run the Bedford Accounting System.

    Since business began, people have depended upon accounting to make sense of their transactions. However, as business became more complex, so did accounting. It became a profession. Before computers appeared, accounting was an arduous process requiring a large staff for entering business transactions and updating ledger books. Accountants had to pour over the company books, making sure that all business transactions were recorded so that regular financial statements could be released to the owners telling them about the profitability of their business and their financial standings.

    Computers were obviously suited to handle the many daily business transactions in an efficient manner. At first, because of the expense of the machinery (hardware) and the programs (software), only large companies could afford to computerize. However, with the development of microcomputers in the 1980s, small businesses are now able to computerize their accounting function. Many desktop computers are as powerful today as the mainframes of twenty years ago. There are also many inexpensive accounting packages available for small and medium sized businesses. Much of this accounting software is easy to learn and use. Today, virtually any business can afford to computerize their accounting function.

WHO SHOULD COMPUTERIZE?

Today, many business owners are asking: "Should I computerize my business?" The answer is actually simple. A common business rule says that a cost should not be incurred unless the benefits provided are greater than that cost. Although some of the benefits of computerizing an accounting system cannot be measured in dollar terms, many can. With the relatively low cost of microcomputers and computerized accounting packages today, a business can not afford *not* to computerize.

The cost of *not* computerizing depends to a large extent on the competition. If a competing firm is computerized, its managers will get more accurate accounting information faster than the managers in a firm that is not computerized. In a highly competitive environment, business success often depends on getting information about the business's operation as quickly as possible. To make accurate forecasts about sales and costs managers need information from the past year regarding sales, labor costs, raw material cost and the various expenses involved in the manufacturing of their product. A computerized accounting system can therefore help managers tremendously. As you are working through this book, you will better understand how a computerized accounting system can provide information much faster than a manual system. In particular, Chapter 3, which compares a manual accounting system to a computerized system, should indicate the benefits of computerizing.

THE BEDFORD ACCOUNTING SYSTEM

The Bedford accounting package is particularly suited to small businesses. Accountants and non-accountants alike will find the package easy to use and easy to understand. It is a full featured, integrated accounting package which includes general ledger, accounts receivable, accounts payable, inventory, payroll and job costing. Being integrated means that you have to enter particular business transaction data only once. For example, if you record a sale through accounts receivable, the inventory will be adjusted automatically to reflect the sale, and both accounts in the general ledger will be updated to reflect the sale as well. Even though the Bedford accounting package is integrated, you can also use each of the modules independently if you so desire.

General Ledger

As in any accounting system, the general ledger module is the focal point of the system. All financial reporting statements as well as the detail of the ledger accounts originate from this module. A balance sheet and/or an income statement can be printed as soon as the last entry has been recorded into the general ledger.

general ledger

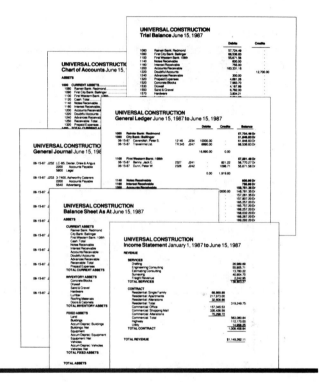

- user can define chart of accounts with flexible 4 digit design or choose from 6 starter companies
- entries can be applied to prior periods within the current fiscal year
- reports can be displayed, printed or exported including:
  - balance sheet (any date)
  - income statement (any period)
  - trial balance (any date)
  - chart of accounts
  - general journal (any period)
  - all ledgers (any period)
- automatically posts from receivables, payables, inventory and payroll making reports as current as the last entry
- journal entries may contain up to 100 ledger accounts
- a journal entry can distribute revenue or expenses to up to 100 projects, profit centers or departments
- produces full audit trails
- account balances up to $20,000,000
- zero balance accounts can be suppressed in some reports

Accounts Receivable

The accounts receivable module is designed to produce invoices for sales of merchandise or on billing of services. These invoices are then tracked by customer and date. An aged receivable listing of the amount owing by each customer can be produced. Monthly statements can be produced for each customer. This helps to improve cash flow.

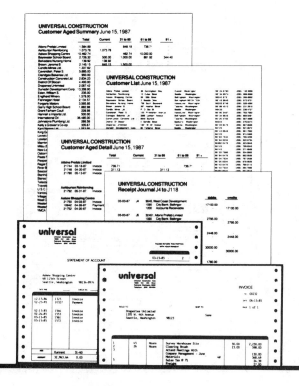

receivables

- uses open invoice method to keep track of full or partial payments against any customer invoice
- invoices that are fully paid may be purged or retained
- automatically updates project records, inventory records and ledger accounts
- user can define aging periods
- reports can be displayed, printed or exported including:
  - address - customer list
  - aged summary
  - aged detail
  - sale journal
  - receipt journal
- on-screen lists automatically provide customer names, inventory items and stock levels when required for program input
- prints customer invoices on computer form stock or supports manual invoicing
- prints customer statements with remittance stubs on computer form stock

Accounts Payable

The accounts payable module is similar to the accounts receivable module. Good control over accounts payable is important to ensure that all bills are paid on time to maintain a good credit rating and avoid service charges by suppliers. Another important reason is to take advantage of discounts offered by suppliers. The accounts payable module also provides a listing of amounts owing to help the user determine the cash needs of the business in the near future.

payables

- uses open invoice method to keep track of full or partial payments against any vendor invoice
- invoices that are fully paid may be purged, or retained
- automatically updates project records, inventory records and ledger accounts
- user can define aging periods
- reports can be displayed, printed or exported including:
  - address - vendor list
  - aged summary
  - aged detail
  - purchase journal
  - payment journal
- on-screen lists automatically provide vendor names and inventory items when required for program input
- prints checks on computer form stock or supports entry of manual checks

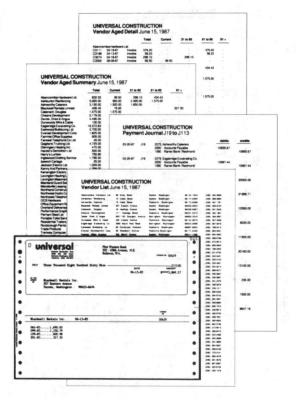

Payroll

The payroll function is probably one of the most time consuming accounting functions. Bedford significantly reduces the time required to process payroll. It will handle many different kinds of pay structures and calculate tax payable based on built-in tax tables. This feature eliminates the need for the user to input the relevant tax tables.

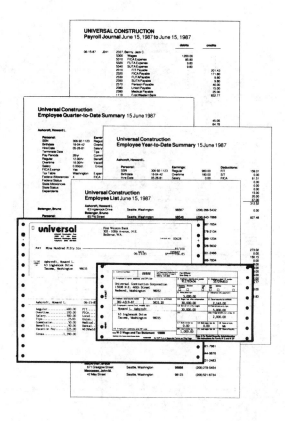

payroll

- supports either automatic or manual calculations
- automatically calculates federal taxes (FIT, FICA, and FUTA) as well as state taxes (SIT, SUTA) and State Disability Insurance
- uses built-in payroll formulas; no user-maintained tables
- automatically posts all payroll expenses to General Ledger and Jobcost
- five income fields - two are user definable
- includes a pay advance field
- user can set employer Federal and State unemployment rates, and State Disability insurance rates
- deducts for taxable benefits
- prints paychecks on computer form stock, or supports manual checks
- automatically retains QTD and YTD employee earnings, deductions and associated payroll expenses
- accumulates 940, 941, W-2 and state tax information
- reports can be displayed, printed or exported including:
  - employee summary
  - payroll journal
  - W-2 forms for each employee

Inventory

The inventory module is used to track inventory and maintain adequate levels, as well as transfer the cost of goods sold to expense accounts. The revenue generated by sales is entered through the accounts receivable module, which automatically transfers the appropriate amount to cost of sales and reduces inventory accordingly. Existing inventory is always available and as current as the last entry.

inventory

- suitable for manufacturers, retailers and wholesalers
- updates from receivables and payables
- up to 2,000 inventory items
- uses average weighted cost method
- handles adjustments and transfers
- automatically flags re-order points
- reports can be displayed, printed or exported including:
  - quantity report
  - synopsis report
- reports on either a margin or markup basis
- expresses selling and cost price to three decimals
- accepts user's own 7 digit alphanumeric code for numbering inventory items

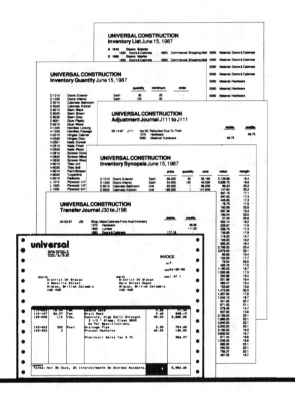

Job Costing

The jobcost module allows a company to track revenues and expenses by project or department. Many companies want to know specific costs associated with a particular job or department. For example, a contractor may be building three houses at one time. He would be interested in knowing the costs of building as well as the profit made from each house. The jobcost module will allow him to assign an invoice or payment to each job, or even part of an invoice or payment to a job. A report can then be produced comparing the income and expenses for that particular job.

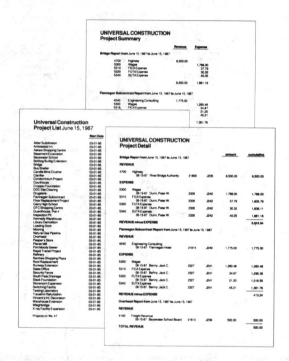

jobcost

- any revenue or expense transaction can be allocated to profit centers, divisions or projects
- paycheck expenses include the company's portion of FICA, FUTA, SUTA and State Disability Insurance expenses
- handles up to 1,000 active projects at any one time
- produces summary and detail reports on revenue and expenses for any project or department
- reports are also available for single or multiple projects for single or multiple revenue and expense accounts
- reports can be displayed, printed or exported

General Program Features

As mentioned, the Bedford Accounting System is a fully integrated package including all of the above modules. It is not necessary to use all of the modules. You can choose any combination of the modules that suit your business. When first computerizing your accounting system, it may be valuable to get advice about which of the modules to use for your particular business.

All reports in Bedford can be displayed on the monitor or printed out on the printer. This is a feature few other accounting packages provide; it is particularly useful for small businesses which want to take a quick look at particular information without always having to print everything out.

Most of the reports can also be exported to a spread sheet such as Lotus 1-2-3. By exporting the reports you can manipulate the data more easily to determine business ratios, do regression analysis or to compare the results from year to year. Data can also be exported in text format to be used in a document created with a word processor.

Finally, Bedford is not copy protected, which means that the program can be copied to a hard drive to improve speed of operation and efficiency of data entry.

SYSTEM REQUIREMENTS

The Bedford Accounting System requirements in terms of computer hardware are simple and so do not require a large outlay of money. You need an IBM PC or compatible using MSDOS operating system, version 2.0 or higher and a minimum of 256K of ram, although the more RAM available, the more data the program will support. Although a hard drive makes program operation more convenient and significantly faster, two floppy drives are sufficient. If you want a hard drive, the smallest one available is sufficient, but you will still need one floppy drive to load the program and to back up the accounting data.

You also need a monitor. Bedford supports both a monochrome monitor and a color monitor with CGA or EGA capability.

A printer is also necessary to print out the various reports and maintain a hardcopy audit trail. A narrow carriage printer is all that is necessary.

Program Capacity

The Bedford Accounting System program is fast and easy to use. Its capacity restrictions are as follows:

Number of ledger accounts	500
Number of vendors	999
Number of transactions	limited by RAM
Number of employees	999
Number of projects	999
Number of journal entries	limited by disk space
Number of customers	999
Inventory items	999

Every accounting program has particular advantages and disadvantages and limitations. Before acquiring such a program and computerizing the accounting function you must be sure to have a program that will work for you. The Bedford Accounting System has all the attributes of a larger and more expensive package, at a significantly lower price. If the above program parameters, restrictions, and limitations fit your business, then Bedford is for you. If your company's accounting tasks exceed the limits of the Bedford package then this package will not work for you, since there is no way to expand it. However, most small and some medium sized businesses will find Bedford more than adequate for their accounting needs.

Chapter 2
BASIC ACCOUNTING CONCEPTS AND TERMINOLOGY

Chapter 2
BASIC ACCOUNTING CONCEPTS AND TERMINOLOGY

PREVIEW

In Chapter 2 you will learn some basic accounting concepts and principles. Accounting refers to the recording of business transactions and the summarizing of the data to provide the business owner or manager with information about how the firm is doing financially. Financial information is presented in the form of a balance sheet which lists the assets, liabilities and the owner's equity in the business. Another major financial statement is the income statement, which provides a summary of the business transactions over a period of time — a month or a year — to show whether or not the business has been profitable.

Business transactions are summarized in accounts, which are generally named in a standard manner. A chart of accounts lists the accounts used by a particular company. Business transactions are recorded and distributed across various accounts in a standard manner. The concept of double entry accounting means that each transaction is recorded in two accounts, one is a debit and the other a credit.

Before financial statements are prepared, all data in the accounts is compiled into a trial balance. Because of the double entry concept, the total number of debits in these accounts must equal the total number of credits. If the trial balance does in fact balance, then we can prepare adjusting entries as necessary and then prepare the yearly financial statements.

OBJECTIVES

After reading this chapter you should be able to explain:

1. The function of accounting and the meaning of entity concept and books of account;

2. The function of the general ledger and subsidiary ledgers;

3. The composition of the chart of accounts and the meaning of the various categories of accounts — assets, liabilities, owner's or shareholder's equity, revenue and expense;

4. The accounting equation and how the owner's or shareholder's equity is influenced by revenue and expenses;

5. How accounts are numbered in the chart of accounts;

6. How transactions are recorded and what is meant by debits and credits and double entry accounting;

7. What a trial balance is and why a trial balance must be developed before financial statements are actually printed;

8. Why adjusting entries are required, and why the trial balance must be recreated after the adjusting entries are made before the final preparation of financial statements;

9. The makeup of a balance sheet and income statement and what each indicates about the financial condition of the business;

10. The accounting process in summary form.

The function of accounting is to record, measure and communicate quantitative information.

Recording

Individual business transactions must be recorded and entered into the accounting books. With a manual accounting system, transactions are written into a ledger or synoptic. The same data may have to be recorded again in subledgers. With a computerized accounting system, a program provides the input form on a computer monitor. Business transactions are entered in a systematic manner according to accepted accounting principles. With most accounting programs, transactions have to be recorded only once with the program automatically transferring transactions to appropriate subledgers and updating them as required.

Measuring

Measuring means monitoring the accumulated sum of transactions, by account, so that the information can be used to make business decisions. For example, you might want to monitor the sum of all cash transactions to determine the amount of cash on hand for additional purchases of inventory.

Communicating

Once business transactions have been accumulated, the various account totals are presented in a standard form known as *financial statements*. These statements indicate the overall financial position of an organization and help management make better decisions.

The financial information generated by the accounting function about a business organization may be required by shareholders for investment purposes, by creditors for lending requirements, or by governments for tax assessment. Other financial information is generated for management decision-making for future undertakings. Before the days of electronic computers, it was said that 80 percent of the time was spent gathering information and 20 percent of the time spent using this information to manage the businesses. Today managers spend 20 percent of the time gathering information and 80 percent of their time analyzing it to manage the business. As a consequence, managers generally make better decisions.

If financial information is that crucial for decision making, then it is of utmost importance that the information gathered is accurate. With a manual accounting system, errors in posting, addition, and transcribing (e.g., changing the number around when copying it from one place to another — $86.40 becomes $84.60) occur frequently, regardless of the safeguards attached to the manual system. Although the computer and the program cannot determine if the data entered is accurate or not, a computerized accounting system will prevent mistakes once the information is entered because all transaction transfers and mathematical calculations are performed by the computer. Most programs also incorporate a series of checking devices that catch some of the operator input errors that might otherwise occur.

ENTITY CONCEPT

The entity concept means that data is gathered and reported for each economic entity. An economic entity controls particular resources and employs them to achieve specific ends. This may be profit in the case of a business entity or achieving a breakeven point for a non-profit organization. For example, the corner grocery store uses fridges, shelves, counters and so on to sell groceries and produce revenue. Under the entity concept, the store is accounted for separately from the personal assets of the owners.

Another entity is a corporation. A large corporation may be broken down into smaller economic units called departments or divisions, each selling different products such as computers, typewriters and photocopiers. Each division or department is a separate economic entity and is accounted for within the larger corporation. This is also called divisional reporting; each unit being a division within the larger economic unit. Nevertheless, a shareholder of a large company wants to see the financial statements of the whole corporation, not just one of the divisions. Without knowing the financial standing of the entire corporation, it is impossible for a shareholder to decide whether to buy more shares, sell the ones she already has, or leave her portfolio as it is.

BOOKS OF ACCOUNT

A company's accounting records are summarized in the books of account which include the following:

a. general journal
b. general ledger
c. subsidiary ledgers (accounts receivable, accounts payable, inventory, and payroll)

General Journal

The general journal is a listing of all transactions made. These entries consist of the various transactions entered into by the economic entity.

General Ledger

A summary of the entries made in the journal is posted to the general ledger. The general ledger is the only permanent record and provides an ongoing summary of the business, from its inception for as long as the business exists. The general ledger provides the basic information from which financial statements are generated.

Subsidiary Ledgers

Subsidiary ledgers are similar to the general journal. They are used to record certain types of entries. For example, all the entries concerned with accounts receivable are recorded in the accounts receivable subsidiary ledger, which includes the sales invoices and payments of specific customers. (We will discuss subledgers in more detail later in this chapter.)

CHART OF ACCOUNTS

The general ledger consists of a series of accounts. The chart of accounts for a particular firm is a listing of these accounts along with a numbering system that indicates the relative position of each account. For example:

100	Cash
115	Accounts Receivable
200	Accounts Payable
250	Income Taxes Payable
"	
"	
"	
510	Telephone Expense
520	Rent Expense

The chart of accounts is used primarily to identify each and every account. Accounts are categorized as one of the following five groups:

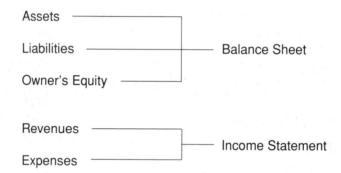

Assets

An asset is something that has value and is expected to benefit the future operation of the business. An asset may be tangible, such as a building, machinery or merchandise for resale. Other assets such as account receivable, a patent, or a franchise agreement are called intangible assets.

At present, accounting bodies follow the **cost principle** in recording assets. Business transactions are recorded in the books at their original cost to the business and no changes are made as long as the business owns the asset. Although the value of the asset may go up or down because of market demand or inflation, no adjustment is made in the books to reflect these changes.

The cost principle is used because this is the only objective method of valuing an asset. The price paid for the asset when it was originally purchased at arms length (meaning the purchase price of the asset was determined by market demand and supply and not by any special relationship that existed between the transacting parties) was the value placed on this asset because it was what someone else was willing to pay for it. Whether assets should be valued according to the cost principle, or based on market value, is a highly controversial topic among accountants today.

Liabilities

All assets belonging to a business are owned by someone, either the owners of the business or its creditors — those that sold the asset to the business or lent the money to buy it. When an asset is owned by a creditor it is said that the company has a *liability* or a *debt*.

These debts or liabilities may be either short-term or long-term liabilities. Short-term liabilities, commonly called current liabilities, are those which will be repaid within the current fiscal year. An example of a current liability is accounts payable. Rather than paying cash for every merchandise order, it is more convenient for a firm to purchase goods on account and pay for them all at once at some convenient time such as at the end of the month. This is also known as *trade credit*.

Long-term debts or long-term liabilities are debts that will take longer to repay than the current fiscal year. They are usually in the form of mortgages or notes payable. For example, a company may need a new building but does not have enough cash to buy it outright. By getting a mortgage from a bank or financial institution, the firm can spread the payment out over many years just as a private home buyer.

Equity

The value of the assets of the business that are not liabilities belong to the owners of the business. It is called *owner's equity* or in the case of a corporation, *shareholder's equity*. Owner's equity is created either by the owner investing money into the business or through the operation of the business when it earns a profit. It is decreased when the owner takes money out of the business or if the business looses money in its operation.

The Accounting Equation

The following equation represents the above discussion about the ownership of a business' assets.

Assets   = Liabilities + Owner's Equity

This is a basic accounting equation. You can always solve for one of the variables in the equation if you know the other two. If you know the following amounts, for example,

Assets	=	$ 1,000
Liabilities	=	$ 400
Owner's Equity	=	?

then the owner's equity is found by subtracting the liabilities from the assets, $1,000 - $400 = $600. In other words, the owner has a $600 equity in the company.

Consider a second example:

Assets	=	?
Liabilities	=	$ 750
Owner's Equity	=	$ 450

We can solve this equation by adding liabilities and owner's equity together, $750 + $450 = $1,200.

Profit

In our society, the primary objective of a business is to earn a profit. As mentioned above, a profit results in a change in owner's equity. For this reason, owner's equity is broken down further into a series of accounts that will tell the owner what contributed to an increase in owner's equity, *revenue*, and what contributed to a decrease in owner's equity, ***expenses***.

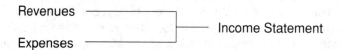

Revenue

Revenue represents the price for which a service is rendered to a customer or the price at which goods are sold to a customer. It is important to note that revenue does not mean collecting money. When revenue is earned, payment sometimes follows immediately in the form of cash or as a promise to pay at a later date, known as an account receivable.

Revenue is recorded at the point of revenue recognition. If the company is selling goods, that recognition comes when the good has been delivered to the customer. If the company is selling services, the revenue is recognized when the service has in fact been performed. Revenue represents an increase in owner's equity.

Expense

Expenses represent the cost to the company incurred in earning revenue. An expense may have been incurred long before the goods or service have been actually paid for by the customer. Expenses represent a decrease in owner's equity.

It is important in measuring the company's net worth that expenses incurred are matched with the appropriate revenues in the same accounting period. The ***matching principle*** allows us to properly match up all those assets that were consumed in the process of earning revenues. By using the matching principle we can accurately calculate net profit.

THE ACCOUNTING EQUATION — REVISITED

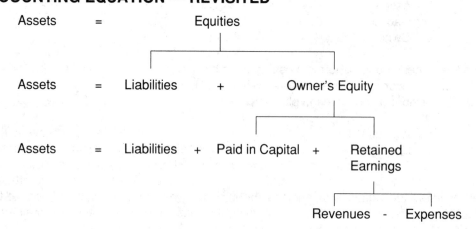

Sequence of Accounts

In creating the chart of accounts, the accounts are always sequenced in financial statement order — assets are first, followed by liabilities, owner's equity, revenues and finally expenses. The following is an example of a typical chart of accounts for a hypothetical firm.

Assets

100	Cash
110	Term Deposits
120	Accounts Receivable
130	Inventory
140	Office Supplies
150	Land
151	Buildings
155	Equipment
190	Other Assets

Liabilities

200	Notes Payable
210	Accounts Payable
220	Accrued Liabilities (amounts owing such as salary)
230	Long Term Debt

Owner's Equity

390	Capital Account — Partner A
391	Capital Account — Partner B

Revenue (most frequent sale item first)

401	Sales Income
402	Commission Income
490	Interest Income

Expenses (no standard order for listing exists)

510	Automotive
520	Advertising
530	Salaries
540	Rent
550	Telephone
560	Depreciation
570	All Other Expense Items

The actual number of accounts in the chart of accounts depends on several things. First, the accountant must determine the number of accounts needed to adequately differentiate the transactions. For example, one account for utilities in a business might be sufficient if utilities are not a significant part of the business. On the other hand, a bakery might want to break down utilities into three accounts, one for general utilities, one to record the cost of heating the ovens, and another one to record the cost of heating the sales area. Since each cost may represent a significant part of expenses, it will allow for better planning for the future.

Second, the number of accounts are often based on whether the accounting system will be done manually or by computer. If done by computer, the accounting program may limit the number of accounts that can be used. In the Bedford Accounting System, the number of accounts are limited to 500, a limit greater than most small businesses will encounter.

In addition to limits on the number of accounts available, a program may also insist on a particular numbering system that must be used. This is often done to make it easier for the computer to generate financial statements. The Bedford Accounting System uses this technique and assigns the following numbering system:

Asset Accounts	100 — 199
Liability Accounts	200 — 299
Equity Accounts	300 — 399
Revenue Accounts	400 — 499
Expense Accounts	500 — 599

A computerized accounting system also has accounts which do not have dollar amounts in them. These are used for headings, subheadings, subtotals and totals. We will discuss this further in Chapter 5 when we talk about *creating the chart of accounts*. You should read this section before you attempt to create the chart of accounts for a company using Bedford.

RECORDING TRANSACTIONS

As mentioned previously, a major aspect of accounting is recording business transactions in the books of account. Whether done manually or electronically, accurate recording of transactions is a most critical function because ultimately all financial decisions will be based on the information compiled by this data. Unfortunately this aspect of accounting also has the greatest potential for error because it is where human interaction with the computer occurs. To minimize human errors in this area an accounting system employs methods of checking input data for errors. This is known as the *audit trail* and uses the system of debits and credits.

Debits and Credits

Every business transaction is recorded in two or more accounts, each entry made up of debits and credits. Because of the accounting equation, the total of all debits must equal the total of all credits. The word *debit* has no particular meaning other than signifying entering a number on the left side of the ledger. Conversely, the word *credit* means that we are entering a number in the right side of the ledger.

The chart in Figure 2.1, also called the accounting window, indicates whether you have a debit or a credit.

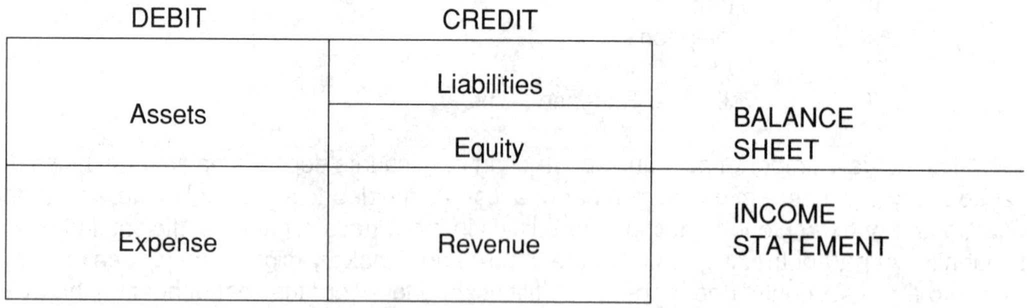

DEBIT	CREDIT	
Assets	Liabilities	BALANCE SHEET
	Equity	
Expense	Revenue	INCOME STATEMENT

Figure 2.1   Accounting window

Both assets and expenses are on the left hand side of the above accounting window. Any additions to these accounts are normally debits, while deductions are normally credits. Liabilities, capital and revenues are on the right hand side of the window and any additions to these accounts are normally credits, while deductions are normally debits.

For example, if you have $20 in cash, cash being an asset, and you wanted to add $10 to your cash balance, you would **debit cash by $10.** If a following transaction decreased cash by $5, we would add a negative amount to the account, or **credit cash by $5.**

To increase a liability account, we add a credit since a liability is normally on the credit side.

In summary, the accounts have the following properties:

To increase a(n):	Add a:
Asset	Debit
Liability	Credit
Shareholder's Equity	Credit
Revenue	Credit
Expense	Debit

To decrease a(n):	Add a:
Asset	Credit
Liability	Debit
Shareholder's Equity	Debit
Revenue	Debit
Expense	Credit

Double Entry Concept

When a business purchases an item for resale, sells an item, receives money, or pays out money, these transactions are recorded in the books with journal entries according to the **double entry system of bookkeeping.** A double entry bookkeeping system means that a business transaction is recorded in two different accounts, one being a debit and the other a credit. Thus for each transaction, the total debits and the total credits will be equal in terms of dollars.

For example, the following describes a company's purchase of some office items on January 5, along with some other transactions.

$ 300   to purchase supplies (an expense item)

700   to purchase stationery (an asset item)

1,000   to purchase a computer (an asset item)

paid $500 in cash (an asset item)

put the remainder on account (a liability item)

The accounting entries in the books would be as follows:

Dr. Supplies Expense	$300	(increase in expense)
Dr. Stationery Inventory	700	(increase in asset)
Dr. Computer	1,000	(increase in asset)
Cr. Cash	$500	(decrease in asset)
Cr. Accounts Payable	$1,500	(increase in liability)
$2,000	$2,000	

Notice that the total of all the debits equals the totals of all the credits. The listing of the transactions is called a *journal entry* and we say the entry balances because the total debits equals total credits.

Each entry of the transaction would be recorded in this way. As the entries are recorded, they are *posted* to an account in the ledger. The ledger is made up of *T-accounts,* which carry information on date, source, description and amount of the transaction. The T-account also allows the accounting person to calculate the total dollar amount of the transaction. (See Figure 2.2.)

In our example, we spent $500 in cash. The $500 must therefore be posted to the cash account as shown in Figure 2.2.

Date	Balance Forward Description	Dr.	Cr.	Dr. 1,256.73
Jan 5	Check 5 ABC Store		500.00	756.73

Figure 2.2   T-account for cash

After adding a number of other transactions, our cash ledger account card will look like the one shown in Figure 2.3.

Date	Description	Dr.	Cr.	Balance Forward Dr. 1,256.73
Jan 5	Check 5 ABC Store		500.00	756.73
Jan 5	Sale to Mr. Smith	300.00		1,056.73
Jan 5	Check 6 Telephone		20.00	1,036.73
Jan 6	Check 7 Salary		100.00	936.73
Jan 6	Loan from owner	500.00		1,436.73

Figure 2.3   Modified T-account for cash.

Each of the other accounts would contain similar information. Each time an entry is recorded, it must be posted to the account. This provides a summary of the increases and decreases for each account during the year.

TRIAL BALANCE

Before financial statements are made up from the ending balances, at a given point in time we have to prepare a *trial balance.* A trial balance is a listing of the chart of accounts along with the balances in each account. It does not contain any details about the transactions, but may include budget figures or figures from the previous year.

		Dr.	Cr.
100	Cash	$ 500	
110	Accounts Receivable	200	
200	Accounts Payable		$ 300
210	Income Taxes Payable		400
"			
"			
"			
500	Telephone Expense	250	
510	Rent Expense	350	

Once the listing has been prepared, showing debits (on the left) and credits (on the right), the two columns are added up. If all entries have been entered correctly, the two columns will balance, or the debits will equal the credits (See Figure 2.4).

ABC Company
Trial Balance
January 6, 19—

100	Cash	450.00	
110	Term Deposit	4,225.00	
120	Accounts Receivable	1,655.00	
130	Inventory	540.00	
140	Office Supplies	125.00	
150	Land	6,000.00	
151	Buildings	12,000.00	
155	Equipment	7,500.00	
190	Other Assets	125.00	
200	Notes Payable		1,295.00
210	Accounts Payable		3,455.00
220	Accrued Liabilities		567.00
230	Long Term Debt		18,546.00
390	Capital Account - Partner A		1,855.00
391	Capital Account - Partner B		1,975.00
401	Sales Income		30,655.00
402	Commission Income		1,250.00
490	Interest Income		500.00
510	Automotive	2,655.00	
520	Advertising	3,477.00	
530	Salaries	13,458.00	
540	Rent	6,100.00	
550	Telephone	356.00	
560	Depreciation	1,256.00	
570	All Other Expense Items	176.00	
		60,098.00	60,098.00

Figure 2.4 Trial balance showing debits equal to credits

Adjusting Entries

Once the trial balance has been prepared, the financial statements can be prepared. Before this can be done however, the *adjusting entries* must be recorded.

As mentioned earlier in this chapter, accountants follow the *matching principle* when recording expenses. At year end there may be many outstanding expenses for revenues received, or revenues may still be outstanding although an expense to generate that revenue has been incurred. To take care of these outstanding charges, you must adjust the trial balance to account for *accruals,* as they are called. The accountant can record:

a) changes in the entries made since the time they were recorded;

b) items not yet transacted but are expenses incurred while producing revenue.

Changes in Entries

We have seen that entries are recorded when they first occur. For example, if we had purchased insurance at the beginning of the year, we would have made the following entry:

Dr. Prepaid Insurance $ 600
     Cr. Cash $600

At the time of entry, the insurance represented an asset that would have value for the next twelve months. At the end of the year however, the prepaid insurance is no longer an asset because it has been used up. Instead it has changed into an expense and therefore we must prepare an adjusting journal entry to record this change as follows:

Dr. Insurance Expense $ 600
     Cr. Prepaid Insurance $600

Other common items that must be adjusted for in this manner include office supplies, bad debts and depreciation. In each case, although no cash is changing hands, an expense is being incurred.

Items Not Yet Transacted

The other type of adjusting entry is made to set up accruals. These are items for which no original transaction has yet taken place. For example, ABC Company borrowed $5,000 on December 1. Interest payments are to be made monthly on the first day of each month. The money was used to finance the company's operation.

At the end of December, no interest has been paid as the amount does not have to be paid until January 1. However, an expense has been incurred as the money has been used in the operation of the company for the month and therefore must be *matched* to the revenue produced. An adjusting entry would then be recorded as follows:

Dr. Interest Expense $ 50
     Cr. Interest Payable $50

When we actually pay the interest in January, we cannot record it again as an expense. The entry we will make then is:

Dr. Interest Payable $ 50
     Cr. Cash $50

Other common accruals include wages incurred but not yet paid, and interest income and deposits received before income is earned.

Adjusted Trial Balance

Once the adjusting entries have been recorded, another trial balance is created with the balances adjusted for accruals. Now the figures can be used to develop financial statements.

FINANCIAL STATEMENTS

Financial statements are used to communicate financial information to various groups of people, such as shareholders, lenders, management, government, and so on. Financial statements consist of two major types, the balance sheet and the income statement.

Balance Sheet

The balance sheet shows the financial position of a business as a whole at a specific date. This statement lists the assets, liabilities and owner's equity.

A balance sheet only reflects a firm's financial position for a particular point in time so its accuracy diminishes after that point has passed, as changes will occur beginning with the next accounting cycle. Nevertheless, it remains a useful tool for financial analysis. Figure 2.5 shows a balance sheet for ABC company.

ABC Company
Balance Sheet
December 31, 1989
(Unaudited)

	1989	1988
ASSETS		
CURRENT ASSETS		
Cash	$1,848	$1,500
Bank - General	4,851	8,423
Accounts Receivable	564	-
Inventories	9,114	7,485
Prepaid Expenses	8,117	4,686
Term Deposits	9,000	-
Investments	9,100	-
	42,594	22,094
FIXED ASSETS		
Land	150,000	150,000
Building	56,425	56,425
Furniture and Fixtures	40,441	55,701
Equipment	15,260	-
Parking Lot	2,615	2,615
	264,741	264,741
TOTAL ASSETS	$307,335	$286,835

LIABILITIES

CURRENT LIABILITIES

Accounts Payable	$3,883	$1,568
Bank Loan	9,631	6,560
	13,514	8,128

LONG TERM LIABILITIES

Mortgage Payable	125,000	130,000

TOTAL LIABILITIES	138,514	138,128

EQUITY

Capital - M. Risto	168,821	148,707

TOTAL LIABILITIES AND EQUITY	$307,335	$286,835

Figure 2.5   Balance Sheet for ABC Company

Statement of Income

The statement of income (Figure 2.6) is a statement of all revenue and expense items only, incurred over a given period of time (i.e., year, month, etc.). This statement defines the net income of the business over that time. It does not list the assets, liabilities or equity of the business.

ABC Company
Statement of Income
For the Year Ended December 31, 1989
(Unaudited)

	1988	1989
REVENUE		
Sales	$278,125	$225,900
Other	5,875	4,100
Total Revenue	284,000	230,000
COST OF SALES		
Purchases	175,000	142,600
Commission	49,400	42,400
	225,000	185,000
GROSS MARGIN	59,000	45,000

EXPENSES		
Advertising	$1,189	$286
Bank Charges and Interest	357	418
Building Repair and Maintenance	329	2,148
Convention Expense	653	-
Insurance	3,754	2,952
Office Equipment Rental	331	-
Office and Postage	3,775	3,070
Security and Pest Control	1,376	-
Professional Fees	825	1,149
Property Taxes	4,727	4,585
Utilities	7,206	6,667
Janitor and Cleaning	6,603	5,130
Wages and Benefits	6,692	2,670
Sundry	1,069	1,886
Total Expenses	38,886	30,961
NET INCOME	$20,114	$14,039

Figure 2.6 Statement of income

Statement of Changes in Financial Position

A third statement — ***the statement of changes in financial position*** — is also an integral part of any financial reporting. This statement represents the inflow and outflow of cash in the business over a given period of time. Since it is not directly applicable to the Bedford Accounting System we will not discuss its makeup here.

SUMMARY OF STEPS IN THE ACCOUNTING PROCESS

The following is a summary of the accounting process regardless of whether you are using a manual or computerized accounting system.

1. **Journalize transactions**

   Enter the transaction data, thus creating a chronological record of events.

   Dr. Cash $ 100.00
       Cr. Sales $100.00
           (to record the sale of a widget to Mr. Smith for cash)

2. **Print listing of transactions**

   Create a listing of the transactions in permanent form. This will be used for the audit trail.

3. **Post ledger accounts**

   This creates a permanent record which is classified by account, rather than by transaction entry.

4. **Prepare trial balance**

   This proves the equality of the debits and the credits in the ledger.

5. Prepare adjusting entries

Used to correct any errors found in the trial balance.

6. Prepare and distribute financial statements.

Chapter 3
MANUAL AND COMPUTERIZED ACCOUNTING

Chapter 3
MANUAL AND COMPUTERIZED ACCOUNTING

PREVIEW

In Chapter 3 we want to look at the accounting cycle and then examine how a business transaction would be recorded under a manual and a computerized accounting system.

OBJECTIVES

After reading this chapter you should be able to explain:

1. What a management information system is and what kind of information it provides;

2. The steps in the accounting process;

3. The advantages of using a computerized accounting system compared with a manual accounting system.

Effective management of a business depends on the information managers can gather about the firm's operation, and how the environment may affect the future of the operation of the firm. To provide this information requires a management information system.

MANAGEMENT INFORMATION SYSTEMS

An effective management information system must provide managers with necessary information to know where the firm is heading and correct problems if necessary. A **management information System, MIS** for short, requires the use of an organization's human and capital resources to collect and process data to produce information that is useful to all levels of management in planning and controlling the activities of the organization. The following characteristics are essential.

1. The information must be timely. It is little help to a manager to find out in July that sales were down in May if it is too late to correct the problem.

2. The information must be reliable. Although computers can accurately compile data into meaningful information rapidly, their output can only be as correct as the data that is fed into them. If that data is not accurate, it is of little value.

3. The information must be objective and allow managers to draw the proper conclusions from it. Figures can be presented in any number of ways, depending on their intended effect. Sheer numbers must not be allowed to hide a drop in quality — as in the old story of the plant manager who consistently exceeded his production quota of manhole covers because he made them thinner, and slightly smaller in size.

4. Information must be channelled to the manager who is responsible for the operation and has the authority to make the necessary changes.

5. The amount of information gathered must not be so great as to make it difficult for managers to decide what is important. Information should be gathered only from those points in the organization where deviations from standards would cause the greatest harm. A few strategically placed controls can provide all the information required for determining harmful conditions, without necessarily using a sophisticated data processing system.

6. Gathering and distributing information which is of little consequence is a waste of money. Even though computers can tabulate information quickly, someone must convert the raw data and feed it into the computer; the computer's printouts must be distributed to management before managers can even begin to interpret the data. If the control system costs the organization more to operate than it saves, it must be redesigned.

A MIS system may or may not include electronic data processing. Medium and large organizations have usually computerized certain aspects of their operation, particularly the accounting function, inventory management and purchasing. With the advent of relatively inexpensive micro computers, even small businesses can computerize parts of their information system, which usually starts with the accounting function. Accounting software, such as the Bedford Accounting System provides relatively sophisticated accounting and financial information for a low price. It is also easy to learn and use. Remember, however, that a computer and software alone cannot provide financial information. People are required to input the raw business transaction data.

THE ACCOUNTING PROCESS

The process of turning accounting data into useful information is called the data processing cycle (See Figure 3.1.). The cycle has five stages:

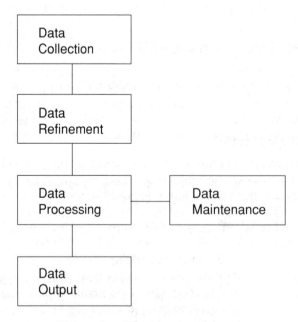

Figure 3.1 The accounting cycle

The primary elements of the accounting cycle and their relationship to the stages of the data processing cycle are illustrated in Figure 3.2. The accounting cycle starts when a business transaction occurs. Transactions are formal or informal agreements between two entities to exchange goods or services having some specific economic value. In most cases, the transaction results in an immediate exchange of assets. Sometimes the exchange may not happen until a future date, such as the signing of a contract for future services.

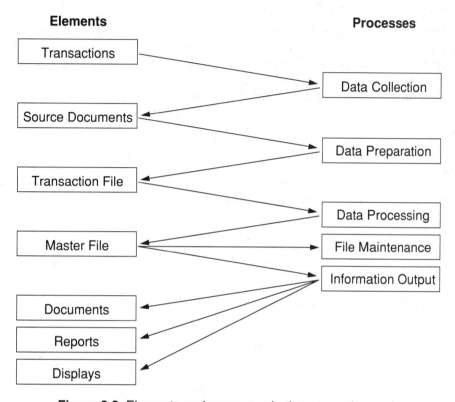

Figure 3.2 Elements and processes in the accounting cycle.

Let's examine how this cycle is accomplished in both a manual and a computerized setting.

Manual Accounting Systems

In a manual accounting system, all transactions are recorded and processed by people. This significantly reduces the speed at which information becomes available to management. For example, all business transactions are entered manually into a general ledger's accounts at the end of a reporting period, i.e., monthly, semi-annually or even annually.

Let's look at a company that accepts and delivers packages to see how a manual process works.

Transaction   The transaction begins when a customer brings a package to the express counter in Westcoast City to be delivered to an address in Eastcoast City. This starts the *data collection* process where the express company's employee gets information from the customer about shipment.

Source Document

The *preparation* **of the source document** begins when the employee takes a standard bill of lading form. This form is filled in with information about the sender, the receiver, how large the package is, what the charges are and who will pay for the freight charges.

Some of the information will be provided by the customer. Data on how much the shipment will cost to ship from one place to another is found in a table prepared by the company. The customer number, and information about the customer, may be found in a permanent *master* file if the customer has used the company before. The employee will likely have to look up some of this information from various books.

Entering this information on the bill of lading finishes the preparation of the *source document* which contains the relevant data about the shipment.

Transaction File

Once the source document has been prepared, it will be entered into a transaction file. In a manual system, this is a journal or synoptic. A journal is a large book with a number of columns. The journal entry is then *posted* into the ledger by debiting cash or accounts receivable and putting a credit into a column marked revenue-freight. The entering of each of these documents is merely a record and does not update the general ledger until a reporting period passes. Entries are *batched* for later posting.

Master File

With the data recording complete, the data is then *processed* for updating the *master* file. This will include adding up the total of the columns for a period, usually one month, and posting those totals into the master file, or the general ledger. The master file will then be updated by taking a calculator and adding the old balance in the account with the new posting to give the final balance. It is this updated balance that will be used to prepare a current trial balance.

The general ledger is not the only master file that must be updated for a sale. If the sale is made on credit, then the *customer* **master** file must also be updated. This involves finding the customer card in a file, and entering on it the amount of the sale and updating the balance owing. If the sale also involved an inventory item, the *inventory* master file for each part would have to be updated showing that one item had been taken from stock. And lastly, if profit centers are used, the item would have to be entered into the *jobcost* master file for the profit center. This updating is the *file maintenance* process.

**Documents
Reports
Display**

Once all the master files have been updated, the balances from the files can be used to create the various documents, reports and displays necessary to allow the user of the accounting system to make decisions. For example, a listing of customers and the amounts they owe from the customer master file may be used to ensure that the money owing is collected from customers on time.

Because of the amount of physical work involved, reports and displays provided by a manual system are not likely to show comparative data with previous years. It is possible to keep old copies of statements or reports and compare current data to them. This however is cumbersome and may not allow accurate comparisons since the way information is grouped or the method of reporting may have changed from year to year.

Another shortcoming of a manual accounting system, is that current financial information is only available when a worksheet is prepared which includes the adjusting entries necessary to bring unrecorded items up to date. Because of the large amount of manual work, this is usually only done once a month, or even once a year. With a computer system, reporting can be done at any time.

Computerized Accounting Systems

Let's look at the above business transaction when a computerized system is used. The transaction and data collection process will start out the same but the cycle will change quickly from there on.

Transaction

The transaction again begins when a customer brings a package to the express counter in Westcoast City to be delivered to an address in Eastcoast City. This starts the *data collection* stage where the express company's employee gets information from the customer about shipment.

Source Document

The *preparation of the source document* is accomplished by the employee entering data collected from the customer directly into a computer. This data includes the name of the sender, the name of the receiver, the size and weight of the package, and who will pay for it. The remainder of the data will be provided by table files and master files in the computer system. Instead of looking up freight rates from a book, the rates will be displayed automatically as the destination and size and weight are entered. Once this data has been entered into the computer, the source document is printed automatically, providing the shipper with the relevant data about the shipment.

Transaction File

As information is entered into the source document it is also automatically entered into a transaction file. No other recording of the item is necessary.

Master File

With the recording of source document information complete, the data is then processed to *update all master files.* This process is performed entirely by the computer either immediately or on a daily basis. If an *integrated accounting system* is used, usually all master files are updated automatically. However, there are computerized accounting systems that still use the *batch* system. These systems do not update the master files until all transaction for a specific period have been entered. The difference is that with the batch system, accounting information is only as current as when the last batch of data was processed. In either case, the computer handles the processing and updating with little or no intervention by the user.

Regardless of whether the updating of master files is done manually or electronically it is still known as the *file maintenance* process.

Documents   With a computerized system, reports and displays of the most current transactions can be created immediately. The master files are always updated, so financial statements are available containing the most current information.

THE BEDFORD ACCOUNTING SYSTEM

The Bedford Accounting System is an integrated accounting information system. Each of the modules — general ledger, accounts payable, accounts receivable, payroll, inventory — are integrated with each other so that when a transaction is entered, all modules will be updated immediately. This is also known as an **online system** (although it is only online to the extent that the data entered is current).

An integrated system does have some drawbacks. The most important of these is that when an entry is made, it is accepted and cannot be changed. If you made a mistake you must enter first a transaction to offset the previous one, and then reenter the original transaction. Although this may seem like a disadvantage, it really is not. It provides a certain amount of protection from fraud and theft because all entries are shown. From the auditors point of view, it is not desirable to be able to change entries once they are made.

The integration of the Bedford Accounting System is one of its major strengths. Once you become familiar with the package, you will find that the ease of data entry, the availability of instant reports and the value of up to date information will allow your business to run much more smoothly and profitably.

Chapter 4
PREPARING TO COMPUTERIZE

Chapter 4
PREPARING TO COMPUTERIZE

PREVIEW

In this chapter you will learn about some basic computer operations that are necessary to first install the Bedford accounting system onto your computer. Then you will make working copies of your master disks and learn why and how to make backup copies of your accounting data files in case they should ever be destroyed accidentally.

You will also learn about the best time for converting your manual accounting system to a computerized one.

OBJECTIVES

After reading this chapter you should be able to explain:

1. The basic operation of a computer — the hardware and software required;

2. How the disk operating system works and how a computer prepares a disk for storing information;

3. Why and how to backup program and data files;

4. How to use the format and copy programs of the disk operating system to create working copies of your master disks;

5. Why you should use subdirectories if you have a hard drive, and how to set them up;

6. When it is best to convert your manual accounting system to the Bedford computerized system.

Before you actually begin to computerize your manual accounting system, you must perform the following two steps:

1. First you must get the accounting program ready for use with your computer. This is called **installation**. It involves setting up the program and data files on the proper drives so that the program can find them later.

2. Second, you must actually change over from a manual accounting system to a computerized one. This is called **conversion**. The changeover may pose many problems and unless done properly can cause errors and lost time. After the initial changeover, the person operating the system must become thoroughly acquainted with it. This can also turn out to be a trying time. But eventually when all the bugs have been removed, you should have an information system that can get you accounting information much quicker, speed up business transaction entry, and make the whole process more enjoyable for the accounting person.

We will now cover these two steps at some length.

INSTALLATION

When you purchase your Bedford Accounting System, you get two manuals and a diskette that contains the accounting program. The Bedford Accounting System is available for the IBM personal computer and compatibles and for the Macintosh computer. We will discuss only the use of the accounting program on IBM or compatible computers. Obviously, except for hardware differences, the Bedford Accounting System will operate much the same on the Macintosh computer.

Not all people or businesses have the identical computer system even though it may be an IBM or compatible computer. A computer may be configured in a variety of ways; in other words, different computers will have different hardware attached to them. Some will have a color monitor while others will have a monochrome monitor. Similarly, many business computers today have a hard disk, while others have one or two floppy disk drives. If you have a hard disk, you can set up individual directories so that the data files of various companies can be kept separate. Different computer systems may also have different printers attached, about which the program must have information in order to provide the various printouts that are available. In other words, the Bedford Accounting System must know what hardware it is dealing with.

Some Computer Basics

You do not have to become a computer guru to use the Bedford Accounting System. However, you should have some basic knowledge about how a computer operates, and how the disk operating system works. You should know how to make a disk bootable, how to copy and rename files, and how to back up your data files onto diskettes for safekeeping in case of a computer crash. In what follows we discuss the disk operating system (DOS) and the various DOS program files. If you are familiar with computer operation and DOS, then you should skip to the section that discusses program configuration.

Turning on a computer is not difficult. You simply flip a switch. But getting the computer to boot up is more difficult unless the system has already been set up for you. Regardless of whether you have a hard disk or one or more floppy disk drives, you have to either make the hard disk bootable or create a bootable diskette that you insert in one of the disk drives before you turn the computer on.

Before you can actually interact with a computer through the keyboard or some other device, the computer must read into its electronic memory a series of programs. This series of programs is called the *disk operating system* or *DOS* for short.

▪ *Disk Operating System*

DOS does not come with your Bedford Accounting System. You must purchase it separately, usually when you purchase the computer. MS-DOS and PC-DOS are the most popular operating systems at this time. The latest version commonly in use now is Version 3.3. Version 4 has just been released and promises some major improvements over previous versions. A more extensive operating system called OS2 has also been released. Its primary function is to allow multitasking on the IBM AT and its compatibles and on the newer, faster 386 computers. It will take a few years before OS2 will be a useful operating system because there are very few application programs available today that can take advantage of this powerful operating system. No doubt in coming years it will be the dominant operating system.

In any case, the disk operating system controls the computer. When the computer is turned on, or *booted*, a short program tells the machine to check Drive A for a bootable **DOS** disk. If you have a hard drive that has been made bootable, after checking Drive A and not having found a disk, the computer goes to the hard drive, usually Drive C, where it looks for the appropriate system program. If Drive C has been made bootable, then you will hear a series of blurbs which simply means that the disk operating system programs are being read into the computer's memory from the hard disk. Once these programs are loaded, they instruct the computer to look for another disk operating system program called COMMAND.COM. This program is then also loaded into the computer's memory. It is this program that gives you the familiar prompt in the upper left corner of the screen to tell you the computer is ready to accept your commands.

COMMAND.COM contains a number of additional programs that allow you to perform a variety of functions. It is these disk operating system programs that allow you to interact with the hardware of the computer and give it commands to perform various functions. Most of the disk operating system programs, including a large portion of the COMMAND.COM program, stay in memory — remain resident — even after you load other programs such as the Bedford accounting program. But this is true only as long as the computer remains turned on.

▪ *Backing up the Program Disks*

The Bedford disk that you received with this book is the only disk you will receive with the program files on it. If it were destroyed while being used you would be severely inconvenienced. Therefore you should never use the original disk as your working disk. Instead, make a copy of it, work with the copy, and store the original in a safe place. If the working copy gets damaged, you can easily make another copy from the original disk.

Making a backup copy with two disk drives

To make a backup copy, you use a DOS program called DISKCOPY. This program allows you to make an exact duplicate of the original disk. You simply place the DOS diskette, with the diskcopy program on it, in Drive A and type

```
DISKCOPY A: B:
```

You will then see a message on the monitor screen asking you to insert the source disk, which is the Bedford program disk, in Drive A, and the destination disk, a new disk, in Drive B. Then you press the return key and the original disk will be copied onto the new disk. A word of caution is in order. Be sure that you have placed the correct disk into the destination drive. If you reverse the two disks, then you will copy the blank disk onto the disk containing the Bedford program and erase it.

Making a backup copy with one disk drive and a hard disk

If you have a hard disk and only one floppy diskette drive, then the procedure is slightly different. You can make a backup copy if you wish, but you can also simply copy the contents of your original Bedford disk into a directory on your hard drive.

To do that, first go to the root directory of your hard drive and issue the command,

```
make dir BEDFORD, or md BEDFORD
```

for short. This creates a subdirectory on your hard drive called Bedford. When you issue the command

```
cd\BEDFORD
```

you will then be in a subdirectory that at present contains no other files. To copy the Bedford files into it, simply place your Bedford disk in Drive A: and type copy A:*.* The asterisks tell the computer that all files on the disk in Drive A should be copied. When you have copied the contents of the Bedford diskette, you can put it away for safekeeping.

If you want to make a backup copy of your original disk but have only one drive, you can still use diskcopy, but you have to specify the following:

```
DISKCOPY A: A:
```

This command tells the computer that you want to use Drive A as both the source and the destination drive. The computer then asks you to insert the source disk in Drive A. A new message tells you that it is reading the source disk. After this procedure is completed, the message tells you to take out your source diskette and insert the blank diskette into Drive A. The blank diskette will then be formatted, after which the files from your Bedford disk are copied to the newly formatted diskette. We will discuss what *formatting* means in a moment. Depending on the amount of memory in your computer, you may be asked to remove your source disk a few times and replace it with your destination disk until the entire disk has been copied.

Making a Working Copy

Once you have made a backup copy of your program diskette, you should put the original program disk away in a safe place and continue working with the copy. If you have a hard disk on your computer, simply copy all of the program files from the Bedford disk to a subdirectory on your hard drive as already mentioned. Then create another subdirectory to contain the data files for your particular company. If you have only two floppy disk drives, then one diskette with the program files on it has to be in Drive A, while another disk with the data files has to be in Drive B.

If you are using floppy disk drives, the wear and tear caused when the drive head reads data off the diskette could eventually damage your program diskette. Therefore, in addition to the backup disk that you have already created, you may want to create one or more working diskettes for daily use. Should a working diskette become damaged, you can always replace it with a new one.

To make a working copy you have to take a blank diskette, format it, make it bootable, and then copy the Bedford program files from the original diskette onto the formatted blank diskette. While this may sound like a formidable task, it is really quite simple. Let's go through the process.

▪ The Format Program

One of the first programs from the disk operating system that you will use is the Format program to make a blank diskette ready for use on the computer.

Since there is a variety of disk drives, you must ensure that you have the correct diskette for your particular drives. The two common disk drives are 5.25 inches or 3.5 inches. The 5.25 inch floppy diskette is flexible and can store approximately 360K or 368,640 characters (360 times 1,024 bytes per K) on it. If you have an IBM AT or compatible computer you will also generally have a high-density disk drive that can store 1.2 megabytes of data (approximately 1,200,000 bytes). A 3.5 inch disk drive uses different types of disks. They are not flexible and are encased in a hard shell which makes them safer to carry around. A regular diskette in this size can hold 720K (720,000 bytes). The high density version can store 1.44 megabytes (1,440,000 bytes).

Regardless of what type of drive you have, to make a new disk usable you have to format or initialize it. The format procedure partitions the diskette electronically so that it can be used to store program or data files and retrieve them again when needed. If you accidentally format a disk that contains data or program files on it, these files are lost.

To format or initialize a diskette, you use a DOS program called FORMAT.COM or FORMAT.EXE. Even if you have a hard drive in your computer you will have to format diskettes on a fairly regular basis. The formatting procedure that follows is therefore described for those who have a hard drive as well as for those who have a two drive system.

Two floppy diskettes	**Hard disk**
	(Assuming hard Drive is C)
Place your operating system diskette in Drive A and close the drive door	
Turn on the computer	Turn on the computer
The computer will make a start up sound and display the following message:	
`Enter date:`	`Enter date:`
Enter the current date as required. The system will respond as follows:	
`Enter time:`	`Enter time:`
Enter the current time as requested.	
You will then see the system prompt:	
`A>`	`C>`

The letter of the prompt will tell you which drive you are *logged* onto. The current logged drive, also called the *default* drive, is where DOS will look for the program that you want to execute. To execute a program, simply type its name. Only files with the extension .EXE, .COM, or .BAT will actually execute. The Bedford program is called BEDFORD.EXE. To execute it, you simply type BEDFORD at the system prompt in either capital or lower case letters.

The drives have been given standard letters to identify them. If you have one or two floppy diskette drives, one will be Drive A and the other will be Drive B. A hard disk usually has the letter C, although you may have more than one hard disk in the computer, in which case the other drives would be identified by the letters D, E, and so on. A single hard disk can also be partitioned to act as one or more individual hard disks. In that case, each partition would be identified by a letter. For further information you should consult your computer manual.

For operating the Bedford program, not only do we want to know which drive we are logged onto, but we also want to know which subdirectory we are logged onto. (See below for a discussion on subdirectories.) We can tell DOS to give us this information as follows:

At A> type   At C> type

PROMPT PG [Ret]	**PROMPT PG** [Ret]

The computer will respond as follows:

A:\>   **C:\>**

This means we are logged onto the drive designated by A: or C:, and that the directory that the directory we are presently logged onto is the ***root directory*** as indicated by the \ with no subdirectory name following the slash. If we were in a subdirectory, the indicator would read

A:\BEDFORD\DATA

indicating that we are logged onto a subdirectory called DATA, which is a subdirectory of a subdirectory called BEDFORD, which is a subdirectory of the root.

To format the blank diskette, place the diskette as follows:

Two floppy diskettes   **Hard disk**
Drive B   Drive A

With the system disk still in   Logged on to the subdirectory
Drive A, type   containing the DOS program files, type

FORMAT B:	**FORMAT A:**

The drive will start spinning and then a message will be displayed on your screen as follows:

Place diskette to be formatted in   **Place diskette to be formatted in**

Drive B: **Drive A:**

Place the diskette in the drive indicated and press [ENTER]. The drive will begin to spin and you will hear the formatting process as a series of soft clicks.

You can think of formatting as being similar to putting addresses on a new housing division in a suburb. Without addresses on the houses it would be difficult, if not impossible, to deliver mail. Formatting a diskette puts electronic addresses on the disk so that the computer, when told to place the contents of a file on the diskette, will be able to find that file later when needed.

After you have formatted one disk, continue the process to format another. This second diskette will be made bootable, so the process is slightly different. A bootable disk is one that will contain the program COMMAND.COM plus some hidden files that will allow us to boot the computer without having to use the system disk.

Place a blank disk in Drive

B: A:
At A:\>, type   At C:\>, type

```
FORMAT B:/S                          FORMAT A:/S
```

the **/S** tells the format program to place the system program files on the diskette after the formatting process has been completed. The diskette will operate as before and show the track that is
being formatted. At the end of the format procedure, there will be a pause. Then the screen will
indicate that the diskette has been formatted and the system has been transferred successfully.
     If you check the space on the diskette, you will notice that there is less room on the
bootable diskette than on the diskette that you only formatted. This is due to the DOS system files
that are required on a bootable disk. Because these files take up space, we do not want all disks
to be bootable, only those that contain program files. Program files are those files which allow us
to carry out a certain task, such as accounting. Data files, on the other hand, are files that contain
only data to be used by the program files. Data files cannot be used without a program and,
therefore, do not need to be on a bootable disk.

▪ The Copy Program

The Copy program will allow you to copy one or more files from one disk to another. It is different
from the diskcopy program that we used earlier, which makes an identical copy of the entire disk.
The disk from which we are copying files is called the **source** disk and the disk to which the files
are copied is called the **destination** disk. To use the Copy program we must indicate which files
we want to copy from the source disk to the destination disk. The * (asterisk) is used as a wild
card, meaning that it can represent any name or letter in a file name.
     For example, if we type

```
COPY A:*.DAT B:
```

then files with any name (*) and extension "dat" (.dat) on the source drive (A:) will be copied to
the destination drive (B:) and added to those already existing on Drive B.

We will want to copy all the files on the program disk included with this book to a second disk to use for everyday computing (working disk). At the system prompt:

Two floppy diskettes
Place the program disk in Drive A: and the formatted disk with the operating system in Drive B.

At A:\>, type

Hard disk
Place the program disk in Drive A.

At C:\>, type

```
COPY A:*.* B:                      COPY A:*.* C:
```

(You may want to put the program files in a subdirectory; see subdirectories in this chapter)

Notice that you typed *.*. This means that any file name with any extension will be copied. In this way, we can copy all files without having to know the names of any of them.

The computer will begin the copy process, and drive lights will come on. Do not open the drive door when the light is on. If you do, you may damage the diskette or the files.

Once all the files have been copied, you may put the original disk(s) in a safe place so that they are not destroyed accidentally but remain available if needed. You will not be using them in normal day to day operation.

Subdirectories

The Bedford Accounting System allows you to work with more than one company's accounting records. Furthermore, each set of accounting records can be kept in its own disk partition known as a *subdirectory*.

The diskette that we formatted but did not put the system files on will be used to contain our data files. After formatting, the disk contains only one directory, called the *root directory*. However, we can partition the root directory into subdirectories and each subdirectory can in turn contain sub-subdirectories. Into each of these sub-subdirectories, we can copy the accounting data files of a particular company.

To better understand the concept of subdirectories, we can use a desk drawer as an analogy. You could put all your papers into the drawer regardless of what they pertain to, but you would wind up with a hodgepodge in which it would be difficult to find any particular paper or set of papers. It would make more sense, and give you easier access to specific papers, if you purchased some hanging file folders with each file folder reserved for a particular subject. There might be one for accounts payable, another for information on finance, and yet another for personnel. Within each file folder you could have other folders containing a subset of the main category of files. In the accounts payable file there may be a subfile for bills yet to be paid, another subfile for bills not yet due, and a third subfile for bills in dispute.

The set up would look like this:

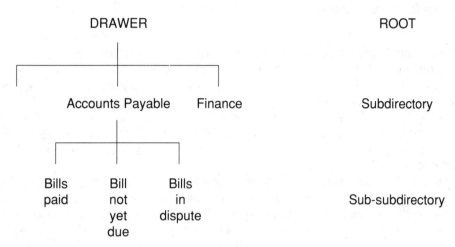

DRAWER   ROOT

Accounts Payable   Finance   Subdirectory

Bills   Bill   Bills
paid   not   in   Sub-subdirectory
            yet   dispute
            due

When you make a subdirectory for your accounting data files, you must give the subdirectory a name so that you can identify the files contained therein. Let's pick the name FASTDEL, short for Fast Delivery, Inc. Note that the name must be eight characters or less and cannot include any blank spaces or punctuation.

To create the subdirectory, make sure you are at the root directory:

Two floppy disks   **Hard disk**
A:\>   C:\>
Place your formatted data disk   Type
in Drive B: and type

```
MD B:\FASTDEL                    MD C:\FASTDEL
```

The command MD is short for "make directory" followed by the drive indicator and the name of the directory to be created. (Remember, you can type these commands in either upper or lower case.) The diskette drive will start to spin shown by the drive light that comes on as the directory is being created. When completed, the system prompt will reappear on the screen. If no error message shows on the screen, then the subdirectory has been successfully created. However, the root directory is still the default drive.

Now let's see if it is really there. To do so, we want to log onto that subdirectory (make the subdirectory the default drive). Ensure that your disk is in Drive B: if you are using diskette drives (hard drive users need not worry about the floppy drive) and type the following:

Two Floppy Diskette Drives   **Hard disk**
B:\   C:\

CD\FASTDEL   CD\FASTDEL

The command CD is short for CHANGE DIRECTORY. After pressing the ENTER key, you will see the following on the screen:

`B:\FASTDEL>`   `C:\FASTDEL>`

with the cursor blinking after it. You are now logged onto the default Drive B: or C: and logged into the subdirectory called FASTDEL, where you will put the data files. When you want to run a program or save a file, the computer will automatically look in this subdirectory for the program or save the data files in this subdirectory unless you command it to do otherwise.

By using subdirectories, you can partition the diskette into many divisions. Each time you make a subdirectory, however, you are limiting the space available to save data. Bedford is particularly sensitive to space limitations, so you do not want to cause too many restrictions. Use different diskettes for different companies or divisions.

For those with hard disks it is a different story. Because a hard disk can hold so much data, many subdirectories can be created on it. You must make sure that you give some thought to naming the subdirectories properly. Once you get more than five or six subdirectories, you will find it impossible to remember the contents unless each name means something to you.

▪ *The Path*

If you have a hard disk, you must look at another DOS command. As mentioned above, the computer will look in the default drive and default directory to find the program you wish to run. You now have the Bedford accounting programs in the root directory but you are logged onto the subdirectory called FASTDEL. Try to run the program from this subdirectory by typing

```
BEDFORD
```

You should get the following response:

`BAD COMMAND OR FILE NAME`

This simply means that the computer could not find the program you wanted to run. The reason is that the computer was looking in the directory containing the data files instead of in the directory containing the program files. BEDFORD is in the root directory. To allow the computer to find the program, you tell the computer where the *path* is that leads to the right directory. You would type:

```
PATH C:\
```

meaning that the computer should look in the root directory (C:\) to find the program. After you enter the information about the path, type

```
BEDFORD  [Ret]
```

You should now hear the program start up and see the following screen:

```
GENERAL     PAYABLE     RECEIVABLE     PAYROLL     INVENTORY     JOBCOST     SYSTEM


    Company:      ...............d:\[path]

              V3.24bR (C) Copyright 1986-1989 Bedford Software
                        All rights reserved.
```

So that you don't always have to type in the path command each time you start up the accounting program you can place the command in the AUTOEXEC.BAT file.
(See AUTOEXEC.BAT later in this chapter.)

We do not want to do anything with the Bedford program at this point so let's get out of it. We can escape by pressing a special key marked ESC. In many programs, including Bedford, this key takes the user back from one menu to a previous menu. As we are only one screen deep into the program, pressing ESCape should take us back to the system prompt.

```
Press the  Esc  key
```

You should now be out of the program.

■ *Showing the Subdirectory*

Now let's look at the files on the disks. Make sure that the BEDFORD disk is in Drive A or that you are logged onto the root directory of the hard disk containing the program files. Type

```
CD\  Ret
```

To get a listing of the files on the disk, type:

```
DIR  Ret
```

This will give you a listing of the files in the directory that you are logged onto, or of the files on the diskette in Drive A. You should now see the following:

BEDFORD.EXE

This is the only file on the disk. The first name indicates the actual accounting program. The four characters that follow, .EXE, mean that the program is executable, or that it will run when it is typed on the command line next to the drive prompt. We cannot take a directory of the data disk or data subdirectory because nothing is there. We will look at the directory later, when it contains data files.

Backing up Your Data Files

The accounting data you will generate is very important to your business. If you lose your accounting files, you may have a difficult time recreating them. Therefore you must take steps to secure them.

The best way to protect computer generated data is to make backup copies. If your data files are kept on a floppy diskette you can simply use the DISKCOPY program discussed earlier to make one or more duplicates and store them in a safe place.

Use one of the two following procedures depending on whether you have two floppy diskette drives or a hard disk.

Two floppy diskettes	Hard disk (Assuming hard Drive is C)
Place your data disk in Drive A	Disk already C
Place your backup disk in Drive B	Place backup disk in Drive A
Type	

```
COPY A:*.* B:                    COPY C:\FASTDEL\*.* A:
```

This will copy the data files from your original data diskette to a backup diskette in Drive B. / This will copy the data files from the hard disk to a backup diskette in Drive A.

The diskette must be formatted in either case.

The timing of a backup is as important as the backup itself. A backup should be done at least weekly; daily if you process a lot of transactions. A good system to use is the grandfather-father-son method. Back up the files on one disk at the end of the first week; this disk is the grandfather. At the end of the second week back up the files on a second disk; this is called the father disk. At the end of the third week, back up the data on a third disk; this is called the son disk. You now have three copies, each one a week later than the other. In the fourth week, you would use the disk used in the first week — the grandfather disk — for backup. The grandfather disk now becomes the son.

This method is safe because even if one disk is destroyed, you still have two others from which you can recover data.

Besides backing up your data on a regular basis it is a good idea to keep a backup of your data for each year on a set of disks that you file away. At some point, you may want to recall the data of a previous year. If you have a backup, you can load it into the computer and use the files to produce printouts of the financial information for that particular year.

This backup procedure is simple to use. There are many backup utility programs on the market today that make backing up data and program files much more convenient. There are also hardware backup solutions that are fast and almost automatic. For larger businesses with large amounts of data, efficient backup systems are important.

Whatever process you use, it is crucial that you back up your data regularly.

CONVERTING YOUR MANUAL SYSTEM

Now that you have the Bedford accounting program installed on the hard disk or on a working floppy diskette, you are ready to start the conversion process. Conversion means taking the present set of accounting records from the manual system and entering them into the Bedford accounting program.

Each of the modules in the accounting program must be converted separately but the process is similar for each module. We will go through the conversion process for each module as we discuss it in the chapters that follow.

Bedford provides a fail safe method for conversion. Since you do not want to start working with any module until the conversion process is complete, Bedford has established a NOT READY and a READY mode of operation. When you call up the Bedford Accounting System for the first time for any company, it is in NOT READY mode. The conversion procedures must be made while in this mode. Anything you enter will not affect any of the working files. For example, you may have been operating with the Bedford general ledger program for some time and then decide to convert the accounts payable from a manual system to Bedford. You can do so without worrying about the existing general ledger files. If you make a mistake in the conversion process of the accounts payable module it will not affect the current general ledger data if the accounts payable module is NOT READY.

The Bedford Accounting System will stay in the NOT READY mode until you are sure that the conversion is complete and correct. Once this is done, you manually switch the program to the READY mode and begin to make actual entries to the accounting records. When you have changed to the READY mode, you cannot return to the NOT READY mode.

Time of Conversion

The timing of a conversion requires some planning as well. The most convenient time to convert is at the year end. This is the time when all balances in the accounts are correct and reconcilable. In this way, you ensure that the information that you are starting with is accurate information.

While year end is the most convenient time, it is not the only time. If you purchase your computer in the middle of the year, it makes sense to computerize your accounting system immediately. However the conversion process will require more planning for a smooth transition.

Bedford Accounting Forms

The Bedford Accounting System makes use of standard forms for payroll checks, accounts receivable statements and invoices.

These forms have been created specifically for use with the Bedford Accounting System and can usually be obtained from a leading stationery store. Although it is not mandatory to use these forms it will simplify your procedures and ensure that your business correspondence looks as professional as possible.

Chapter 5
SETTING UP THE BEDFORD ACCOUNTING SYSTEM

Chapter 5
SETTING UP THE BEDFORD ACCOUNTING SYSTEM

PREVIEW

In Chapter 5 you will begin to work with the Bedford Accounting System. First, you will learn about the function of some of the keys on your keyboard, particularly the three function keys used in the Bedford Accounting System. Then you will begin to set up the accounting files for the company that we will use in this tutorial. In the latter part of the chapter you will learn how to customize the Bedford Accounting System for your particular computer hardware.

OBJECTIVES

After reading this chapter you should be able to explain:

1. The purpose of the various keys on your keyboard, particularly the three function keys used by the Bedford Accounting System;

2. How to set up the computer files for a particular company for use with the Bedford Accounting System;

3. How to access the various accounting modules from the Bedford main menu;

4. The major function of the SYSTEM module;

5. How to enter information about a company into the Bedford Accounting System;

6. How to customize the Bedford Accounting System for your particular hardware including monitor and printer.

Before you can use the Bedford Accounting System you have to set up certain files which will contain the accounting data that you enter into the computer. But before doing that you should understand the function of the various keys on your keyboard, particularly those that have been designated in the program to perform particular functions. Let's look at these keys first.

SPECIAL KEYS USED BY BEDFORD ACCOUNTING SYSTEM

To make the Bedford Accounting System easy to use, various keys on the keyboard perform special functions. The keyboard shown indicates the special keys used. As we discuss each of them you should locate them on your own keyboard.

The Arrow Keys

The arrow keys are located on the right hand side of the keyboard. On most keyboards they are superimposed on the numeric keys, 8, 6, 2, and 4. If this is the case, you should know how to change from using the arrow keys to using the number keys. In most instances you simply depress the key called NUM LOCK, also located in the same area of the keyboard. If you don't have a NUM LOCK key check your computer manual.

When the Bedford main menubar is showing, then the right and left arrow keys move the large cursor highlight left or right. To activate (execute) a major module you press the down arrow key which opens a submenu on the left side of the screen.

Once the main modules have been activated then the up and down arrow keys are used to select items from the various submenus of the Bedford Accounting System by moving a little cursor highlight next to the menu item. When you press the right arrow key you will activate (execute) the appropriate menu item, or if you are in a data insert screen, the right arrow clears fields for data entry. When you press the left arrow key the program accepts the data entered or any changes made and also posts transactions.

The ESCape Key

The ESCape key is usually located in the upper left hand corner of the keyboard. In the Bedford Accounting System the ESCape key allows you to back out of any menu as well as cancel any data entered.

The ENTER or RETURN Key

The ENTER key, called the RETURN key by the Bedford Accounting System, is found on the right hand side of the alphabetical key board as well as on the bottom right side of the numeric key pad on those keyboards with a separate numeric key section. When you press the RETURN or ENTER key you are telling the Bedford program to accept the data keyed into the various fields. For example, if you are entering $1,234.00 as the amount of a journal entry, you would type 1234 [ENTER]. You do not have to type .00 as there are no cents involved in this entry.

The SHIFT Key

The SHIFT key is found on either side of the alphabetical keyboard, and is used to type capital letters. The Bedford accounting program will automatically capitalize the first letter of an alphabetical entry. Therefore you do not need to hold down the SHIFT key when typing a name. However, to make the first letter a lower case letter, or to capitalize a second letter you must hold down the SHIFT key when you type that letter.

The BACKSPACE Key

The BACKSPACE key is found on the top right hand side of the alphabetical keyboard. This key is used to erase the character directly to the left of the cursor.

The INSERT and DELETE Keys

These two keys are used to insert and delete data. When you press the INSERT key you add a row in a computer generated invoice for entering items purchased. Similarly, when you press the DELETE key you delete a row in a computer generated invoice. Depending on the keyboard, these keys may be found in more than one place.

The NUM LOCK Key

The NUM LOCK key is found on the top row of the numeric keypad. The numeric keypad is designed to let you enter numbers more easily as well as access keys that perform specific functions. When you press the NUM LOCK key you change the functioning of the numeric keypad from entering numbers to performing other functions. Usually a little green light indicates if the number entry function is on or off.

The Function Keys

The function keys are found either across the top of the keyboard or at the left edge of the keyboard and are shown as F1...F10 or F12 depending on the keyboard. The Bedford accounting program only uses the first three function keys, F1, F2 and F3.

These three function keys allow you to access particular information in the program.

The F1 key displays general help information
The F2 key displays a journal entry
The F3 key displays a document

The program displays one or more of these three function keys in the upper right-hand corner of the screen when they are available for use. Unless visible, the function key will not work.

After pressing one of the three function keys to access information you can return to where you left your previous task by pressing the key again.

HOW THE COMMANDS YOU SHOULD CARRY OUT ARE INDICATED IN THIS BOOK

In this tutorial you will be guided through the procedures for each module in the Bedford Accounting System. The following graphic symbols will be used to indicate what you should do.

The arrow keys on the numeric keypad on the left side of the keyboard perform particular functions in the Bedford program. To indicate which key you should press you will see the following symbols:

⬆	to move cursor highlight up to access a menu item or an item in a data entry screen, or to scroll through more than one screenful of data on your monitor.
⬇	to move cursor highlight down to activate a Bedford accounting module, to move cursor down to access a menu item or an item in a data entry screen, or to scroll through more than one screenful of data on your monitor.
➡	to activate (execute) a menu item or clear a field in a data entry screen. When the Bedford main menubar is dis-

```
                          played the right or left arrow key
                          allows you to move the cursor highlight
                          to a particular accounting module so it
                          can be activated.

        ⬅              to have the program accept entered data
                          or changes to it as well as back out of
                          particular entry screens or submenus.

        [Esc]             to cancel commands and back out of all
                          Bedford menus and data entry screens.
                          This key discards data entered and does
                          not save it.

        [Ret]  or
        [ENTER]           to tell the program that data entry is
                          completed. This key is shown on some
                          keyboards as the RETURN key. The Bed-
                          ford program always refers to the ENTER
                          key as the RETURN key.

        [Shift][Ret]      to accept the default information dis-
                          played on the screen next to where data
                          is to be entered.
```

GETTING YOUR COMPUTER SYSTEM READY

Before you can use the Bedford Accounting System you have to boot your computer and have the system prompt showing on the screen (A:\> if you are using a floppy diskette system and C:\> if your computer has a hard disk). Be sure that you have created the necessary subdirectory for your company files on your hard disk or on the data disk in Drive B. The company used in this tutorial is called Fast Delivery Inc., so an appropriate subdirectory name is FASTDEL.

Place your working copy of the Bedford Accounting System in Drive A and a formatted data disk in Drive B with the subdirectory FASTDEL. (If you have a hard disk, you will probably use it for both program execution and data storage. Or you can have the data disk in Drive A, but execute the program from Drive C, your hard drive.) These disks will be left in the drives while you are working with this book. If you wish to stop at any time, simply go to the exit menu of the Bedford program and save the work you have done. Be sure to back up the data files each time.

STARTING THE BEDFORD ACCOUNTING SYSTEM

With your program and data disks in Drive A and Drive B respectively and logged on to the drive which contains the program disk, or with the program in a subdirectory on your hard disk, type

You can type the name in either upper or lower case characters. If you have a monochrome display — one color, you should start the program as follows:

After a few seconds, the display shown in Figure 5.1 will appear on your screen.

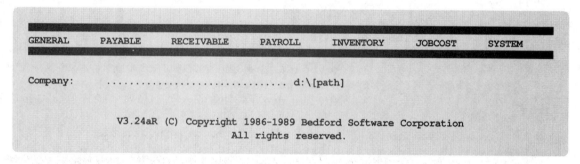

Figure 5.1 Bedford opening screen

You must now tell the Bedford program where the data files are located. If the data files are located on a diskette in Drive B, then entering the drive letter and the colon — B: — is sufficient. If the files are in a subdirectory, then you must indicate the drive letter and the name of the subdirectory. A hard disk is always designated as the C drive, although a large hard disk could be further partitioned into drives D and E. The following are examples.

Floppy Disk Users   **Hard Disk Users**

B:\FASTDEL   C:\FASTDEL

If you enter a directory that does not exist, the Bedford program will beep and continue to display the opening screen. You should re-enter the drive, path and subdirectory information ensuring that the spelling is correct. If the program reacts as before, you should return to DOS by pressing the ESCape key, and check the path and subdirectory to see that they are properly set up. Then re-enter the information.

Subdirectories are very useful if you wish to keep the accounts for several companies. You can create a number of subdirectories on the hard disk, each subdirectory name indicating the name of a different company. The files for that company are then kept in that particular subdirectory.

Once you have indicated the drive and subdirectory where the data files are located, press the ENTER key and you will see the display as shown in Figure 5.2.

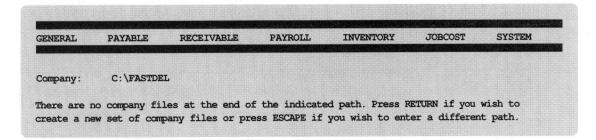

Figure 5.2 Message to indicate that no company files exist

The program reminds you that there are as yet no company files present in the directory. If you want to leave the program without entering company information you can do so by pressing the ESCape key.

Setting up Company Files

Since we want to create our company files, press ENTER. (The Bedford program refers to the ENTER key as the RETURN key). The program will now set up the company data files so that it can store the accounting data that you will enter later.

Before creating these data files, however, the program asks you to enter three dates; the **Start** date, the **Conversion** date, and the **Finish** date (See Figure 5.3).

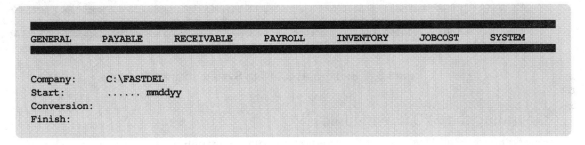

Figure 5.3 Entering the company start, conversion and finish dates

The **Start** date is the first day of the company's fiscal year. For our fictitious company we have chosen the first day of January 1, 1988 as the Start date. The following prompt appears on the monitor:

mmddyy

This means that you must enter a two digit number, beginning with the month, followed by a two digit number for the day, and finally a two digit number for the year. In our case, we will type in

```
010188
```

The program will take care of the spaces, dashes or commas.

The **Conversion** date is the day within the year on which you will convert your manual system to a computerized one. This date can be any date on or after the Start date. If you are converting your manual accounting system to a computerized one at the year end, the Conversion date will be the same as the Start date, otherwise these dates will not be the same. This allows you to convert to the Bedford Accounting System at any time. In our case, the Conversion date will coincide with our Start date. So again enter

```
010188
```

The **Finish** date is the fiscal year end date. For our company this will be December 31, 1988, so we enter

```
123188
```

As soon as the last date is entered, the program creates the data files. The display on the monitor will change as shown in Figure 5.4. This is the Bedford Accounting System main menubar which lists all the accounting modules. You will notice that the word, **GENERAL**, is highlighted. When you press the right arrow key the cursor highlight moves from left to right highlighting each module. If you press the left arrow key, the cursor highlight moves backwards. Use the arrow key which will get you most quickly to the module you want.

Figure 5.4 Bedford Accounting System main menubar

Operating the SYSTEM module

Our first task in Bedford is to tell the program something about the company for which we will use the program and about the particular computer system we are using. This is done through the **SYSTEM** module. Move the cursor highlight on the main menubar to the word **SYSTEM** by pressing either the right or the left arrow key (Figure 5.5).

Figure 5.5 Cursor highlight on SYSTEM

To enter information into the **SYSTEM** module, press

You now see the **SYSTEM** submenu on the left side of the screen (See Figure 5.6).

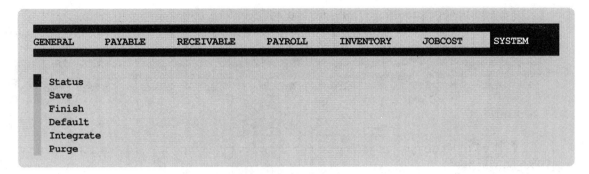

Figure 5.6 SYSTEM submenu

There are six items in this submenu. If you press the down or up arrow key you can move the cursor highlight from item to item on the submenu.

Each module in the Bedford Accounting System contains this type of pull down menu which lists the options available in each respective module. To move to an item in the submenu you press the down or up arrow key. Once the cursor highlight is next to that item you can execute it by pressing the right arrow key once.

We want to move the cursor highlight to the word **Default**. You can use either the up or the down arrow key depending on which one will get you to the item quickest. Press

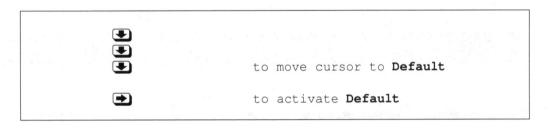

The display will change to resemble Figure 5.7.

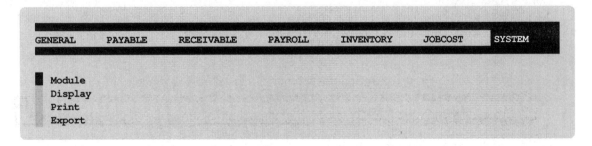

Figure 5.7 Default submenu

You are now in the **Default** submenu with the cursor highlight next to the word **Module**. Press

By activating **Module**, you will see another submenu as shown in Figure 5.8.

| GENERAL | PAYABLE | RECEIVABLE | PAYROLL | INVENTORY | JOBCOST | SYSTEM |

General
Payable
Receivable
Payroll
Inventory
Jobcost
System

Figure 5.8 The Module submenu

The items in this submenu correspond to each of the modules in the Bedford Accounting System. The cursor highlight is now on the word **General**. Press

➡   to activate **General**

Another new menu appears which looks like the one in Figure 5.9. This display should be familiar to you because it looks like the one you entered the various dates into when you first started the program.

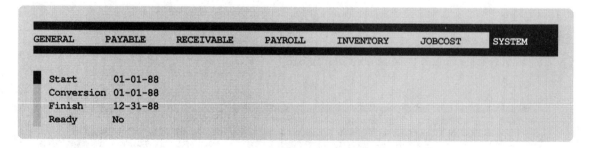

| GENERAL | PAYABLE | RECEIVABLE | PAYROLL | INVENTORY | JOBCOST | SYSTEM |

Start   01-01-88
Conversion   01-01-88
Finish   12-31-88
Ready   No

Figure 5.9 General submenu in the SYSTEM module

Notice that the word READY is added at the bottom of the screen with a **No** beside it. The Bedford Accounting System has two modes, READY and NOT READY. We are in the NOT READY mode because we are in the conversion stage. Once we have converted one part of our manual system to the Bedford Accounting System, we will change the program to READY mode.

You now want to get back to the submenu of the **SYSTEM** module. You can press either the left arrow key or the ESCape key to do so. If you press either of the keys once more you will be back to the Bedford main menubar with the names of the various modules across the top. Always press the left arrow key when data or changes have to be saved.

⬅	
⬅	
⬅	cursor now on **Default**
⬅	to return to the Bedford main menubar

CUSTOMIZING THE BEDFORD SYSTEM

At this point the Bedford Accounting System is not set up for entering a company's business transactions. It also doesn't have any information about the computer hardware we are using or how this system is set up (the configuration of the system). We use the **SYSTEM** module to give the Bedford program this information.

Entering Company Information

First we will enter information about our company — name and address. With the main cursor highlight on **SYSTEM** press

⬇	to activate **SYSTEM** submenu. Cursor is on **Status**
⬇	
⬇	
⬇	to move cursor next to **Default**
➡	to activate **Default** submenu. Cursor is on **Module**
➡	to activate **Module** submenu. Cursor is on **General**
⬆	to move cursor next to **System**. (Note the up arrow causes the cursor to jump to the bottom of the list of menu items and gets you there quicker than if you had used the down arrow repeatedly to get to the same point.)
➡	to activate **System** menu item which provides input screen for entering company data.

The display will be as shown in Figure 5.10.

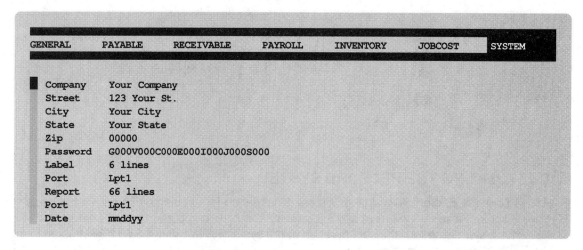

| GENERAL | PAYABLE | RECEIVABLE | PAYROLL | INVENTORY | JOBCOST | SYSTEM |

```
Company     Your Company
Street      123 Your St.
City        Your City
State       Your State
Zip         00000
Password    G000V000C000E000I000J000S000
Label       6 lines
Port        Lpt1
Report      66 lines
Port        Lpt1
Date        mmddyy
```

Figure 5.10 Company information screen

You can now enter the company name. The cursor is next to the first item, **Company**. Press

to open **Company** input area

Then type in the following

Fast Delivery Inc. [Ret]   to enter company name

If you make a mistake while typing, use the BACKSPACE key to erase the incorrect characters and then retype the correct ones. If you have already entered the information and accepted it by pressing the enter key, just repeat the above and type in the entire correct name.

Notice you do not have to hold down the SHIFT key to capitalize the first letters of the company name. The program does that for you. When you have entered the name, press the ENTER key. This signals to the program that you have entered the information for that line. Any remaining dots will disappear leaving the name on the top line. Continue to enter other company information. Press

⬇️	to move cursor next to **Street**
➡️	to activate **Street**
1251 Bel Red Road Ret	to enter the street Address
⬇️	to move cursor next to **City**
➡️	to activate **City**
Bellevue Ret	to enter the city name
⬇️	to move cursor next to **State**
➡️	to activate **State**
Wa. Ret	to enter the state name
⬇️	to choose **Zip** code
➡️	to activate **Zip** code
98625 Ret	to enter the zip code

Do not enter a password at this point. We will discuss the use of passwords in Chapter 12.

When you have entered the above information into the system you must save it so that the program can recall it later. To do so press

⬅️	to save data
⬅️	to return to **Default** submenu
⬅️	to return to the **SYSTEM** submenu. (See Figure 5.6)

NOTE: You must always press the left arrow key to save the data entered. If you press the ESCape key instead it tells the program to discard the data entered and the company information that you entered will not be saved. If you have already done that, repeat the steps for entering the above data and be sure to use the left arrow key to return to the SYSTEM submenu.

■ *Setting the Display Defaults*

We now have to tell the program some other information about our particular computer system. Let's set the display defaults first which depend on the monitor that you are using. You are in the **SYSTEM** submenu. Press

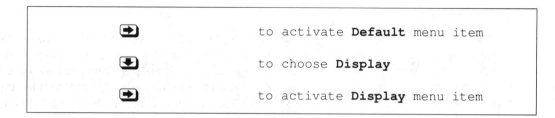

➡	to activate **Default** menu item
⬇	to choose **Display**
➡	to activate **Display** menu item

You will now see the default display screen information as shown in Figure 5.11.

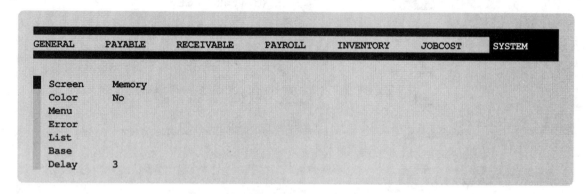

GENERAL	PAYABLE	RECEIVABLE	PAYROLL	INVENTORY	JOBCOST	SYSTEM
Screen	Memory					
Color	No					
Menu						
Error						
List						
Base						
Delay	3					

Figure 5.11 Display **Default** screen when using a monochrome monitor

- **Setting the Screen Save Option**

The cursor highlight is now next to **Screen**. Press

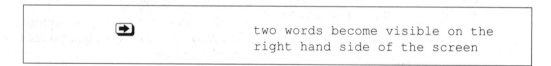

➡	two words become visible on the right hand side of the screen

These words are **Bios** and **Memory**, and they refer to how the program saves the screen image when you press one of the three function keys to get a quick look at information that you entered. When you press that function key again, you are returned to the previous screen. The program can use either the bios or memory method to save the screen image. The memory setting is extremely fast, but is dependent to some extent on the hardware you have. Because it is suitable for most computers and because it is extremely fast, it is the default setting.

The bios setting is compatible with virtually all computers systems, but may not be as fast as the memory method. If you find that using the memory method of saving the screen image does not work well, then try the bios method.

Leave the program in the **Memory** setting for now. Type

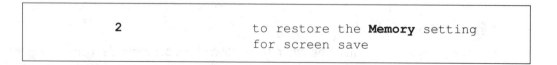

2	to restore the **Memory** setting for screen save

▪ *Setting the Color Option*

The next setting is the **Color** of your monitor. If you are using a monochrome monitor (one color) then the word beside **Color** is automatically set to **No**. The program will not allow you to change **Color** to **Yes**. If you press the right arrow key when your cursor is next to **Color**, you will hear a short beep, but nothing else happens. If you are using a color monitor then the program will be in color when you start it up. You can then change the display to monochrome or set the colors for the various categories of display to your liking.

The various default color settings are as follows:

Menu   The default color for menu displays is white.

Error   The default color for warning messages is red.

List   The default color for displayed lists is light green.

Base   The default background color is blue.

To change the color display on a color monitor, press

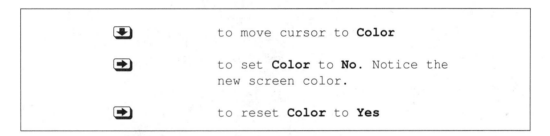

⬇	to move cursor to **Color**
➡	to set **Color** to **No**. Notice the new screen color.
➡	to reset **Color** to **Yes**

To change the colors for the various categories of display move the cursor highlight next to the item you want to change and press the right arrow key. You can then select the color you like from the color menu that appears on the right side of the monitor.

When you have set all of the colors to your liking, press

⬅	to save your choice of colors.

To retain the default color setting, press

Esc	to retain the default settings

▪ Setting the Delay Option

The **Delay** in Figure 5.11 refers to how long messages are displayed on the screen. You can have them flash on quickly (1) or stay on for a considerable period of time (9). The default is (3). With your cursor next to **Delay**, pressing the right arrow key allows you to change this default.

To get out of the **Display** default section press

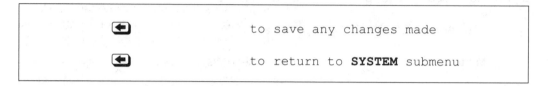

Setting the Printer Port and Default Printer

Our next task is to tell the program what make of printer we have. But before we do that we must select the printer port through which the printer is connected to the rest of the computer system.

To choose a printer port and the printer, you should be in the **SYSTEM** submenu with your cursor highlight next to **Default**. Press

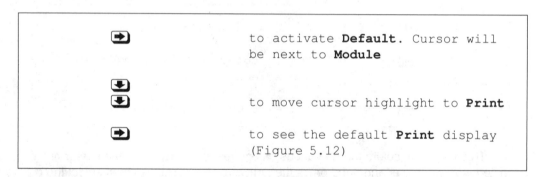

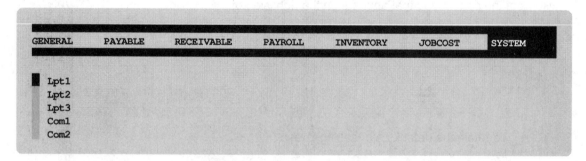

Figure 5.12 Various printer port options

Figure 5.12 shows that you can have a printer connected to each parallel port (**Lpt1, Lpt2,** or **Lpt3**) or to two communications ports (**Com1** and **Com2**). Since most printers have a parallel interface, your printer is in all likelihood connected to **Lpt1.**

Now, you can select your printer. Press

to display default printer
connected to **Lpt1**

The program will show an EPSON printer as the default printer since they are very popular. Many other printers emulate (act as) an EPSON printer in which case you can use the default EPSON printer. If you do not have an EPSON printer or compatible then press

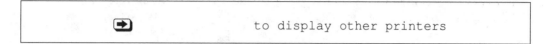

to display other printers

The listed default printer disappears and a list of other printers appears on the right hand side of the screen as shown in Figure 5.13. Use the up or down arrow keys to scroll through the list of printers until you find yours. Then type that printer's number where the two dots are.

```
??          to enter the number of your printer
            if it is not the default Epson printer
```

GENERAL	PAYABLE	RECEIVABLE	PAYROLL	INVENTORY	JOBCOST	SYSTEM

```
Printer      ..                    Admate  100,150..............1
   Select                          Anadex  9500,9501...........2
   Setup                           Apple Daisy Wheel...........3
   Bold                            Apple Dot Matrix............4
   Compress                        Brother Daisy Wheel.........5
   UnderLine                       Brother Dot Matrix..........6
   FormFeed                        C.Itoh Daisy Wheel..........7
   LineFeed                        C.Itoh Dot Matrix...........8
   Laser                           Canon Daisy Wheel...........9
Compress    Yes                    Canon Dot Matrix...........10
Emulation   Yes                    Canon Laser Beam...........11
                                   Canon Type Writer..........12
                                   Centronics 352.............13
                                   Centronics 739.............14
                                   Corona LP300...............15
                                   Corona LP300(Epson)........16
                                   Diablo.....................17
                                   Epson......................18
                                   Epson Graftrax.............19
                                   Epson LQ...................20
                                   Fujitsu....................21
                                   Gemini.....................22
                                   HP LaserJet................23
                                   IBM Graphics...............24
                                   IBM ProPrinter.............25
                                   IBM QuietWriter............26
```

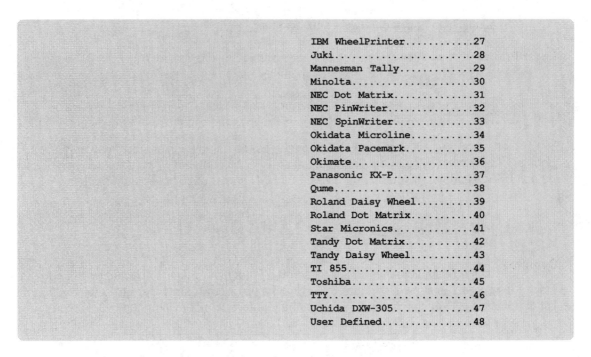

```
IBM WheelPrinter...........27
Juki......................28
Mannesman Tally...........29
Minolta...................30
NEC Dot Matrix............31
NEC PinWriter.............32
NEC SpinWriter............33
Okidata Microline.........34
Okidata Pacemark..........35
Okimate...................36
Panasonic KX-P............37
Qume......................38
Roland Daisy Wheel........39
Roland Dot Matrix.........40
Star Micronics............41
Tandy Dot Matrix..........42
Tandy Daisy Wheel.........43
TI 855....................44
Toshiba...................45
TTY.......................46
Uchida DXW-305............47
User Defined..............48
```

Figure 5.13 Setting the printer default

If your printer is not among those listed then you would choose the last category in the list — *User Defined*. When you insert that number then some of the other default options slightly indented on the left side of the screen in Figure 5.13 can also be changed.

Select   When you choose this option the list of printers reappears and you can enter a printer whose codes you want to modify in the subsequent fields.

Setup   In this field you have to set the ASCII codes that initialize your printer. For example, most printers print at six lines per inch. You could place a code in this setup field to have the printer start with printing 8 lines per inch. The appropriate ASCII codes are available from your printer manual.

Bold   In this field you would place the ASCII codes that turn the bold feature on and off, separated by a space.

Compress   Insert two ASCII codes that turn the compress feature on and off separated by a space.

Underline   Insert two ASCII codes to begin and end the underlining process, separated by a space.

Formfeed   If your printer does not allow a form feed character (ASCII FF) to advance the paper to the next page, then this option has to be set to **No**. The program will then issue a series of linefeeds to move the printhead to the top of the next page. Most printers do allow a formfeed, so this option can be left as **Yes**.

Linefeed   Some printers produce an extra linefeed when they receive the command for a carriage return. Your reports would then be double spaced. If that happens then set this field to **No**, otherwise set it to **Yes**.

Laser Printer   If you have a laser printer then change this default to **Yes**. This issues a formfeed at the end of each check, statement or invoice printed on that printer.

In case there are alignment problems when printing checks, invoices or statements on the laser printer, you will have to make the following changes:

i. Change the printer to **User Defined** from the list, (48), and set the **Select** menu item to your chosen printer.

ii. Adjust the **Setup** control codes to change the left and top margins for your printer. The required control codes for the setup field are in the laser printer manual. They may be preceded by the code to re-initialize the printer.

Compress   A dot matrix printer comes in either wide or narrow carriage form. For accounting purposes a wide carriage printer is better, but you can get wider output even on a printer that accepts 8.5 by 11 inch paper by setting the **Compress** option to **Yes**. This will give you 16.6 characters per inch. If this field is set to **No**, your printer will print at 10 characters per inch across 14 inch wide paper. The **Compress** feature is automatically overridden when printing checks, statements or invoices.

Emulation   If you set this field to **Yes** you can print foreign language characters which contain accents. These characters are emulated by using standard ASCII characters. If you set this field to **No**, then the program will print foreign language characters according to codes established by IBM. If you have an IBM printer or compatible, or a printer that filters out these codes, then set this field to **No**.

Figure 5.14 shows how this default setting might look after an Epson printer was customized by changing some of its default settings.

```
GENERAL      PAYABLE      RECEIVABLE      PAYROLL      INVENTORY      JOBCOST      SYSTEM

  Printer       User Defined
    Select      Epson LQ
    Setup
    Bold        ^[G ^[H
    Compress    ^O ^R
    UnderLine   ^[-1 ^[-0
    FormFeed    Yes
    LineFeed    Yes
    Laser       No
  Compress      Yes
  Emulation     Yes
```

Figure 5.14 An example of printer codes customized for an Epson printer

When you have finished defining your printer, save the entry. Press

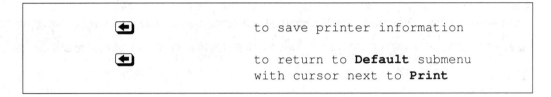

⬅	to save printer information
⬅	to return to **Default** submenu with cursor next to **Print**

Setting Export Defaults

If you want to manipulate existing accounting data by calculating various percentages and key ratios, then you can **Export** a file. A spreadsheet is ideal for this purpose, but the data has to be changed from the form used by the Bedford Accounting System to a spreadsheet format.

You can export files from the Bedford Accounting System into a Lotus 1-2-3 spreadsheet, or into any spreadsheet that uses the Lotus file format such as SuperCalc. Alternatively you can export a Bedford report as a text file for inclusion in a report prepared with a word processor. Figure 5.15 shows the default export screen for creating a Lotus compatible spreadsheet file. Press

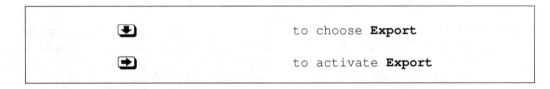

⬇	to choose **Export**
➡	to activate **Export**

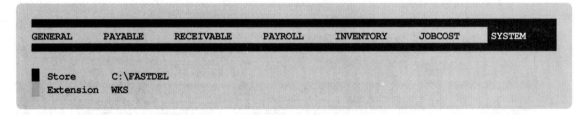

Figure 5.15 File export submenu showing the subdirectory for storing exported files and the file extension

The default format, with file extension WKS, is for exporting files to version 1 of Lotus 1-2-3. If you have Lotus 1-2-3 version 2, then you would choose WK1. Many other spreadsheets can use a Lotus 1-2-3 spreadsheet file. Check your spreadsheet manual as to its capabilities. If you want files compatible with Lotus Symphony you would choose WR1 as the file extension and format. If you want files that can be read into a report by a word processor you would choose the TXT format.

To change the default format from WKS (version 1A of Lotus 1-2-3) to one of the other formats, press

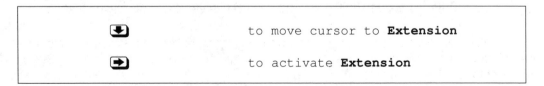

⬇	to move cursor to **Extension**
➡	to activate **Extension**

You will see the screen display shown in Figure 5.16.

GENERAL	PAYABLE	RECEIVABLE	PAYROLL	INVENTORY	JOBCOST	SYSTEM

Store   C:\FASTDEL   WKS.............1
Extension   .   WK1.............2
                                                        WR1.............3
                                                        TXT.............4

Figure 5.16 Choices of Lotus 1-2-3, Symphony and text file formats for exporting Bedford files

Let's restore the **Default** setting; type:

```
        1                    to elect WKS extension
```

The **Store** option tells the program what drive and directory you want the exported files to be in after they are exported. The **Default** setting is the drive and directory where your company files are stored.

> *NOTE: Be sure when you work with exported files that you do not accidentally alter the Bedford accounting files which hold your data. Otherwise they could be damaged. These files should only be used by the Bedford program or copied to another disk for backup.*

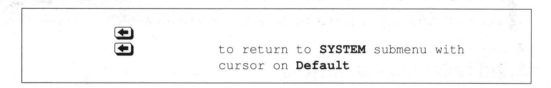

```
                     to return to SYSTEM submenu with
                     cursor on Default
```

A Look at Status

You should still be in the **SYSTEM** submenu with the cursor highlight next to **Default**. **Status** is the first item in this menu. Press

```
                     to choose Status

                     to activate Status
```

You will now see the display as shown in Figure 5.17, the **Status** screen. This provides basic information about the program. As you are working on the Bedford Accounting System you will want to return to this screen from time to time. It shows the number of existing accounts, the number of accounts that can still be used, the amount of room left for new transactions, and if there is an asterisk next to the word RAM under the column, **Residing**, it indicates that the data has not been saved to disk yet. The status screen in Figure 5.17 shows the capacity of a computer with 640K memory. If you have less than 640K then the **Remaining** column will show smaller totals.

GENERAL	PAYABLE	RECEIVABLE	PAYROLL	INVENTORY	JOBCOST	SYSTEM

	Existing	Remaining	Limiting		Residing
Ledger Accounts:	40	460	Program	*	RAM
Vendor Accounts:	0	999	Program		RAM
Transactions:	0	16365	RAM		RAM
Customer Accounts:	0	999	Program		RAM
Transactions:	0	16365	RAM		RAM
Employee Records:	0	859	RAM		RAM
Inventory Records:	0	999	Program		RAM
Project Records:	0	999	Program		RAM
Memory:	640 K	319 K			

Version V3.24aR

Figure 5.17 System status screen for 640K memory capacity

When you have completed viewing the **Status** display, return to the **SYSTEM** submenu by pressing

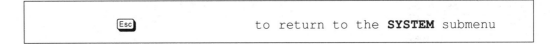

Esc   to return to the **SYSTEM** submenu

SAVING YOUR JOURNAL ENTRIES

When you record business transactions in the Bedford Accounting System these entries are stored in the RAM (Random Access Memory) of your computer. If you were to get a power or machine failure, you would loose the data that you entered up to now. Since you do not want to needlessly enter data twice, it is important periodically to save all entries to disk. Saving data is a fairly quick procedure. Use your own judgement as to how often to save data. Sometimes a computer can hang-up for no apparent reason, which would require you to re-boot the system. You would then loose all entries made since the last time you saved to disk.

You should still be in the **SYSTEM** submenu. To save your data to disk, press

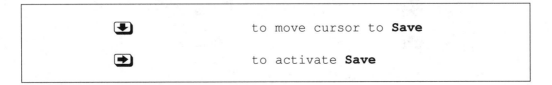

⬇   to move cursor to **Save**

➡   to activate **Save**

FINISHING THE SESSION

When you are finished with the program you can eliminate the step to save your data by pressing the right arrow key when the cursor highlight is next to **Finish** in the **SYSTEM** submenu. The **Finish** command will save all journal entries currently stored in RAM memory to disk, and exit the Bedford Accounting System.

To end this session and save your data at the same time, press

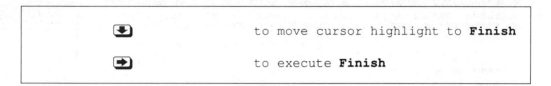

Whenever you have worked through a chapter in this tutorial you should exit the program using the **Finish** command. Start the program in the regular manner described earlier in this chapter when you are ready to start the next tutorial chapter.

BACKING UP YOUR TUTORIAL DATA

As you work through the tutorial starting with this chapter you should back up the data files. Use the COPY or DISKCOPY program described in Chapter 4. An alternative method is to back up the accounting data files for each chapter so you can work through a particular chapter again if you want more practice or if you make a mistake. For example, if you get to the PAYROLL module in Chapter 9 and then make a mistake or experience a power failure, your data files may be hopelessly out of balance or even destroyed. You may have to return to Chapter 5 and reenter all the journal entries, which might be a tedious process.

To overcome this problem, format a diskette and create various subdirectories on it as follows.

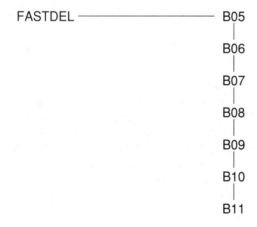

The main subdirectory, FASTDEL, contains your working data files. You should create 7 subdirectories from the main FASTDEL subdirectory corresponding to each of the chapters in this tutorial. As you complete each chapter, quit the program with the **Finish** command that saves your data files. Then copy these data files to the respective subdirectory on the diskette or hard disk. Then start the Bedford program again and carry on with the tutorial. If you make a serious mistake, for example, while entering journal entries in Chapter 8, the accounts RECEIVABLE module, you can simply end the program, copy the completed Chapter 7 data files from the B07 subdirectory over the existing files in FASTDEL, then start the Bedford program again in the regular manner and reenter the data for Chapter 8. In this way you do not lose all the work that you have done since Chapter 5.

Chapter 6
THE GENERAL LEDGER

Chapter 6
THE GENERAL LEDGER

PREVIEW

In this chapter you will learn about the general ledger — its purpose in the accounting system. The general ledger accounts provide the information for the two major financial statements — the balance sheet and the income statement. The key to the general ledger is the chart of accounts and its general makeup. In working through this chapter, you will get a good understanding of the types of accounts in the chart of accounts, how Bedford handles these accounts, and how to add, delete, modify and print the chart of accounts. As an exercise you will print the financial statements for the hypothetical company, Fast Delivery, Inc. After entering historical balances into a number of accounts you will change the Bedford general ledger to the READY mode, and make a number of journal entries.

OBJECTIVES

After completing this chapter you should be able to explain:

1. The importance of the general ledger in accounting and its relationship to the balance sheet and the income statement;

2. What a default chart of accounts is and how it can be customized for individual firms;

3. How to assign types of accounts to the chart of accounts in the Bedford Accounting System;

4. How to add, modify, and delete accounts from the Bedford default chart of accounts;

5. How to print out the balance sheet, income statement, chart of accounts, and the trial balance;

6. How to enter the opening balances into the general ledger and how to make the system ready for entering daily business transactions;

7. How to enter a number of journal entries into the general ledger;

8. How to view the accounting data entered during a particular time period or session;

9. The importance of maintaining an audit trail.

      After learning how to install the Bedford Accounting System in Chapter 5, you can begin to use it. We will begin with the general ledger, which is the cornerstone of any accounting system.

PURPOSE OF THE GENERAL LEDGER

The general ledger is the heart of any accounting system. It contains all of the major accounts from which information is taken to generate the financial statements. You can update these accounts through regular journal entries, which represent the business transactions that have taken place over a period of time. By using the double entry accounting system, debits and credits, you can always check to make sure the accounts are in balance. This means that the total dollar amount of assets must equal the total dollar amount in the liabilities section plus the equity section. Balancing accounts is done through a trial balance to which adjusting entries can be made prior to printing the financial statements. Because the general ledger is the most important part of an accounting system and often the only module a business needs to computerize, it is necessary to have a good understanding of what that module does.

Let's take a look at the cash account in the general ledger. In this account you keep track of all deposits made to the bank account (debits) and all the checks, charges and withdrawals (credits). In addition you keep track of the date that each transaction took place, the nature of the transaction, and how it originated. The dollar value of each transaction is either added or subtracted from the previous balance. The cash balance at the end of the year represents the amount of money left in the company.

If the company started with a balance of $250.00 on December 1, deposited $500 from sales during the day and wrote a check out to the telephone company with check #44, for $142.50 the general ledger account for cash would resemble the following:

CASH		DR.	CR.	BALANCE
Opening balance				250.00
September 1	Sales Sept 1.	500.00		750.00
September 1	Check #44 Telephone Co.		142.50	607.50

The general ledger keeps track of all accounts that belong to one of the major categories shown on the balance sheet and income statement — assets, liabilities, owner's equity, revenues and expenses. At fiscal year end the balance in each account will be the amount shown in the appropriate place on the balance sheet and on the income statement.

COMPUTERIZING THE GENERAL LEDGER

In converting a manual accounting system to the Bedford Accounting System we must start with the chart of accounts. As we discussed in Chapter 2, the chart of accounts lists each business account along with its assigned number. This chart of accounts must contain every account in the business to which transactions will be posted during the year. Although we can add accounts as needed, it is more cumbersome to add accounts during the data input stage, as opposed to doing so at the beginning.

Establishing the Chart of Accounts

In a manual accounting system we often group a number of accounts together to keep the system and data entry manageable. For example, you may have a number of telephone bills, one for the regular business line, one for the facsimile line and one for the computer data line. In a manual system you might put all three into the telephone account. However, a computerized accounting system such as Bedford, with easy access to 500 accounts, means that expenses can be distributed over more accounts without making the system unmanageable.

By keeping accounts separate, management will have more specific information about the operation of the business. Separate accounts also quickly tell us what cost are too high. It may turn out, for example, that the computer data line in the above example is the culprit responsible for high line charges.

Before we begin the conversion process we must therefore consider how detailed we want our accounting system to be. The first step is to design a complete chart of accounts before we enter any transactions into the Bedford program. The makeup of the chart of accounts must comply with the parameters established by the Bedford Accounting System.

The Default Chart of Accounts

The Bedford Accounting System contains a pre-defined (default) chart of accounts when you first create a set of files for a company. The default chart of accounts contains the basic accounts needed by virtually all businesses. It also contains specific accounts necessary to use the other modules in the system — accounts receivable, accounts payable, inventory, payroll and job costing. By setting up these accounts in the beginning, you are spared the possible problems associated with establishing these accounts at a later time. The Bedford Accounting System assumes that a business will ultimately use all available modules.

Let's look at the default chart of accounts provided by the Bedford Accounting System. We can add additional accounts for our particular type of business later.

If you exited the Bedford Accounting System after working through Chapter 5, then you must reload the program now. If you are using a hard disk, you should be in the subdirectory containing the Bedford program. If you are using a floppy disk system you should have your Bedford system disk in Drive A and your data disk in Drive B. Then type the following:

The opening Bedford screen will appear asking you to enter the location of data files. Enter one of the following:

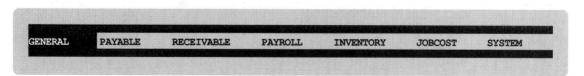

After a few seconds, the main menu of the Bedford program will appear as shown in Figure 6.1.

GENERAL	PAYABLE	RECEIVABLE	PAYROLL	INVENTORY	JOBCOST	SYSTEM

Figure 6.1 The Bedford main menubar

The word **GENERAL** is highlighted. Press

to activate the **GENERAL** ledger module

Your screen will now display the **GENERAL** submenu as seen in Figure 6.2.

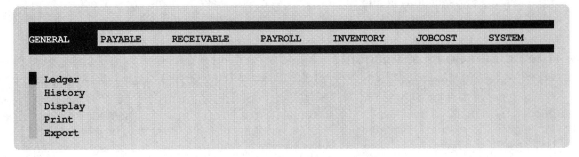

Figure 6.2 The GENERAL submenu

With the cursor next to the word **Ledger** as shown in Figure 6.2, press

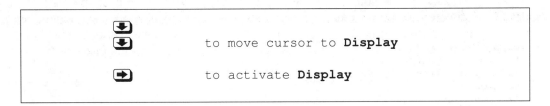

to move cursor to **Display**

to activate **Display**

You will now see the **Display** submenu as shown in Figure 6.3.

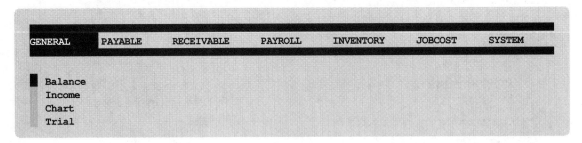

Figure 6.3 GENERAL display submenu

To look at the default chart of accounts created by the Bedford Accounting System press

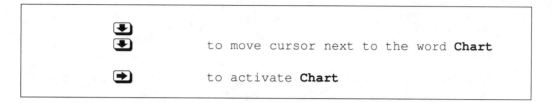

Your screen will now display the default chart of accounts (Figure 6.4) set up by the Bedford Accounting System. Some of these accounts are set up by the Bedford Accounting System to make the integration of accounts possible. Specific accounts allow the other system modules — payable, receivable, payroll, inventory and jobcost — to interface with the general ledger. You can scroll around the chart of accounts by using the up and down arrow keys. When you press the down arrow key one time, you will see the second page of the chart of accounts, and so on. To move to a previous screen, use the up arrow key. When you reach the last page of the chart of accounts, pressing the down arrow key again will take you back to the first page. For now just scroll through the chart of accounts using the up and down arrow keys to become familiar with them.

GENERAL	PAYABLE	RECEIVABLE	PAYROLL	INVENTORY	JOBCOST	SYSTEM

```
100  CURRENT ASSETS................H
106    Bank A - Payable............L
108    Bank B - Receivable.........L
110    Bank C - Payroll............L
112    Cash: Total.................S
120    Accounts Receivable.........R
124    Advances Receivable.........R
126    Inventory...................R
139  TOTAL CURRENT ASSETS..........T

200  CURRENT LIABILITIES...........H
220    Accounts Payable............R
231    FIT Payable.................R
232    SIT Payable.................R
233    FICA Payable................R
234    FUTA Payable................R
235    SUTA Payable................R
236    SDI Payable.................R
237    Local Tax Payable...........R
240    Deduction A Payable.........R
242    Deduction B Payable.........R
244    Deduction C Payable.........R
260    Sales Tax Payable...........R
269  TOTAL CURRENT LIABILITIES.....T

300  EARNINGS......................H
356    Retained Earnings...........R
360    Current Earnings............X
369  TOTAL EARNINGS................T
```

```
400  REVENUE.....................H
402    General Revenue.............R
410    Freight Revenue.............R
439  TOTAL REVENUE................T

500  ADMINISTRATION...............H
502    General Expense.............R
520    Freight Expense.............R
530    Wages.......................R
531    FICA Expense................R
532    FUTA Expense................R
533    SUTA Expense................R
534    SDI Expense.................R
539  TOTAL ADMINISTRATION.........T
```

Figure 6.4 The Bedford default chart of accounts

When you have finished viewing the listing, press the following keys to return to the Bedford main menubar.

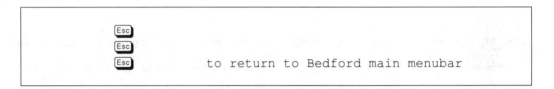

Esc
Esc
Esc   to return to Bedford main menubar

■ *Defining the Integration Accounts*

The Bedford Accounting System is a totally integrated accounting system. **Integration** means that when an entry is made in one of the submodules (i.e., accounts payable, accounts receivable, etc.), the general ledger is updated automatically. There is no need to make another entry into the general ledger or to manually make a transfer of an entry from the other modules. Similarly, the Current Earnings account automatically records the difference between the total year-to-date revenues and the total year-to-date expenses. The Current Earnings balance is then automatically added to the Retained Earnings account when a new accounting year is started. In order for the Bedford Accounting System to be able to make these entries, it must know which accounts the entries are to be posted to.

The allocation of the integration accounts is done automatically when you set up a default chart of accounts. If you wish to look at these accounts, move your cursor to **SYSTEM** and choose the integration option from the menu. For each of the four modules you will find a listing of the default integration accounts preset by the system as shown in Figure 6.4A .

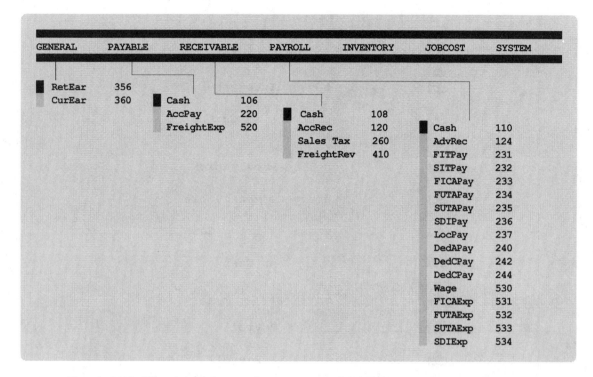

GENERAL	PAYABLE	RECEIVABLE	PAYROLL	INVENTORY	JOBCOST	SYSTEM

RetEar 356
CurEar 360

Cash 106
AccPay 220
FreightExp 520

Cash 108
AccRec 120
Sales Tax 260
FreightRev 410

Cash 110
AdvRec 124
FITPay 231
SITPay 232
FICAPay 233
FUTAPay 234
SUTAPay 235
SDIPay 236
LocPay 237
DedAPay 240
DedCPay 242
DedCPay 244
Wage 530
FICAExp 531
FUTAExp 532
SUTAExp 533
SDIExp 534

Figure 6.4A The default integration accounts of the Bedford Accounting System for the GENERAL, PAYABLE, RECEIVABLE and PAYROLL modules.

▪ Changing The Default Integration Accounts

The default integration accounts provided may not be the ones that you wish to have in your system. As shown above, the system sets up a different bank account for payroll, accounts receivable and accounts payable. For example, the accounts receivable module uses account #108 as its default bank account. When a customer payment is recorded the program automatically adds this payment to the balance in that account. Similarly, when an invoice payment is recorded through accounts payable, the amount of the check is automatically deducted from account #106. A payroll check issued to an employee is automatically deducted from account #110.

It is not necessary to keep the account numbers set up by the system. If you set up account #106 and give it the name of your bank, then you would enter that account number for each of the above accounts and delete the other two bank accounts.

Fast Delivery Inc. only has one bank account, #106 currently called Bank A - General. The default chart of accounts has three bank accounts — #106 Bank A - Payable, #108 Bank B-Receivable, and #110 Bank C - Payroll. Since you want all bank entries to be recorded in account #106 this means you will have to change the bank accounts for both Receivable, #108, and Payroll, #110, to account #106. Start with the Bedford main menubar. Press

➡ or ⬅   to place large
            cursor highlight on **SYSTEM**

⬇   to activate **SYSTEM** submenu

⬇	
⬇	
⬇	
⬇	to choose **Integrate**
➡	to activate **Integrate**
⬇	
⬇	to choose **Receivable**
➡	to activate **Receivable**
➡	to erase existing **Cash** account number
106	to enter new **Cash** account
⬅	to accept the change
⬇	to choose **Payroll**
➡	to activate **Payroll**
➡	to erase existing **Cash** account number
106	to enter new **Cash** account #106
⬅	to accept change
⬅	
⬅	to return to Bedford main menubar

With the integration accounts changed, all deposits and checks will be posted to account #106.

▪ Adding and Deleting Accounts from the Default Chart

Some of the integration accounts provided may not be required by your business. The bank accounts that you changed, #108 and #110, could be erased because they are no longer required as integration accounts. Some of the others are required later as you begin to use the other accounting modules. For now let's not erase any of the accounts.

You are however free to add new accounts to the system, up to a total of 500 accounts including the ones already provided. You can later delete any accounts you added if you find you don't need them. You can also modify any of the accounts that you added as well as some of the default accounts created by the Bedford program.

▪ *How the Accounts Are Set Up*

Return to the **GENERAL** module and redisplay the existing chart of accounts. When you look at the current asset accounts, you see that they are numbered from 100 to 139. The numbers keep the descriptive names that identify each account in a specific sequence. For example, the first account, 100, is labelled CURRENT ASSETS followed by a capital letter **H**.

The number, 100, determines the position of this account in relation to all others. This is important, because the accounts in the financial statements are printed in numerical order based on where they are in the chart of accounts. Normally, balance sheet accounts are printed according to their liquidity. Since cash is the most liquid asset, it is listed first, followed by the item that is most easily converted into cash. This would be securities, followed by accounts receivable, inventory, prepaid expenses and so on.

The number in the chart of accounts also indicates whether the item is an asset, a liability, owners equity, a revenue or an expense account. The Bedford Accounting System uses a set of predetermined numbers to identify each category of account:

Asset Accounts	100	to	199
Liability Accounts	200	to	299
Equity Accounts	300	to	399
Revenue Accounts	400	to	499
Expense Accounts	500	to	599

If we wanted an account for OTHER ASSETS, and we wanted that item to be printed out last on the asset side, we would have to give that account a number close to account 199. The label CURRENT ASSETS indicates the contents of the account. The **H** means that this account is a heading only. All of the other accounts in the chart of accounts are defined in the same manner.

The easiest way to create a chart of accounts for the Bedford Accounting System is to take a set of your detailed financial statements and, using the numbering parameters above, assign a number to each account. This will ensure that you will not miss any accounts and that all the accounts are in the correct order.

Figure 6.5 shows a balance sheet and an income statement to which account numbers have been assigned. Notice that the account types have also been assigned according to the position of the account balance on the financial statements.

Fast Delivery Inc.
Balance Sheet
December 31, 1987

234 FUTA Payable R

ASSETS			
100 CURRENT ASSETS			*H*
104 Petty Cash	300.00		*L*
106 First Interstate Bank	1,243.33		*L*
Total Cash		1,543.33	*R*
120 Accounts Receivable		555.00	*R*
126 Inventory		100.00	*R*
135 Prepaid Insurance		55.67	*R*
139 TOTAL CURRENT ASSETS		2,254.00	*T*
150 FIXED ASSETS			*H*
154 Buildings	15,000.00		*L*
156 Accm Depn - Building	(2,500.00)		*L*
164 Automotive	26,000.00		*L*
166 Accm Depn - Auto	(5,500.00)		*L*
170 Subtotal		33,000.00	*S*
172 Land		18,000.00	*R*
175 TOTAL FIXED ASSETS		51,000.00	*T*
TOTAL ASSETS		53,254.00	—

LIABILITIES			
200 CURRENT LIABILITIES			*H*
220 Accounts Payable		260.00	*R*
233 FICA Payable	256.66 →		*R*
232 State Tax Payable	195.00 →		*R*
231 Federal Tax Payable	568.00 →		*R*
265 Withholding Tax payable		1,019.66	*S*
266 Short Term Loan		2,000.00	*R*
269 TOTAL CURRENT LIABILITIES		3,279.66	*T*
271 LONG TERM DEBT			*H*
275 Mortgage payable		22,500.00	*R*
280 TOTAL LONG TERM DEBT		22,500.00	*T*
TOTAL LIABILITIES		25,779.66	—
SHAREHOLDER'S EQUITY			*H*
301 SHARES			
302 Class A Common		5,000.00	*R*
303 Class B Common		2,000.00	*R*
310 TOTAL SHARES		7,000.00	*T*
350 EARNINGS			*H*
356 Retained Earnings		20,474.34	*R*
369 TOTAL EARNINGS		20,474.34	*T*
TOTAL SHAREHOLDER'S EQUITY		27,474.34	—
TOTAL LIABILITIES AND EQUITY		53,254.00	—

FAST DELIVERY INC.
Statement of Income
For the year ended December 31, 1987

REVENUE			
401 SERVICE REVENUE			*H*
406 General Delivery	55,456.00		*R*
407 Special Delivery	35,126.00		*R*
410 TOTAL SERVICE REVENUE		90,582.00	*T*
419 OTHER REVENUE			*H*
426 Insurance Income	5,685.00		*R*
427 Interest Income	1,255.00		*R*
430 TOTAL OTHER REVENUE		6,940.00	*T*
TOTAL REVENUE		97,522.00	—

502 GENERAL EXPENSE L

EXPENSES			
500 OPERATING COSTS			*H*
506 Truck Rental	2,500.00		*L*
507 Fuel	10,456.00		*L*
508 Insurance	2,999.00		*L*
509 Truck Repairs	1,456.00		*L*
510 Permits	1,356.00		*L*
519 Total Trucking Costs	18,767.00		*S*
530 Wages	36,896.00		*R*
536 Employee Benefits	8,966.00		*R*
538 Warehouse Rent	7,533.00		*R*
540 TOTAL OPERATING COSTS		72,162.00	*T*
560 OVERHEAD			*H*
561 Accounting	1,255.00		*R*
562 Advertising	2,548.00		*R*
563 Telephone	4,588.00		*R*
570 TOTAL OVERHEAD COSTS		8,391.00	*T*
TOTAL EXPENSE		80,553.00	—
INCOME		16,969.00	—

520 FREIGHT EXP. R
531 FICA Exp R
532 FUTA Exp R

Figure 6.5 Working copy of balance sheet and income statement.
Account numbers have been assigned and new accounts have been noted.

▪ *Types of Accounts*

When assigning the account numbers, you must also indicate the type of account. In the Bedford Accounting System there are six definable types of accounts, each indicated by a letter as follows:

H This indicates a **block heading**. This account is printed in bold face form. It is not a postable account, meaning that no dollar amounts can be assigned to it. It is simply a subheading for a group of accounts.

R This is a postable account, meaning it can have an opening balance and have journal entries posted to it. The balance of the account will be printed in the **right** hand column within a particular category of accounts.

L This is also a postable account which will be printed in the **left** hand column within a particular category of accounts.

S This is a subtotal account and is used to provide a **subtotal of all left sided accounts** immediately above it. The subtotal is calculated and automatically printed in the field to the right within the section.

X The X account signifies the account that will be used to **summarize the current revenues and expenses**, or the current earnings of the business. Each time a journal entry is made that affects a revenue or expense account the value of current earnings changes. It is not a postable account and there can be only one of these types of accounts in the chart of accounts. Its balance is printed to the field at the right within the section.

T This represents a block total. It represents the **total balance of all Right accounts and all Subtotal accounts above it or since the last block total.** It is not a postable account so you cannot assign opening balances to it or enter journal entries into it. The program automatically calculates the total and prints it to the right within a section.

▪ *Section Totals*

There are five main section totals — TOTAL ASSETS, TOTAL LIABILITIES, TOTAL EQUITY, TOTAL REVENUE and TOTAL EXPENSE — which correspond to the five main sections of the balance sheet and income statement. Section totals are printed automatically by the program, so it is not necessary for you to define them. Furthermore, you cannot alter or change these section totals.

Now lets look at an example of a section within a typical balance sheet and assign account types to them. We will use a small fixed asset section of a typical balance sheet.

For example:

1	H	Fixed Assets		
2	L	Building	15,000	
3	L	Accm Depn - Building	(2,500)	
4	L	Automotive	26,000	
5	L	Accm Depn - Automotive	(5,500)	
6	S	Total		33,000
7	R	Land		25,000
8	T	Total Fixed Assets		58,000

The first line is a heading and has no dollar amount assigned to it.

The second to the fifth lines are accounts to which dollar amounts can be posted. These are printed to the left within the fixed asset section. This is typical of this type of account.

The first total in line 6 is a subtotal of all the left items above it.

Line 7, Land is printed to the right. The last line is the total of the block and includes left and right accounts.

By following this approach we can group accounts together in a set of financial statements as shown in Figure 6.5 . As you look through the accounts displayed on your screen, you can tell what section each individual account belongs to. For example, if you look at the asset section you can almost visualize what the balance sheet will look like when it is printed out.

You must take care when developing the chart of accounts to ensure that you have included proper subtotals and block totals. The program will not print out the reports for you until this has been corrected. Because the program is "user friendly" it will tell you where the mistakes are and allow you to correct any errors before going on.

In defining any chart of accounts, you should keep in mind one of the rules of good coding. It is important that you leave space between the numbers so that you can add other accounts later if necessary. For example, if you used the following account numbers at the beginning you may have serious problems later if you wanted to add additional accounts.

100	Current Assets
101	Bank
102	Bank 2
103	Bank 3
104	Total Cash
105	Short Term Investments

With this number system, you couldn't add a fourth bank account because you couldn't fit it in. You must always leave room between the numbers to fit in future accounts as needed. You only get one chance to define the accounts so a little more time spent now can save some problems later on.

Adding to the Chart of Accounts

Using the financial statements shown in Figure 6.5, we will add the missing accounts to the default chart of accounts. Let's start by entering the fixed asset section as it is not included with the default chart of accounts. The accounts to be added in this section are as follows:

Account Number	Description	Type	Purge
150	FIXED ASSETS	H	N
154	Building	L	N
156	Accm Depn - Building	L	N
164	Automotive	L	N
166	Accm Depn - Automotive	L	N
170	Subtotal	S	N
172	Land	R	N
175	TOTAL FIXED ASSETS	T	N

To add these accounts start from the Bedford main menubar with the cursor highlight over the word **GENERAL**. Press

        to activate **GENERAL** module

        to activate **Ledger** submenu

You will now see the **Ledger** submenu as shown in Figure 6.6. This menu is used to **modify** an existing account. With the exception of the account number itself, we can change any account item. From this menu we can also **insert** a new account or **delete** an account that we have previously added or one that we do not need from the default chart of accounts. Remember that you cannot delete an account that the system created for integration of the other modules.

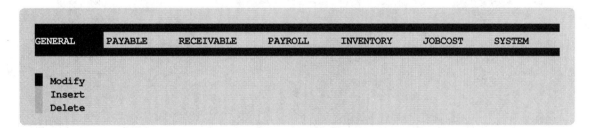

Figure 6.6 Ledger submenu from which accounts can be added, deleted or modified

To insert the new accounts press

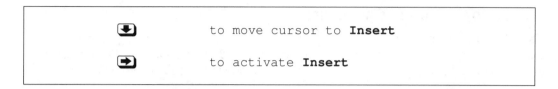

You will now see the **Insert** screen displayed on your monitor (See Figure 6.7). This is called a prompting menu, as the cursor is waiting for you to insert data. You will also see the existing accounts displayed to the right of the screen.

GENERAL	PAYABLE	RECEIVABLE	PAYROLL	INVENTORY	JOBCOST	SYSTEM

Account .... CURRENT ASSETS............100
Number   Bank A - Payable..........106
Type   Bank B - Receivable.......108
Suppress   Bank C - Payroll..........110
                                 Cash: Total...............112
                                 Accounts Receivable.......120
                                 Advances Receivable.......124
                                 Inventory.................126
                                 TOTAL CURRENT ASSETS......139
                                 CURRENT LIABILITIES.......200
                                 Accounts Payable..........220
                                 FIT Payable...............231
                                 SIT Payable...............232
                                 FICA Payable..............233
                                 FUTA Payable..............234
                                 SUTA Payable..............235
                                 SDI Payable...............236
                                 Local Tax Payable.........237
                                 Deduction A Payable.......240
                                 Deduction B Payable.......242
                                 Deduction C Payable.......244
                                 Sales Tax Payable.........260
                                 TOTAL CURRENT LIABILITIES..269
                                 EARNINGS..................300
                                 Retained Earnings.........356
                                 Current Earnings..........360
                                 TOTAL EARNINGS............369
                                 REVENUE...................400
                                 General Revenue...........402
                                 Freight Revenue...........410
                                 TOTAL REVENUE.............439
                                 ADMINISTRATION............500
                                 General Expense...........502
                                 Freight Expense...........520
                                 Wages.....................530
                                 FICA Expense..............531
                                 FUTA Expense..............532
                                 SUTA Expense..............533
                                 SDI Expense...............534
                                 TOTAL ADMINISTRATION......539

Figure 6.7 Account insert screen and complete default chart of accounts

Your cursor is blinking at the beginning of the dotted line to the right of the word **Account.** Here you will insert the name of the new account, FIXED ASSETS. Type

```
FIXED ASSETS Ret        to enter the name of the new account
```

Note that you do not have to type a capital letter at the beginning. The program assumes that all first letters are capitals and automatically capitalizes it for you. To make the subsequent letters capitals, you must hold down the SHIFT key and at the same time press the letter. If you wanted to make the first letter a lower case letter you would have to press the SHIFT key first before typing the letter.

It is a good idea to adhere to the program's method of capitalizing the first letter with the remaining letters in lower case mode. You will find that it speeds up data entry considerably.

Let's return to our task of adding accounts. After you type the name, pressing the ENTER key will automatically advance you to the next item.

You are now prompted for the account number. As soon as you enter the account number, the program automatically advances the cursor to the next item.

```
150             to enter account Number.
                (Pressing Ret is not required)
```

Now the program asks you to indicate the type of account that you have entered. Refer to the account types that you assigned to the financial statement. You will see that this is a heading account. Type

```
H               to enter Type of account.
                (Pressing Ret is not required)
```

Lastly, you are asked whether you wish to **Suppress** this account. To suppress an account means to avoid printing the account altogether if the balance of the account is zero. Financial statements do not usually contain zero balance items so the answer to this question is most often, **Yes**. Heading accounts never have a balance but you always want them printed so respond **No**, meaning the account will be printed anyway. Type

```
N               to indicate NOT to Suppress the printing of
                the account.(Pressing Ret is not required)

←               to add new account to existing accounts
```

Pressing the left arrow key saves the new account information and adds that account to the existing list of accounts. You are left in the **Ledger** submenu ready to enter another account.

To see that the new account has in fact been added to the others, press the right arrow key again. When the insert menu appears, look to the right of the screen and you will see that the account heading, FIXED ASSETS, has been added to the previous accounts.

■ *Practice Exercise*

Repeat the above steps to add the remainder of the accounts to the chart of accounts. The items to enter are listed below:

NOTE: Be sure to enter all of the following accounts exactly as indicated or you will have problems with the rest of the tutorial. You must also modify and delete the accounts as indicated in subsequent exercises.

Description	Acct No.	Type	Suppress
Petty Cash	104	L	N
Prepaid Insurance	135	R	N
Building	154	L	N
Accm Depn - Building	156	L	N
Automotive	164	L	N
Accm Depn - Automotive	166	L	N
Other Assets	168	L	N
Subtotal	170	S	N
Land	172	R	N
TOTAL FIXED ASSETS	175	T	N
Short Term Debt	266	R	N
LONG TERM DEBT	271	H	N
Mortgage Payable	275	R	N
TOTAL LONG TERM DEBT	280	T	N
SHARES	301	H	N
Class A Common	302	R	N
Class B Common	303	R	N
TOTAL SHARES	310	T	N
EARNINGS	350	H	N
General Delivery	406	R	N
Special Delivery	407	R	N
TOTAL SERVICE REVENUE	412	T	N

OTHER REVENUE	419	H	N
Insurance Income	426	R	N
Interest Income	427	R	N
TOTAL OTHER REVENUE	430	T	N
Truck Rental	506	L	N
Fuel	507	L	N
Insurance	508	L	N
Truck Repairs	509	L	N
Permits	510	L	N
Total Trucking Costs	519	S	N
Employee Benefits	536	R	N
Warehouse Rent	538	R	N
TOTAL OPERATING COSTS	540	T	N
OVERHEAD	560	H	N
Accounting	561	R	N
Advertising	562	R	N
Telephone	563	R	N
TOTAL OVERHEAD COSTS	570	T	N

Modifying Accounts

There are times when you want to modify something about the existing accounts, such as the account title or the type of account. It is a good idea only to modify accounts when there are no transactions posted to them. While just changing the name of an account is simple, there is some danger of loosing data when trying to adjust an active account.

To modify an account, choose **Modify** from the **GENERAL Ledger** submenu. Press

⬆	to get to **Modify**
➡	to activate **Modify**

You are now in the **Modify** screen with the cursor next to the three dots prompting you to input an account name (Figure 6.8). The existing accounts are listed on the right side of the screen. You can see all of the accounts by pressing the up or down arrow keys.

| GENERAL | PAYABLE | RECEIVABLE | PAYROLL | INVENTORY | JOBCOST | SYSTEM |

■ Account   ...
  Number
  Type
  Suppress

```
CURRENT ASSETS............100
Petty Cash................104
Bank A - Payable..........106
Bank B - Receivable.......108
Bank C - Payroll..........110
Cash: Total...............112
Accounts Receivable.......120
Advances Receivable.......124
Inventory.................126
Prepaid Insurance.........135
TOTAL CURRENT ASSETS......139
Building..................154
Accm Depn - Building......156
Automotive................164
Accm Depn - Automotive....166
Other Assets..............168
Subtotal..................170
Land......................172
TOTAL FIXED ASSETS........175

CURRENT LIABILITIES.......200
Accounts Payable..........220
FIT Payable...............231
SIT Payable...............232
FICA Payable..............233
FUTA Payable..............234
SUTA Payable..............235
SDI Payable...............236
Local Tax Payable.........237
Deduction A Payable.......240
Deduction B Payable.......242
Deduction C Payable.......244
Sales Tax Payable.........260
Short Term Debt...........266
TOTAL CURRENT LIABILITIES..269
LONG TERM DEBT............271
Mortgage Payable..........275
TOTAL LONG TERM DEBT......280

EARNINGS..................300
SHARES....................301
Class A Common............302
Class B Common............303
TOTAL SHARES..............310
EARNINGS..................350
Retained Earnings.........356
Current Earnings..........360
TOTAL EARNINGS............369

REVENUE...................400
General Revenue...........402
General Delivery..........406
Special Delivery..........407
Freight Revenue...........410
TOTAL SERVICE REVENUE.....412
```

```
OTHER REVENUE.............419
Insurance Income..........426
Interest Income...........427
TOTAL OTHER REVENUE.......430
TOTAL REVENUE.............439

ADMINISTRATION............500
General Expense...........502
Truck Rental..............506
Fuel......................507
Insurance.................508
Truck Repairs.............509
Permits...................510
Total Trucking Costs......519
Freight Expense...........520
Wages.....................530
FICA Expense..............531
FUTA Expense..............532
SUTA Expense..............533
SDI Expense...............534
Employee Benefits.........536
Warehouse Rent............538
TOTAL ADMINISTRATION......539
TOTAL OPERATING COSTS.....540
OVERHEAD..................560
Accounting................561
Advertising...............562
Telephone.................563
TOTAL OVERHEAD COSTS......570
```

Figure 6.8 Modify screen

Let's change the name of account #301 from its present name, "SHARES" to "SHARE CAPITAL", a more appropriate name. Type the number of the account to modify in the space occupied by the three dots.

301	to change account #301. As soon as you enter the account number, the display changes to show the existing account information.

You can now change the information in the account. Your cursor will be beside the word **Account**. The existing name for account #301, is "SHARES". To change the account name, press

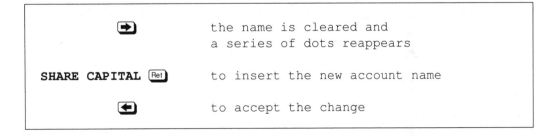

Remember, you must use the left arrow key to save any changes and return to the previous menu.

Check the chart of accounts again to make sure the account name has in fact been changed. You can do this by choosing modify or insert and then using the up or down arrow key to view accounts. When you are satisfied the account name has been changed properly, press

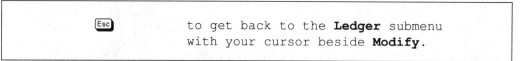

```
[Esc]          to get back to the Ledger submenu
               with your cursor beside Modify.
```

▪ Practice Exercise

As further exercise, modify the following accounts:

Acct No.	Acct Name	Area to Modify	From	To
106	Bank A - Payable	Name	Bank A - Payable	First Interstate - General
500	ADMINISTRATION	Name	ADMINISTRATION	OPERATING COSTS
502	General Expense	Type	R	L

▪ Deleting Accounts

Because the Bedford Accounting System only has room for 500 accounts in the general ledger, it is important that we only keep the accounts that are necessary. When an account is not used, it should be deleted from the chart of accounts. This of course does not apply to the integration accounts which must be retained so the Bedford Accounting System will operate properly. If you attempt to delete one of these accounts, the program will print a message on the screen, saying that it is a protected account and cannot be deleted.

Furthermore, you can only delete an account for which no transactions are entered or which does not have a dollar balance in it. Since you have as yet not entered any transactions, you can delete any unwanted accounts.

To delete one of the accounts that you have inserted but that you will not use, start from the **Ledger** submenu. Press

```
⬇
⬇              to Delete

➡              to activate Delete
```

The screen will again resemble Figure 6.8.

You now have to enter the three digit account number of the account you want to delete. Let's delete account #168, Other Assets. Simply enter the account number, 168, where the dots are.

```
    168           to choose account to delete
```

The program will respond with the following message:

*** press RETURN to proceed or ESCAPE to reconsider ***

By pressing the RETURN or ENTER key the program will go ahead with the deletion. If you are not sure, then press the ESCape key, which gives you a chance to think about it.

In our case we want to proceed, so press the ENTER key. You will be returned to the **Modify** menu. If you go back to look at the chart of accounts, account #168 will no longer be there.

▪ Practice Exercise

Delete the following accounts.

Acct Number	Acct Name
300	EARNINGS
439	TOTAL REVENUE
539	TOTAL ADMINISTRATION

▪ Completing the Chart of Accounts Entry

NOTE: Since each chapter builds on the previous one, it is crucial to this tutorial that you enter the entire chart of accounts listed above, including each section heading and section subtotal. If your chart of accounts is incomplete you may have problems displaying and printing the chart of accounts, as well as entering future transactions.

The Bedford program will help to identify problems in the setup of the chart of accounts if it detects an error. The program will then display the following message:

`General ledger account types are not in logical order near account ???`

The ??? marks indicate the account number where the potential problem exists. If you get this message, display the chart of accounts and review the accounts around the number indicated by the program. To rectify the problem, you have to return to the **Ledger** submenu in the **GENERAL** module and use the **Modify, Insert** or **Delete** function. You may want to print out the chart of accounts to assist you in solving your problem. The following section will explain how to print out the chart of accounts.

We have now finished defining the chart of accounts. Press

```
    ⬅ or Esc    to get back to the GENERAL submenu.
```

Printing the Chart of Accounts

The chart of accounts can be printed from the **GENERAL** submenu. Press

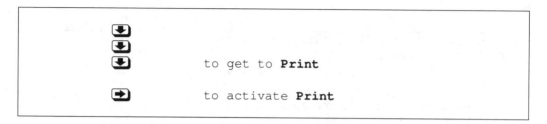

You will now see a listing of the items that can be printed out. See Figure 6.9.

Figure 6.9 Items for which a printout can be obtained

Since we want to print the chart of accounts, press

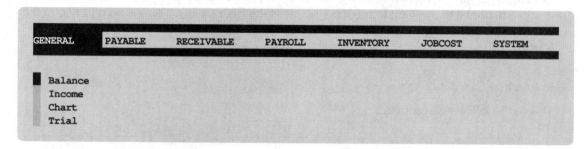

As soon as you do that, the message

processing

appears on the screen. You must have your computer hooked up to a printer and the printer must be on-line. If your printer is not ready to print, your computer system will not respond to your commands. Ready your printer. As soon as you do that the printer will begin printing the chart of accounts which should resemble the print out shown in Figure 6.10. You should save this print out of the chart of accounts and keep it close to the computer so that you can refer to it as necessary.

Now return to the **GENERAL** submenu. Press

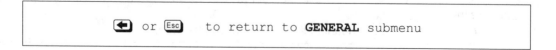

Fast Delivery Inc. FOR INSTRUCTIONAL USE ONLY
CHART OF ACCOUNTS Jan 1,1988

ASSETS

100 CURRENT ASSETS ....H
  104 Petty Cash L
  106 First Interstate - General L
  108 Bank B - Receivable L
  110 Bank C - Payroll L
  112 Cash: Total ....S
  120 Accounts Receivable ....R
  124 Advances Receivable ....R
  126 Inventory ....R
  135 Prepaid Insurance ....R
139 TOTAL CURRENT ASSETS ....T

150 FIXED ASSETS ....H
  154 Building L
  156 Accm Depn - Building L
  164 Automotive L
  166 Accm Depn - Automotive L
  170 Subtotal ....S
  172 Land ....R
175 TOTAL FIXED ASSETS ....T

LIABILITIES

200 CURRENT LIABILITIES ....H
  220 Accounts Payable ....R
  231 FIT Payable ....R
  232 SIT Payable ....R
  233 FICA Payable ....R
  234 FUTA Payable ....R
  235 SUTA Payable ....R
  236 SDI Payable ....R
  237 Local Tax Payable ....R
  240 Deduction A Payable ....R
  242 Deduction B Payable ....R
  244 Deduction C Payable ....R
  260 Sales Tax Payable ....R
  266 Short Term Debt...............................R
269 TOTAL CURRENT LIABILITIES ....T

271 LONG TERM DEBT ....H
  275 Mortgage Payable ....R
280 TOTAL LONG TERM DEBT ....T

EQUITY

301 SHARE CAPITAL ....H
  302 Class A Common ....R
  303 Class B Common ....R
310 TOTAL SHARES ....T

350 EARNINGS.......................................H
  356 Retained Earnings..........................R
  360 Current Earnings X
369 TOTAL EARNINGS ....T

Figure 6.10 Printout of chart of accounts

Fast Delivery Inc. FOR INSTRUCTIONAL USE ONLY
CHART OF ACCOUNTS Jan 1,1988

REVENUE		EXPENSE	
400 REVENUE	H	500 OPERATING COSTS	H
402 General Revenue	R	502 General Expense	L
406 General Delivery	R	506 Truck Rental	L
407 Special Delivery	R	507 Fuel	L
410 Freight Revenue	R	508 Insurance	L
412 TOTAL SERVICE REVENUE	T	509 Truck Repairs	L
		510 Permits	L
419 OTHER REVENUE	H	519 Total Trucking Costs	S
426 Insurance Income	R	520 Freight Expense	R
427 Interest Income	R	530 Wages	R
430 TOTAL OTHER REVENUE	T	531 FICA Expense	R
		532 FUTA Expense	R
		533 SUTA Expense	R
		534 SDI Expense	R
		536 Employee Benefits	R
		538 Warehouse Rent	R
		540 TOTAL OPERATING COSTS	T
		560 OVERHEAD	H
		561 Accounting	R
		562 Advertising	R
		563 Telephone	R
		570 TOTAL OPERATING COSTS	T

Figure 6.10 Printout of chart of accounts (continued)

Entering the Opening Balances

Many businesses start out with a manual accounting system and computerize later. It would be time consuming if not physically impossible to enter all of the transactions since the beginning of the business. Instead we can enter the current account balances that exist on the date that we change from a manual to a computerized accounting system. The Bedford Accounting System refers to this as historical data. In accounting terms it is known as the opening trial balance.

■ The Opening Trial Balance

The only accounts that require historical balances are those accounts to which we can post journal entries. These are the accounts marked with an L (left) or an R (right). The subtotals and totals for these accounts are calculated automatically by the program from the postable accounts. The heading accounts, of course, have no dollar balances.

Be sure that you have the opening trial balance of your company before you attempt to start entering the current account balances, and also make sure that you do not miss entering any of these amounts or the system will not balance. For our illustration we will use the trial balance shown in Figure 6.11.

```
        Fast Delivery Inc.
        Trial Balance
        December 31, 1987

                                           DR.              CR.

    104  Petty Cash                       300.00
    106  First Interstate - General     4,243.33
    120  Accounts Receivable               555.00
    126  Inventory                         100.00
    135  Prepaid Insurance                  55.67
    154  Buildings                      15,000.00
    164  Automotive                     26,000.00
    156  Accm Depn - Building                             2,500.00
    166  Accm Depn - Automotive                           5,500.00
    172  Land                           18,000.00
    220  Accounts Payable                                   260.00
    260  Sales Tax Payable                                1,019.66
    266  Short Term Debt                                  2,000.00
    275  Mortgage Payable                                22,500.00
    302  Class A Common                                   5,000.00
    303  Class B Common                                   2,000.00
    356  Retained Earnings                               23,474.34

                                       64,254.00         64,254.00
```

Figure 6.11 Trial balance

Notice that the total debits and credits for our opening trial balance are equal. This must always be the case as we are using the double entry accounting system described in Chapter 2.

To enter the opening trial balance into the Bedford program we start with the **Ledger** submenu. Notice that the second item in the menu is called **History**. Historical balances can only be entered or changed while the system is in the NOT READY mode. Once we change the general ledger to the READY mode the historical balances are no longer accessible.

To enter the historical balances, press

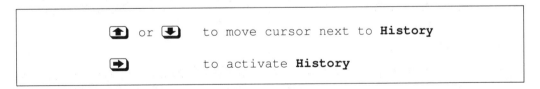

The chart of accounts will now appear to the right of the screen. Some of the accounts will have a square beside it, which indicates that this account is a postable account and can therefore accept a historical balance.

Type in the account number for which you want to enter a dollar balance. As soon as you do the display changes and you can enter the balance for that account. Once you have entered the proper amount, press the left arrow key to save it. Let's try it for the first account. Type

104	to enter account number
300 Ret	to enter the historical balance amount
⬅	to record the entry permanently

As you are entering account balances, the Bedford Accounting System will automatically put the amount into either the debit or credit column based on the type of entry. For example, the cash account is an asset which is usually a debit. If the cash balance is positive, simply enter the amount and the account will be debited. If you have a negative balance, meaning the account is overdrawn, you would enter the amount with a minus sign preceding it.

The reverse is true for liability accounts. For example, accounts payable is a liability and therefore usually a credit. If you wish to enter a credit to the account, you would add a positive number. If you wish to add a debit, you would add a negative number.

- **Practice Exercise**

Enter the remaining balances from the trial balance shown in Figure 6.11.

> NOTE: Be sure to enter the balances for accumulated depreciation as a negative amount (i.e., -2500 for account 156). These amounts are **contra assets,** which means they are negative adjustments to accounts that are normally debited. When you enter a negative adjustment to a debit, you must precede the amount with a minus sign.

Viewing the Trial Balance

Once the remaining historical balances have been entered, you should take a look at the trial balance. This will show that your debits and credits are equal to each other. If they aren't you have made a mistake somewhere. The trial balance will help you find it. Press

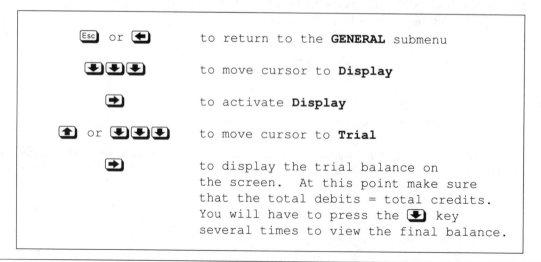

Esc or ⬅	to return to the **GENERAL** submenu
⬇⬇⬇	to move cursor to **Display**
➡	to activate **Display**
⬆ or ⬇⬇⬇	to move cursor to **Trial**
➡	to display the trial balance on the screen. At this point make sure that the total debits = total credits. You will have to press the ⬇ key several times to view the final balance.

When you have finished looking at the trial balance, press

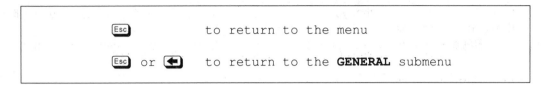

Esc   to return to the menu

Esc or ⬅   to return to the **GENERAL** submenu

Printing the Financial Statements

In the Bedford Accounting System, the financial statements are defined for you based on the chart of accounts that you set up earlier.

To print the financial statements, start from the **GENERAL** submenu and press

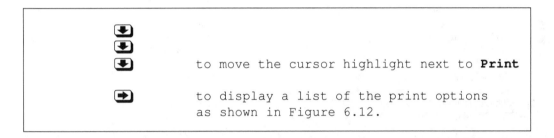

⬇
⬇
⬇   to move the cursor highlight next to **Print**

➡   to display a list of the print options
             as shown in Figure 6.12.

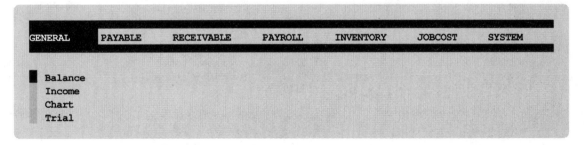

GENERAL	PAYABLE	RECEIVABLE	PAYROLL	INVENTORY	JOBCOST	SYSTEM

Balance
Income
Chart
Trial

Figure 6.12 Items for which printouts can be obtained

A firm's financial statements consist of two main statements: a balance sheet — a representation of the company's financial position at a particular time, and the income statement — a listing of revenues and expenses over a specific period of time. (See Chapter 2.)

Make sure your printer is connected and on-line. With the cursor next to the word **Balance**, press

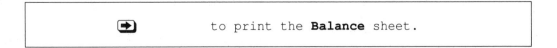

➡   to print the **Balance** sheet.

The message

processing

will appear next to the item that you want to print out. When the printing is finished you will be returned to the Print menu.

Repeat the procedure to print out the income statement. When you have finished, press

---

⬅ to return to the **GENERAL** submenu.

Fast Delivery Inc. FOR INSTRUCTIONAL USE ONLY
BALANCE SHEET Jan 1,1988

ASSETS			LIABILITIES	
CURRENT ASSETS			**CURRENT LIABILITIES**	
Petty Cash	300.00		Accounts Payable	260.00
First Interstate - General	4,243.33		FIT Payable	0.00
Bank B - Receivable	0.00		SIT Payable	0.00
Bank C - Payroll	0.00		FICA Payable	0.00
Cash: Total		4,543.33	FUTA Payable	0.00
Accounts Receivable		555.00	SUTA Payable	0.00
Advances Receivable		0.00	SDI Payable	0.00
Inventory		100.00	Local Tax Payable	0.00
Prepaid Insurance		55.67	Deduction A Payable	0.00
TOTAL CURRENT ASSETS		5,254.00	Deduction B Payable	0.00
			Deduction C Payable	0.00
FIXED ASSETS			Sales Tax Payable	1,019.66
Building	15,000.00		Short Term Debt	2,000.00
Accm Depn - Building	2,500.00-		TOTAL CURRENT LIABILITIES	3,279.66
Automotive	26,000.00			
Accm Depn - Automotive	5,500.00-		**LONG TERM DEBT**	
Subtotal		33,000.00	Mortgage Payable	22,500.00
Land		18,000.00	TOTAL LONG TERM DEBT	22,500.00
TOTAL FIXED ASSETS		51,000.00		
			TOTAL LIABILITIES	25,779.66
TOTAL ASSETS		56,254.00		
			EQUITY	
			SHARE CAPITAL	
			Class A Common	5,000.00
			Class B Common	2,000.00
			TOTAL SHARES	7,000.00
			EARNINGS	
			Retained Earnings	23,474.34
			Current Earnings	0.00
			TOTAL EARNINGS	23,474.34
			TOTAL EQUITY	30,474.34
			LIABILITIES AND EQUITY	56,254.00

Figure 6.13A Balance sheet

Fast Delivery Inc. FOR INSTRUCTIONAL USE ONLY
INCOME Jan 1,1988 TO Jan 1,1988

REVENUE		EXPENSE	
REVENUE		OPERATING COSTS	
General Revenue	0.00	General Expense	0.00
General Delivery	0.00	Truck Rental	0.00
Special Delivery	0.00	Fuel	0.00
Freight Revenue	0.00	Insurance	0.00
TOTAL SERVICE REVENUE	0.00	Truck Repairs	0.00
		Permits	0.00
OTHER REVENUE		Total Trucking Costs	0.00
Insurance Income	0.00	Freight Expense	0.00
Interest Income	0.00	Wages	0.00
TOTAL OTHER REVENUE	0.00	FICA Expense	0.00
		FUTA Expense	0.00
		SUTA Expense	0.00
TOTAL REVENUE	0.00	SDI Expense	0.00
		Employee Benefits	0.00
		Warehouse Rent	0.00
		TOTAL OPERATING COSTS	0.00
		OVERHEAD	
		Accounting	0.00
		Advertising	0.00
		Telephone	0.00
		TOTAL OPERATING COSTS	0.00
		TOTAL EXPENSE	0.00
		INCOME	0.00

Figure 6.13B Income statement

Changing to Ready Mode

Having entered your opening historical balances, you have completed the conversion process. You are almost ready to enter current transaction data into the Bedford Accounting System. All that remains is to change the general ledger from the NOT READY mode to the READY mode.

Keep in mind that once you change to the READY mode, you cannot return to the NOT READY mode to change any of the historical balances. Therefore, you must be absolutely sure that the data you entered is correct. To do so, you should compare your printed trial balance, income statement and balance sheet to those produced manually prior to conversion. If all numbers agree, then you can be fairly sure that your opening balances were correctly entered.

With the **GENERAL** submenu showing, press

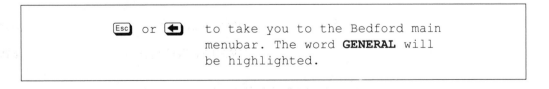

Esc or ← to take you to the Bedford main menubar. The word **GENERAL** will be highlighted.

Figure 6.14 The Bedford main menubar

Press

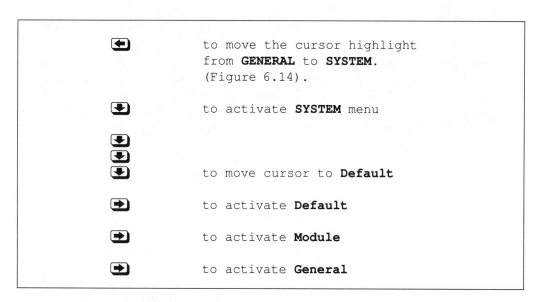

⬅	to move the cursor highlight from **GENERAL** to **SYSTEM**. (Figure 6.14).
⬇	to activate **SYSTEM** menu
⬇ ⬇ ⬇	to move cursor to **Default**
➡	to activate **Default**
➡	to activate **Module**
➡	to activate **General**

You have seen this display before (Figure 6.15). It shows the starting, conversion and finish date that you entered when you first started the Bedford Accounting System. At the bottom of this display is the word READY with **No** beside it. With your cursor highlight at the top menu item, press

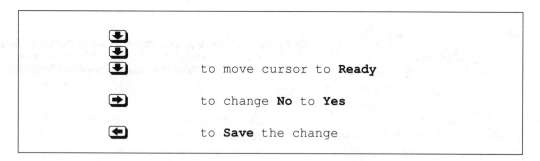

⬇ ⬇ ⬇	to move cursor to **Ready**
➡	to change **No** to **Yes**
⬅	to **Save** the change

The **SYSTEM** is now in READY mode (See Figure 6.15).

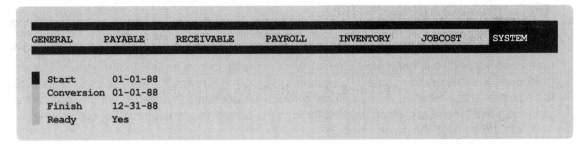

Figure 6.15 General ledger is in READY mode

NOTE: If the trial balance does not balance you will receive an error message (e.g Accounts not in logical order near account number ??? or General ledger debits exceed credits by $xx.xx). Before you can change the general ledger to READY mode you will have to make the necessary corrections. Check your chart of account entries or your historical balances to be sure they are correct.

Now return to the **GENERAL** module. Press

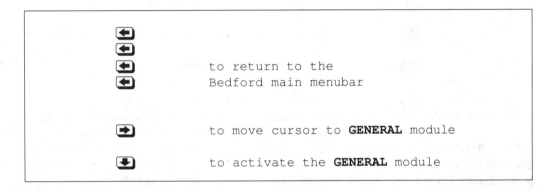

You will notice that the **GENERAL** submenu has changed (See Figure 6.16).

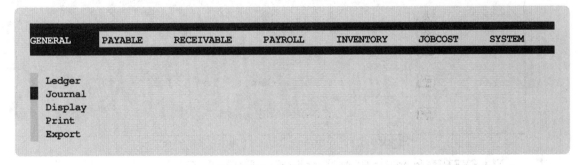

Figure 6.16 General ledger History item is now changed to Journal

The menu item **History** has been changed to the item **Journal**, which is the menu item that will be used to record all journal entries to the system.

ENTERING JOURNAL ENTRIES

All accounting entries are made through a series of journal entries. As discussed in Chapter 2, the general journal is commonly used for special types of entries like adjusting or reversing entries. It is possible to enter all business transactions as journal entries to the general ledger accounts. But that would not make full use of the program. Transactions for common items such as sales and cash receipts will be entered through the accounts receivable module, purchases and cash disbursements will be entered through the accounts payable module, and payroll transactions through the payroll module.

Let's make the following entry:

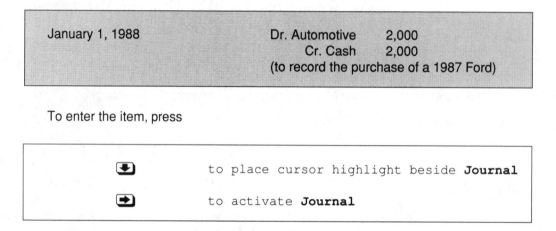

January 1, 1988	Dr. Automotive 2,000
	Cr. Cash 2,000
	(to record the purchase of a 1987 Ford)

To enter the item, press

	to place cursor highlight beside **Journal**
	to activate **Journal**

The journal entry menu will now appear. The cursor highlight is next to **Comment**, with the cursor flashing to the left of the dotted line prompting you to enter the necessary data (See Figure 6.17).

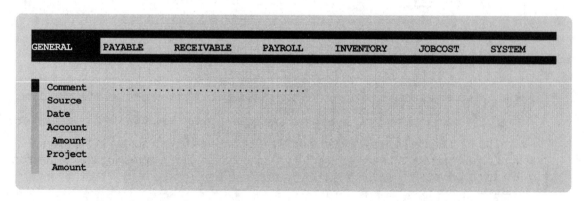

Figure 6.17 General ledger journal entry screen

1987 Ford Ret	the **Comment** is used to indicate a memo about the entry, in this case, 1987 Ford. The memo must be able to fit in the space provided.
1098 Ret	the **Source** area is used to enter information as to the source of the transaction. This could be a journal entry page reference, a check number or a source document such as an invoice number. Let's assume we paid for the vehicle with check number 1098.
010188	to enter the **Date** the transaction took place, January 1, 1988. The range of this entry can only be between the conversion date and the using date. The range of possible dates will appear on the right side of the screen.
164	to enter the **Account** number to distribute the entry to. Since this is an automotive asset it has to go to account number 164. Once you enter the number it will be displayed so you know that you didn't make a mistake in entering the account number.
2000 Ret	to enter the **Amount** to be allocated to that particular account, $2,000. Notice that you do not enter the amount with commas or dollar signs. You would, however, enter the period to indicate cents. Press the Ret key.

The F2 function key now appears on the top right side of your screen in the main menubar highlight. You can review the entry you made at any time by pressing the F2 function key. Do so now. Press

F2	to display particulars about the entry

You will see that the amount $2,000 is listed under debits. As yet there is no amount under credits. To return to the journal entry screen, press

F2	to return to journal entry screen

After you entered the dollar amount and pressed the ENTER key the cursor highlight moved next to the word **Account**. The cursor itself is flashing at the beginning of the dotted line, prompting you to enter the other account (double entry accounting) to which this entry must be credited. This would be account number 106, First Interstate Bank. Press

```
    106              to enter the Account number to which
                     this journal entry is credited

   -2000 [Ret]       to enter Amount of purchase
```

The journal entry now balances. Check by pressing F2 (See Figure 16.18).

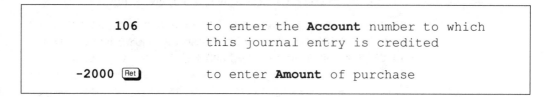

Figure 6.18 Pressing F2 shows the journal entry (J1) pertaining to the Ford purchase. Debits and credits are in balance.

You can only make an entry in the Bedford Accounting System to one account at a time. If you have two entries to make, each affecting the same account, you must make a complete separate entry for each account.

A Review of Debits and Credits

It might help to briefly review the concept of debits and credits and how Bedford handles them. Assets are normally on the left side of the ledger while liabilities and equities are on the right side. Similarly, expense accounts are on the left side of the ledger while revenues are on the right side.

The Bedford program views accounts as being increased when a positive value is entered or as being decreased when a negative value is entered. For example, an increase to cash — an asset — will require a positive entry. In this case a positive entry represents a debit. In another example, when accounts payable is increased — a liability account — a positive entry is also required. The positive entry in this case represents a credit.

Keep the following rules in mind when working with Bedford.

Asset and expense accounts are on the left hand side of the ledger. For these accounts, a debit is a positive entry and a credit is a negative entry.

Liabilities, equities and revenues are negative account categories. For these accounts, a credit is a positive entry, while a debit is a negative entry.

Contra asset accounts, such as accumulated depreciation, and contra revenue accounts, such as sales discounts, are treated in reverse fashion and therefore an increase in these accounts requires a negative entry.

Changing the Journal Entry

Even after you have entered both the debits and credits you may still make changes to the journal entry as long as you haven't pressed the left arrow key to save the entry permanently. If you wish to change any of the items in the journal entry before then, merely type in the account number associated with the entry that you made. This will display the amount again, at which time you can change it.

Accepting the Journal Entry

When you are satisfied that the entry is correct, make sure your cursor highlight is next to the word **Account**. Press

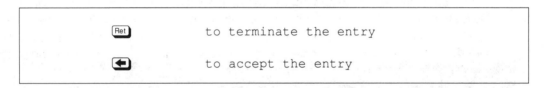

```
[Ret]              to terminate the entry

[←]                to accept the entry
```

Now the entry has been saved and can no longer be changed. It will be posted automatically to the account and will update the general ledger.

■ *Practice Exercise*

Make the following journal entry:

```
January 1, 1988   Dr. General Expense              125.00
                      Cr. First Interstate - General            125.00
                  (check #1099 for payment of paper supplies)
```

Reviewing the Entry

To review the above entries, be sure you are in the **GENERAL** submenu. Press

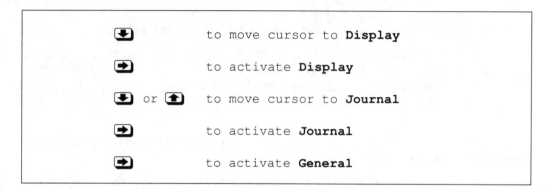

⬇	to move cursor to **Display**
➡	to activate **Display**
⬇ or ⬆	to move cursor to **Journal**
➡	to activate **Journal**
➡	to activate **General**

Now enter dates for which you want to see the entries.

| 010188 | Beginning date |
| 010188 | Ending date |

The journal entries for the appropriate date will be displayed on the screen as in Figure 6.19. This feature allows you to review all of the entries made for a given date or range of dates.

GENERAL	PAYABLE	RECEIVABLE	PAYROLL	INVENTORY	JOBCOST debits	SYSTEM credits
01-01-88 J1		1987 Ford, 1098				
		164 Automotive			2,000.00	–
		106 First Interstate - General			–	2,000.00
01-01-88 J2		Paper supplies, 1099				
		502 General Expense			125.00	–
		106 First Interstate - General			–	125.00

Figure 6.19 Journal entries display

If you do not wish to look at the entries for a specified date, you can instead look at the entries made during the current entry session. Press

Esc	to return to the previous menu
⬆ or ⬇	to move the cursor highlight to **Session**
➡	to view the entries made in this session

Since you only made two entries, the display will be identical to Figure 6.19. After reviewing the display, press

Esc (several times)	to return to the Bedford main menubar.

MAINTAINING AN AUDIT TRAIL

It is important to establish an audit trail for all accounting entries made. An audit trail is a printout of all the entries made to the General Ledger module during a particular session.

To do so, start from the **GENERAL** submenu. Press

⬇	to activate **GENERAL** module
⬇ ⬇ ⬇	to choose **Print**
➡	to activate **Print**
⬆	to choose **Journal**
➡	to activate **Journal**
➡	to activate **General**
010188	to enter **Start** date for session
010188	to enter **Finish** date for the session. The cursor automatically moves to **Print**. Make sure your printer is connected and on-line to receive data from the computer.
➡	to activate **Print**

The journal entries for the session will now be printed. Store the printout of these entries in a binder marked **GENERAL JOURNAL ENTRIES**. You can then use that file to review any of the entries made in the event that the computer should crash or if the disk is destroyed.

EXPORTING GENERAL LEDGER REPORTS

The Bedford Accounting System has the ability to create not only the reports — balance sheet, income statement, general ledger, journal entries, chart of account or trial balance — but also to transfer those reports into a spreadsheet file or a text file.

Exporting these files to a spreadsheet, for example, can be very useful to calculate various ratios or to develop various graphs of the financial data. (Bedford has a utility program to develop graphs. See Chapter 13.) Accounting data can also be exported as a text file for inclusion in a report prepared with a word processor.

Remember that you must set the default file format. If you want to export the same data to two types of files, spreadsheet and text, you would have to reset the default file format each time.

To set the **Default** extension begin at the Bedford main menubar. Press

➡️	to move cursor highlight over the word, **SYSTEM**
⬇️	to activate the **SYSTEM** module
⬇️ ⬇️ ⬇️	to move cursor to **Default**
➡️	to activate **Default**
⬆️	to move cursor to **Export**
➡️	to activate **Export**
⬇️	to move cursor to **Extension**
➡️	to activate **Extension**

You can now see the various file extensions which indicate the type of file to which you can export data. The default is WKS, which is the file format for the Lotus 1-2-3 spreadsheet version 1A. If you want a version 2 compatible file, you would have to change the extension to WK1. Other choices are Lotus Symphony and text files. Set the extension to the one required for your spreadsheet. Then press

```
⬅          to return to main menubar
⬅
⬅

➡ or ⬅     to move cursor to GENERAL

⬇          to activate GENERAL

⬆          to move to Export

➡          to activate Export
```

Now choose the item that you want to export. Let's export the income statement. Press

```
⬇          to choose Income

➡          to activate Income

010188     to enter the Start date
           of transactions to be included
           in the report

010188     to enter the Finish date
           of transactions to be included
           in the report.

➡          to activate Export
```

If you want to actually read the exported file into your spreadsheet, end this session of Bedford and call up your spreadsheet. The file will be located in the same subdirectory or on the same disk as your Bedford files. If you use Lotus 1-2-3 as your spreadsheet program, for example, it would look as shown in Figure 6.20.

```
Fast Delivery Inc.  Income Statement  Jan 1,1988 TO Jan 1,1988

        REVENUE
400     REVENUE
402     General Revenue                                     0.00
406     General Delivery                                    0.00
407     Special Delivery                                    0.00
410     Freight Revenue                                     0.00
412     TOTAL SERVICE REVENUE                               0.00
419     OTHER REVENUE
426     Insurance Income                                    0.00
427     Interest Income                                     0.00
430     TOTAL OTHER REVENUE                                 0.00
        TOTAL REVENUE                                       0.00
        EXPENSE
500     OPERATING COSTS
502     General Expense                   125.00
506     Truck Rental                        0.00
507     Fuel                                0.00
508     Insurance                           0.00
509     Truck Repairs                       0.00
510     Permits                             0.00
519     Total Trucking Costs                              125.00
520     Freight Expense                                     0.00
530     Wages                                               0.00
531     FICA Expense                                        0.00
532     FUTA Expense                                        0.00
533     SUTA Expense                                        0.00
534     SDI Expense                                         0.00
536     Employee Benefits                                   0.00
538     Warehouse Rent                                      0.00
540     TOTAL OPERATING COSTS                             125.00
560     OVERHEAD
561     Accounting                                          0.00
562     Advertising                                         0.00
563     Telephone                                           0.00
570     TOTAL OVERHEAD COSTS                                0.00
        TOTAL EXPENSE                                     125.00
        INCOME                                          (125.00)
```

Figure 6.20 The Bedford income statement exported into a Lotus 1-2-3 spreadsheet. Note that all balances are 0 except for the one supply expense entry that you made earlier.

FINISHING THE SESSION

You have now completed the general ledger tutorial. You should finish this session to save your data to disk. After activating the **Finish** command you will be returned to the disk operating system.

To finish this session, press

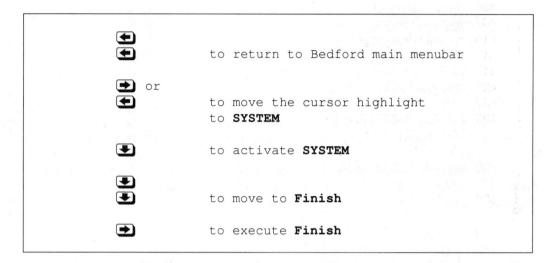

In the following chapters you should always end each session with the **Finish** command. When beginning each chapter in this tutorial start the Bedford accounting program as described earlier in this chapter.

BACKING UP YOUR DATA FILES

Now that you have started your own set of books with the Bedford Accounting System, backup your data. (Review backup procedure in Chapter 4 and 5.) Keep the backup disks so you can start each chapter from the beginning if you wish.

BEDFORD PRACTICE SET
AMERICANA DECORATING SALES AND SERVICE INC.

Americana Decorating Sales and Service Inc. is a practice set covering all six of the Bedford accounting system modules:

1. General Ledger
2. Accounts Payable
3. Accounts Receivable
4. Payroll
5. Inventory
6. Job Cost

You will keep Americana's books for the six-month period July to December. By the end of December, you should have a full understanding of how all six modules apply in a practical business situation.

Americana Decorating Sales & Service Inc., is a custom home decorating and sales business. It is a close (non-public) corporation chartered by and operating in the State of Oregon. The store has five departments:

Sales - Paint
Sales - Wallpaper
Sales - Fabric
Decorating Service
Delivery Service

All sales and purchases are on credit with discounts available for early payment. All sales of merchandise are subject to a 7% sales tax. The sales-tax percentage does not represent the current rate, if any, of the operating state; it is only a working figure to demonstrate how sales tax would be treated if applicable.

The fiscal year for the business is January 1 to December 31 with June 30 (conversion date) the date on which the manual accounting system was converted to the Bedford system. Each month, inventory is counted to calculate the change from the end of previous fiscal period. A balance sheet is generated monthly to show year-to-date financial position. An income statement is generated for each month's activity and for the year-to-date.

Part I — General Ledger

In PART I of the VI PART series covering all Bedford Accounting System modules you will establish the chart of accounts and enter a series of business transactions into the General Ledger. Because this is a continuing case covering all of the Bedford modules, it is essential to save each part's data so that you can continue in sequence without starting from the beginning again.

OBJECTIVE

After completing this practice set for the GENERAL ledger module you should have a good introduction to computerized accounting using the Bedford Accounting System. You should be able to:

1. Create new company files.

2. Enter necessary defaults and integration accounts.

3. Create General Ledger chart of accounts.

4. Enter Historical data to accounts.

5. Set the System to Ready.

6. Enter daily transactions using only the GENERAL MODULE.

7. Print Journals, Ledgers, Trial Balance, and Financial Statements.

INSTRUCTION: 1. Create company files
                     Start Date: 01-01-88
                     Conversion Date: 06-30-88
                     Finish Date: 12-31-88
                     Remember to go to Finish after entering dates

INSTRUCTION: 2. Verify General Defaults
                     - Check to see proper dates have been stored.
                     Remember do not set to Ready
                     Enter company name in System Default.
                          Americana Decorating Sales and Service Inc.
                          123 Bedford Avenue
                          Portland, Oregon
                          89767-5435

INSTRUCTION: 3. Erase all integration accounts for Payable, Receivable and Payroll. Note:
                     You will keep Retained Earnings as 356 and Current Earnings as 360.

INSTRUCTION: 4. Create GENERAL module Chart of Accounts using your own account
                     numbers and enter the historical balances given for 06-30-88 that would
                     display the following financial statements.
                     *Note: You must leave three account numbers free between accounts
                     Opening Inventory 01-01-88 and Purchases - Paint so you can add three
                     new accounts in Part V Tutorial*

Americana Decorating Sales & Service Inc. FOR INSTRUCTIONAL USE ONLY
BALANCE SHEET Jun 30,1988

ASSETS			LIABILITIES		
CURRENT ASSETS			**CURRENT LIABILITIES**		
Petty Cash	100.00		Accounts Payable		5,768.90
Bank of America - General	15,234.67		FIT Payable	2,431.22	
Bank of America - Payroll	0.00		FICA Payable	1,851.16	
Cash: Total		15,334.67	FUTA Payable	0.00	
Advances Receivable		0.00	TOTAL FEDERAL TAXES PAY.		4,282.38
Accounts Receivable		21,675.43	SIT Payable	944.03	
Inventory - Paint	24,536.75		SUTA Payable	0.00	
Inventory - Wallpaper	18,700.76		TOTAL STATE TAXES PAYABLE		944.03
Inventory - Fabric	42,389.75		Company Pension Plan Pay.		616.23
TOTAL INVENTORY		85,627.26	Medical Plan Pay.		270.00
Office Supplies		675.34	Short Term Loan		6,000.00
Prepaid Insurance		2,400.00	Sales Tax Payable		2,216.35
TOTAL CURRENT ASSETS		125,712.70	TOTAL CURRENT LIABILITIES		20,097.89
FIXED ASSETS			**LONG-TERM DEBT**		
Buildings	210,000.00		Mortgage Payable		79,850.69
Accumulated Depr.-Building	10,500.00-		TOTAL LONG-TERM DEBT		79,850.69
Automotive	13,320.00				
Accumulated Depr. - Auto.	1,110.00-				
SUBTOTAL		211,710.00	TOTAL LIABILITIES		99,948.58
Land		105,500.00			
TOTAL FIXED ASSETS		317,210.00			
			EQUITY		
TOTAL ASSETS		442,922.70			
			SHARES		
			Class A Common		5,000.00
			Class B Common		9,000.00
			TOTAL SHARES		14,000.00
			EARNINGS		
			Retained Earnings		232,047.63
			Current Earnings		96,926.49
			TOTAL EARNINGS		328,974.12
			TOTAL EQUITY		342,974.12
			LIABILITIES AND EQUITY		442,922.70

Americana Decorating Sales & Service Inc. FOR INSTRUCTIONAL USE ONLY
INCOME Jun 30,1988 TO Jun 30,1988

REVENUE

SALES REVENUE		
Sales - Paint	61,987.65	
Sales - Wallpaper	43,098.75	
Sales - Fabric	101,574.89	
TOTAL SALES REVENUE		206.661.29
Sales Ret & Allow - Paint	3,457.89-	
Sales R & A Wallpaper	4,653.23-	
Sales R & A Fabric	5,234.87-	
TOTAL SALES RETURNS & ALL.		13,345.99-
Sales Discounts - Paint	1,254.78	
Sales Discount - Wallpaper	1,189.76-	
Sales Discounts - Fabric	897.65-	
TOTAL SALES DISCOUNTS		3,342.19-
TOTAL NET SALES REVENUE		189,973.11
SERVICE REVENUE		
Decorating Service	85,679.67	
Delivery Service	23,876.05	
TOTAL SERVICE REVENUE		109,555.72
OTHER REVENUE		
Interest Income	1,436.86	
TOTAL OTHER REVENUE		1,436.86
TOTAL REVENUE		300,965.69

EXPENSE

COST OF GOODS SOLD		
Opening Inventory 01-01-88		45,236.89
Purchases - Paint	46,897.65	
Purchases - Wallpaper	34,789.66	
Purchases - Fabric	54,890.75	
Freight Expense	4,765.92	
Purchase Ret & All. - Paint	3,309.86-	
Purchase R & A - Wallpaper	2,309.87-	
purchase R & A - Fabric	1,546.90-	
Purchase Discounts - Paint	1,256.74-	
Purchase Disc. - Wallpaper	987.56-	
Purchase Discount - Fabric	1,456.90-	
NET TOTAL		130,476.15
Ending Inventory 06-30-88		85,627.26-
TOTAL COST OF GOODS SOLD		90,085.78
OPERATING EXPENSES		
Salary Expense		73,948.02
FICA Expense	5,553.48	
FUTA Expense	280.00	
SUTA Expense	560.00	
TOTAL PAYROLL TAXES EXP.		6,393.48
Fuel Expense	6,542.98	
Insurance Expense	2,400.00	
Repair Expense	1,232.59	
Permits Expense	555.65	
TOTAL AUTOMOTIVE EXPENSES		10,731.22
TOTAL OPERATING EXPENSES		912,072.72
OVERHEAD		
Office Supplies Expense		980.75
Telephone Expense		1,324.67
Advertising Expense		1,765.87
Utilities Expense		2,135.67
Depreciation Exp.-Building		10,500.00
Depreciation Exp. -Auto		1,110.00
TOTAL OVERHEAD		17,816.96
OTHER EXPENSES		
Interest Expense		4,808.85
Bank Charges		254.89
TOTAL OTHER EXPENSES		5,063.74
TOTAL EXPENSE		204,039.20
INCOME		96,926.49

INSTRUCTION: 5.   Set the SYSTEM>Default>Module>General>:
Start   01-01-88
Conversion   06-30-88
Finish   12-31-88
Ready   Yes

INSTRUCTION: 6.   Enter the following source document symbols using the first number given as your starting point for transactions.

P234	Purchase Invoice	For all purchases of assets, costs and expenses on credit.
S405	Sales Invoice	For all sales on credit.
R145	Receipt	For all customer payments on account.
Ch345	Cheque	For all payments made by Canadiana.
Dm45	Debit Memo	For all vendor returns & allowances.
Cm56	Credit Memo	For all customer returns & allowances.
DN	Demand Note	For all bank loans **NO SOURCE NUMBER REQUIRED**.
M73	Memo	For all other transactions .

Note: No source document is required for month end adjusting entries.

INSTRUCTION: 7. Enter the following transactions, using only the GENERAL ledger module, for the month of July.

July
1. Paid Fashion Magazine for advertising, $150.00. Ch345.

3. Received on account from John Davidson, $3,458.56. R145

6. Sold merchandise on account to Mary Winston: paint, $789.56; wallpaper, $1,232.40; fabric, $5,678.34; plus sales tax of $539.02; total, $8,239.32. S405.

8. Purchased merchandise on account from Interior Supply: paint, $4,563.89; wallpaper, $3,547.75; fabric, $4,538.78; total $12,650.42. P234.

11. Paid on account to Williams Paint, $1,392.61, covering invoice for $1,435.68 less purchase discount - paint, $43.07. Ch346.

11. Paid on account to Rainbow World Inc., $3,957.14, covering invoice for $4,333.22 less purchase discount - wallpaper, $162.30; less purchase discount - fabric, $213.78. Ch347.

12. Sold merchandise and service on account to J. Gonzalez: paint $789.78; wallpaper, $1,423.90; fabric, $4,563.78; decorating service, $4,123.23; plus sales tax of $474.42; total, $11,375.11. S406.

15. Paid Internal Revenue Service withholding taxes: Federal Income Tax, $2,431.22; Federal Insurance, $1,851.16; total, $4,282.38. Ch348.

15. Paid State Income Tax Payable, $944.03. Ch 349

15. Paid Bell Tel. phone bill, $145.24. Ch350.

16. Paid Texaco Oil Co. gasoline bill, $64.84. Ch351.

16. Record bank transfer from General to Payroll account, $3,697.40. M73

16. Paid middle of month payroll advances, $3,697.40. Ch352-6.

18. Sold merchandise on account to Carolyn Campbell: paint, $1,320.76; wallpaper, $1,254.89; fabric, $5,367.89; plus sales tax of $556.04; total, $8,499.58. S407.

20. Paid Northwestern Hydro Co. utilities bill, $329.65. Ch357.

20. Paid provincial sales tax to State of Oregon, $2,216.35 Ch358.

21. Received on account from Rob Chung, $4,527.56, covering invoice for $5,042.91 less sales discount: paint, $124.67; wallpaper, $165.34, fabric, $225.34. R146.

24. Granted credit to Mary Winston for merchandise returns: paint, $42.30; wallpaper, $56.35; fabric, $230.75; plus sales tax of $23.06; total, $352.46. Cm56.

25. Returned merchandise to Interior Supply: paint, $345.67; wallpaper, $235.89; fabric, $154.89; total, $736.45. Dm45.

29. Paid company pension payable to Merrill Lynch, $616.23. Ch359.

29. Paid medical plan payable to Blue Cross, $270.00. Ch360.

31. Recorded bank transfer from General to Payroll account, $3,440.21. M74.

31. Paid month end payroll, $3,913.76, covering: Salary Expense, $12,324.67; less deductions of Federal Income Tax, $2,431.22; Federal Insurance, $925.58; State Income Tax, $944.03; Company Pension, $616.23,; Medical Plan, $270.00; Advances Receivable, $3,697.40. Ch361-5.

31. Recorded employer's payroll FICA Expense, $925.58. M75.

31. Recorded Bank Reconciliation adjustments: Short Term Loan Payment, $253.46; Mortgage Payment, $345.78; Interest Expense, $604.52; Bank Charges Expense, $53.23; Interest Income, $135.67; net total bank debit, $1,121.32. M76.

31. Recorded adjusting entry for insurance expense incurred, $400.00.

31. Recorded adjusting entry for office supplies expense incurred, $145.78.

31. Recorded adjusting entry for estimated depreciation expense incurred: Building, $1,750.00; Automotive, $185.00.

31. Recorded ending inventory change from end of last period, decreasing: paint, $347.78; wallpaper, $435.65; fabric, $542.50; total, $1,325.93. Note: Modify the description of account Ending Inventory 06-30-88 to Inventory Change July 1-31 before entering transaction.

INSTRUCTION: 8.   Print General Journal entries from 07-01-88 to 07-31-88.
Print Income Statement for 07-01-88 to 07-31-88.
Modify the description of Inventory Change July 1-31 to Ending Inventory 07-31-88.
Print Income Statement for 01-01-88 to 07-31-88.
Print Balance Sheet for 07-31-88.

Chapter 7
ACCOUNTS PAYABLE

Chapter 7
ACCOUNTS PAYABLE

PREVIEW

In Chapter 7 you will learn about the accounts payable subledger and how a subledger in general can benefit the accounting function. After that you will look at the accounts payable function in some detail before actually discussing the conversion process from a manual accounts payable system to the computerized Bedford Accounting System. You will learn how to enter vendor accounts and the historical balances for each vendor. You also learn how to delete vendor accounts, as well as how to modify vendor information. You will then display on the monitor screen, data previously entered into the Bedford Accounting System, and also examine the various printouts available through the accounts payable module. Then you will make the accounts payable module ready for entering current transactions. Finally you will enter a number of journal transactions to record invoices and payments. You are also informed about the importance of providing an audit trail and creating backup copies of your data files.

OBJECTIVES

After completing this chapter you should be able to explain:

1. The importance of an accounting subledger;

2. What the accounts payable module does and how it can help in transaction processing;

3. What has to be done before you can convert a manual accounts payable system to a computerized one — preparing a vendor list and current balances;

4. How to enter vendor accounts and historical balances;

5. How to add or delete a vendor account and how to modify vendor account information;

6. How to make the accounts payable module READY;

7. How to display information about vendor accounts entered into the system and how to prepare various printouts;

8. How to enter journal transactions — purchases and payments — into the accounts payable module;

9. Why it is important to have an audit trail and how to prepare one.

The general ledger is the main ledger in any accounting system. It establishes the trial balance and provides the information for both the balance sheet and the income statement. Why then do we have to be concerned with other modules?

THE PURPOSE OF SUBLEDGERS

It is possible to operate an accounting system using only the general ledger. It is, however, much more convenient and informative to use a subledger for the following reasons:

1. they help to speed up the data entry process into the accounting system.

2. they provide useful information.

Increases Speed of Data Entry

We discussed in the previous chapter that all journal entries are made up of a series of debits and credits that in total equal each other (double-entry bookkeeping). These entries are then posted individually into the general ledger. This method is very cumbersome and slow.

By using subledgers you can speed data entry substantially. Certain types of entries are very similar. For example, when making journal entries for cash disbursements (payments by check) you start to notice a pattern. If you pay the telephone bill for $150 with a check from the bank account, the entry is:

```
Dr. Telephone Expense          $150.00
    Cr. Bank                            $150.00
```

If you pay a salary to one of your employees, the entry is:

```
Dr. Salary Expense             $600.00
    Cr. Bank                            $600.00
```

As you can see, each cash disbursement entry has a corresponding credit entry to Bank, because you are paying by check. Since all credits are to the Bank, why not enter them as one total. This allows you to use the **cash disbursements** portion of a subledger to enter all check payments as debits. At the end of each entry, the total amount debited can be credited to Bank, which is the common credit entry. Entries in other subledgers — payable, receivable, payroll and inventory — are treated in a similar manner.

Provides Useful Information

The second advantage of a subledger is that it can provide useful information about certain aspects of a business. The account balances in the general ledger can be analyzed. For example, the balance in accounts receivable, a control account in the general ledger, only tells us how much money our credit customers owe us, nothing else.

For proper management of accounts receivables, however, we need more information. We would want to know such things as:

-   who owes us the money?
-   what phone number to call to enquire about payment of overdue accounts?
-   who to contact?
-   when to expect to receive the money?
-   how long it has been since the charge was made?
-   who to trust to charge on account?

We can get all of this additional information by using an accounts receivable subledger, which allows us to keep track of such information. We will discuss the accounts receivable subledger in more detail in Chapter 8.

Subledger Listing

To ensure that the subledger agrees with the appropriate control account in the balance sheet, we usually make a listing of the components on a regular basis — each month or each week. This listing can provide us with important information. For example, if we had a balance in accounts payable of $3,150, the control account in the general ledger — accounts payable — would tell us the total amount that we have to pay out, but it wouldn't tell us who receives the various payments. However, an accounts payable subledger provides us with all the following important information:

Acme Delivery	$ 145.00
Falcon's Hardware	116.00
Hallmark Cards	66.00
Jello Desserts	214.00
Land Grow Carriers	1,455.00
Rancho Communications	919.00
Western Freight Carriers	235.00
	$ 3,150.00

The total of the subledger listing must agree with the control account, accounts payable, in the general ledger. Without this listing you could never be sure if your accounts payable were in fact paid, or who to pay it to.

Each of the Bedford Accounting System modules provide the above information. As you work through each chapter that describes one of the modules, you should become very familiar with what each module does, what kinds of entries are included in each module, what the various subledger listings are, and what the control account in the general ledger is.

THE ACCOUNTS PAYABLE SUBLEDGER

Accounts payable is the first of the subledgers in the Bedford Accounting System that we will look at. This module is used to record all credit purchases made by the firm — the amount of the purchase, the date of the purchase, the name of the supplier, and the account to which the purchase should be charged. The module is also used to record cash disbursements made as payments to the various suppliers. In this way, the payables listing will provide you with a record of who the company owes money to and for how long the money has been owing. This information can then be used to determine what the cash requirements of the company will be over the next few months.

Discounts

The information available from the accounts payable ledger can also be used to take advantage of cash payment discounts. Some creditors allow a discount if the invoice is paid within a certain period of time. While the Bedford Accounting System does not keep track of the companies allowing discounts or the amount of the discount, it will keep track of the time since purchase. A manager usually knows which companies will give the discount. By reviewing the **aged listing** —

the list that indicates the number of days since the purchase was made — the payment can be made within the discount period.

Discounts are usually stated in the following fashion:

2/10/n/30 (to be read "two, ten, net, thirty")

This means that if the bill is paid within 10 days, the purchaser may reduce the amount owing by 2 percent (i.e., 2/10). This is intended to entice the buyer to make payment quickly so the supplier can get the cash. If the bill is not paid within the 10 days, the net amount of the purchase is due in 30 days (i.e., n/30).

Credit Rating

Good control over accounts payable will also ensure that the company maintains a good credit rating. A company using a manual accounting system may forget to pay a bill or misplace it after it is recorded. The accounts payable module will not allow this to happen because outstanding bills are listed each time payments are made.

A good credit standing is important. It may allow you to negotiate a discount with the creditor. It may also mean that you get a product in short supply, instead of a competitor who uses trade credit to finance his business. Suppliers shun such firms because they have difficulty collecting their money on time.

OPEN ITEM ACCOUNTING

The Bedford Accounting System uses the **open item method of accounting** for accounts payable and accounts receivable as opposed to the balance forward method. The open item method keeps track of all individual invoices together with any payments made on behalf of that invoice. This tells you how much is owed to a specific vendor, or how much is owed to you by a customer. Furthermore, it tells you which invoices are unpaid or owing. Eventually, when the invoices are fully paid, you can either retain this information or clear it out of the system. This is known as **purging**. If you purge it, the information is lost forever except for the print outs that you made along the way. In most cases this is all that is necessary.

The ability to identify specific invoices is the key to good internal control. This is why the open item method is superior to the balance forward method, which only accounts for the total owing and not for specific invoices. The open item method would be difficult to implement under a manual accounting system because of the many transactions that are required, but for a computerized accounting system such as Bedford implementation is simple.

The open item method of accounting for invoices payable specifically provides the following benefits.

Late Payments Charges

The open item method provides enough detail to allow you to calculate interest charges on overdue accounts receivable. Similarly, you can identify which of your invoices have been paid and which have not. By promptly paying your invoices when due you can also avoid paying interest charges.

If you are charged with interest, you would enter it into the system as an invoice and pay it along with the regular payment. In this case, you would record the charge with a debit to interest expense.

Discounts

The open item method also provides sufficient detail to allow you to take advantage of discounts offered by vendors for early payment. These can be considered as negative invoices and in effect reduce the amount owing. You would credit the account, "Discounts Taken," which is a revenue account. Alternatively, you can consider it as an expense reduction and credit a **contra expense** account.

Bad Debts

The open item method can also identify invoices that have not been paid for one reason or another. As a supplier, you would record this in accounts receivable as a negative invoice with the debit entered into **bad debt** expense.

Prepayments

There are times when you or your customers may be required to make a prepayment for goods or services that will be received at some point in the future. To have this item appear in your records you would enter it as a negative invoice, using the check number as the invoice number.

COMPUTERIZING ACCOUNTS PAYABLE

Converting from a manual to a computerized accounts payable system is much easier if the process is approached in a logical manner. The following discussion will explain what should be done before making the actual conversion.

Organizing Vendor Records

As with the General Ledger module, before you can begin to convert your accounts payable to the Bedford Accounting System you must organize your existing data and have it ready for entry to the system. There are three steps to organizing your data properly:

- *Prepare a Vendor Listing*

Prepare a complete listing of the vendors that provide you with credit when purchasing from them. The list should include the name, street address, city, state, zip code and telephone number. There is no need to assign customer numbers to this listing as the Bedford Accounting System will do this task for you. The program will then sort the customers into an alphabetical listing for easy access.

- *List Outstanding Invoices*

Make a listing of all unpaid invoices for each vendor at the time of conversion. The listing should include the date of the invoice, the invoice number and the amount owing. If you have made any partial payments against these invoices, they should also be listed. The following is an example.

Invoice or check number	date	item	amount
Acme Supply Company			
123	12-15-87	invoice	$ 123.44
4345	12-16-87	partial payment	- 23.44
456	12-31-87	invoice	50.00
			$ 150.00
Didyk, Edwards			
124	12-18-87	invoice	140.00
411	12-30-87	partial payment	- 30.00
			$110.00
Total accounts payable (to agree to control)			$260.00

- *Agree to Control Account*

Total all outstanding amounts and make sure that this amount agrees with the amount showing in the accounts payable account, the control account in the general ledger. It is important to start off with the payables listing equalling the amount in the control account. The two have to balance at the start.

Beginning the Accounts Payable Conversion

With the above information complete you are ready to begin the Accounts Payable Conversion. Start the Bedford Accounting System.

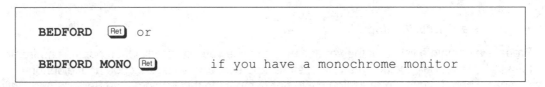

After a few seconds, the opening Bedford menu will appear, as shown in Figure 7.1.

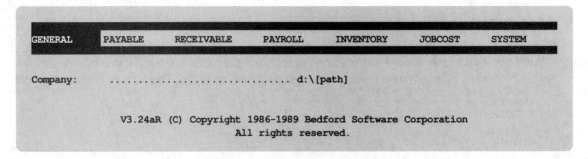

Figure 7.1 Bedford opening menu

Enter the location of the data files as discussed in Chapter 5:

```
B:\FASTDEL          where B: is the floppy drive and
                    FASTDEL is the subdirectory containing
                    the data files

C:\FASTDEL          where C: is the hard drive and
                    FASTDEL is the subdirectory containing
                    the data files
```

Next you are asked to enter the **Using** date.

```
010188              enter the USING date
```

The Bedford Accounting System main menu will now appear as shown in Figure 7.2 with the word **GENERAL** highlighted in inverse video.

Figure 7.2 Bedford main menubar

Move the cursor highlight over the word **PAYABLE**. Press

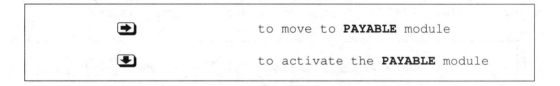

You will now see the accounts **PAYABLE** submenu on your screen as shown in Figure 7.3.

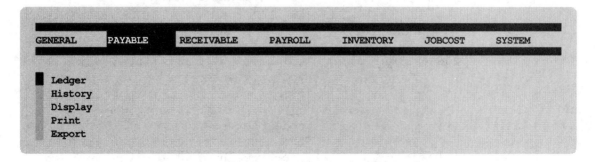

Figure 7.3 Accounts PAYABLE submenu

You are now ready to begin the accounts payable conversion.

▪ *Entering Vendors into the Payable Module*

Using the vendor listing that you created previously you will now have to enter these vendors into the accounts **PAYABLE** module. Let's enter information for the first vendor, Acme Supply Company, as shown below.

<u>Vendor Number</u>	(provided by the system)
<u>Vendor Name</u>	Acme Supply Company
<u>Street Address</u>	123 Johnson St.
<u>City</u>	Seattle
<u>State</u>	Wa.
<u>Zip Code</u>	92469
<u>Phone Number</u>	206-669-1331

With your cursor next to the word **Ledger** press

➡	to activate **Ledger** (Figure 7.3)
⬇	to move cursor to **Insert**
➡	to activate **Insert** for entering information about the vendor.
Acme Supply Company [Ret]	to enter the name of the vendor

Notice again that you do not have to hold down the SHIFT key when you type the first letter of the company name. The program will do that for you. If you make a typing mistake, simply use the BACKSPACE key to erase the error and retype the correct letters.

123 Johnson St.[Ret]	to enter the **Street** address
Seattle [Ret]	to enter the **City**
Wa.[Ret]	to enter the **State**
92469 [Ret]	to enter the **Zip** code
2066691331	to enter the phone number. If you only enter the 7-digit phone number then you have to press [Ret] . If you also enter the area code then the cursor will jump to the next item automatically after you type the last digit.

Your cursor will now be on the word **Purge**. Here you have a choice of retaining the history of invoices and payments for the vendor, in which case you select **No**, or, once the invoices have been fully paid, you would select **Yes**, to purge the data. If you keep too much previous information it will eventually fill the computer's memory and you would not be able to enter any more current data.

In most cases it is advisable to keep the detail information for at least two months so that you can easily access the payment information in case there is a question about a particular payment date or amount. Older information can be purged after printing a hardcopy, preferably at month end. Type

Y	to select **Yes** for **Purge**

GENERAL	PAYABLE	RECEIVABLE	PAYROLL	INVENTORY	JOBCOST	SYSTEM

```
Vendor    Acme Supply Company
Street    123 Johnson St.
City      Seattle
State     Wa.
Zip       92469
Phone     206-669-1331
Purge     Yes
```

Figure 7.4 Supplier information entered into vendor section

When complete your screen should resemble Figure 7.4. When you have entered data in all of the fields, you may then edit the data by using the up and down arrow keys to move to the appropriate field. After making the necessary corrections, press

⬅	to save vendor information

Remember, if you press the ESCape key at this point you will clear the data you just entered. You might want to do this if you entered a wrong customer into the system and realized it just prior to saving the entry. Once you press the ESCape key you must reenter all of the data again.

Once you have accepted the first vendor, the system will automatically assign the number "1" to this vendor. You have no other choice but to accept the number given to this vendor by the program.

■ *Practice Exercise*

Enter the following suppliers:

Vendor Number	(entered by the system)		
Vendor Name	Didyk, Edward	AT&T Telephone Co.	Williams Stationery Inc.
Street Address	3455 Decatur Blvd.	1261 Emerson Blvd.	1419 Cornwall Ave.
City	Bellevue	Seattle	Tacoma
State	Wa.	Wa.	Wa.
Zip Code	96222	98624	92268
Phone Number	206-674-1144	206-683-4396	206-644-9121
Purge	YES	YES	YES

■ *Modifying Vendor Information*

If you want to change information about a vendor already in the system you would use the **Modify** command. You may want to change the address or phone number, or you may wish to change the purge method. Instead of creating another vendor, or deleting the existing one, you can modify the information.

    After entering the vendors in the previous exercise, you should be in the **Ledger** sub-menu with the cursor next to **Insert**. To change vendor information, press

⬆	to move cursor to **Modify**
➡	to activate **Modify**

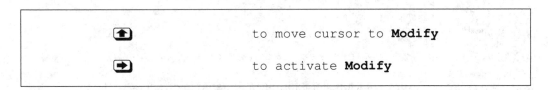

| GENERAL | PAYABLE | RECEIVABLE | PAYROLL | INVENTORY | JOBCOST | SYSTEM |

Vendor ...	AT&T Telephone Co...........3
Street	Acme Supply Company.........1
City	Didyk, Edward..............2
State	Williams Stationery Inc......4
Zip	
Phone	
Purge	

Figure 7.5 Entry screen for modifying vendor information

    Your screen will now resemble Figure 7.5, which contains the same information as the **Insert** input screen, except that on the right side is a listing of the names of the four vendors that you previously entered. To change information for vendor #2, Didyk, Edward, type

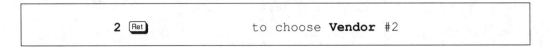

2 [Ret]	to choose **Vendor** #2

The program recalls the vendor information pertaining to that vendor number and displays it beside the respective headings. Now let's change the telephone number to 206-679-1144.

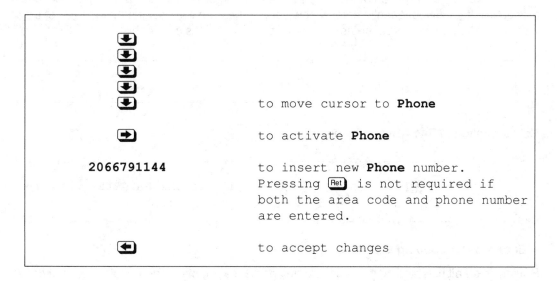

⬇ ⬇ ⬇ ⬇ ⬇	to move cursor to **Phone**
➡	to activate **Phone**
2066791144	to insert new **Phone** number. Pressing [Ret] is not required if both the area code and phone number are entered.
⬅	to accept changes

▪ *Deleting Vendors*

Although the Bedford Accounting System can support 1,000 vendors, there may be times when an existing vendor is no longer required or has gone out of business and should be deleted from the vendor list.

The Bedford program will only allow you to delete vendors that have no current balances in them. If you attempt to delete a vendor with a current balance, the program will print a message on the screen to that effect and not allow you to proceed with the deletion. Otherwise you could easily get out of balance with the control account — Accounts Payable — in the general ledger

To delete a vendor that will not be used, choose **Delete** from the **Ledger** submenu. Press

⬇ ⬇	to move cursor to **Delete**
➡	to activate **Delete**

You will now be prompted for a vendor number. The list of accounts will appear to the right of the screen.

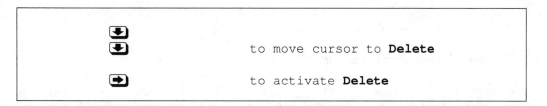

3 [Ret]	to choose vendor #3 (AT&T Telephones)

You will see the following message

Press RETURN to proceed or ESCAPE to reconsider

If you do change your mind at this point you can press the ESCape key to cancel the procedure. If you subsequently enter a new vendor the program assigns the number of the previously deleted vendor to the new vendor. In our case, let's delete this vendor. Press

Now return to the **PAYABLE** submenu. Press

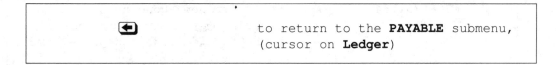

▪ *Entering the Opening Balances*

Having listed all outstanding invoices and any partial payments made up to the time of conversion, you can now enter the historical balances. We start with the opening menu of the **PAYABLE** module. Notice that the second item in the menu is **History** (See Figure 7.3). You can only enter historical data while the module is in the NOT READY mode. Once we change to the READY mode you will not be able to change the historical balances.

When we created the vendor file we did not enter any outstanding balances. We have to enter those now, along with outstanding invoices and partial payments for each vendor. Be sure not to leave one out or the listing will be out of balance.

To enter the historical balances start from the **PAYABLE** submenu with your cursor next to **Ledger**. Press

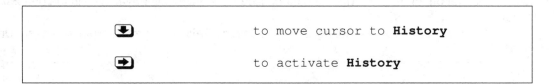

Your screen will now resemble Figure 7.6.

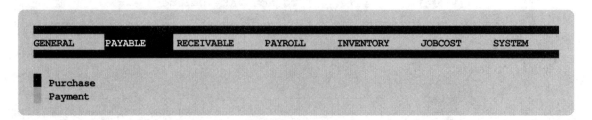

Figure 7.6 History item activated from the PAYABLE submenu

You can now proceed to enter opening invoice balances under **Purchase** and any partial payments under **Payment**. Use the following information:

Acme Supply Company

number	date	item	amount
123	12-15-87	invoice	123.44
345	12-16-87	partial payment	23.44-
456	12-31-87	invoice	50.00
		total	150.00

▪ Entering Purchases

To enter the opening purchases or invoices for Acme Supply Company, place your cursor beside the word **Purchase** and press

Your screen should now resemble Figure 7.7.

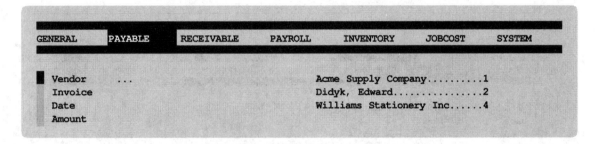

Figure 7.7 Purchase information entry screen

1 [Ret]	to enter **Vendor,** Acme Supply Company. The three dots will now be replaced by the vendor name.
123 [Ret]	to enter **Invoice** #123
121587	to enter **Date.** The date you enter is the date the invoice was created or date of transaction. This must be on or before the conversion date.
123.44 [Ret]	to enter the **Amount**
[←]	to save entry

▪ *Practice Exercise*

Enter the other outstanding invoice, #456, for Acme Supply Company.

▪ *Entering Payments*

To enter full or partial payments you follow the same procedure except that you choose **Payment** from the **History** submenu instead of **Purchase**.

⬇	to **Payment**
➡	to activate **Payment**
1 [Ret]	to choose vendor #1
121687	to enter **Date**. Again this date is on or before the conversion date and represents the date on which the partial payment was received.

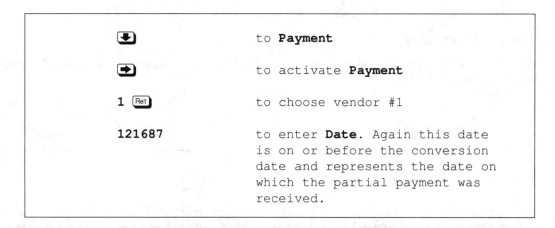

GENERAL	PAYABLE	RECEIVABLE	PAYROLL	INVENTORY	JOBCOST	SYSTEM

purge

```
Vendor    Acme Supply Company              ▶ 123............123.44
Date      12-16-87                           456.............50.00
Amount    .......... ▌123.44▐
Check
```

Figure 7.8 Payment input screen showing outstanding vendor invoices

Now a list of outstanding invoices will appear on the screen (Figure 7.8). If you completed the above practice exercise, the two invoices entered for vendor #1 will appear at the right side of the screen. You can choose the invoice that you want to pay by pressing the ENTER key. Each time you do, the arrow moves down to the next invoice. In our case, we want to allocate the payment to the first invoice, #123. If we wanted to enter a prepayment we would have to enter it as a negative invoice.

With the arrow pointing to invoice #123, type

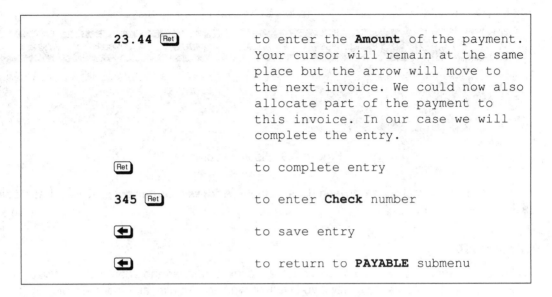

23.44 Ret	to enter the **Amount** of the payment. Your cursor will remain at the same place but the arrow will move to the next invoice. We could now also allocate part of the payment to this invoice. In our case we will complete the entry.
Ret	to complete entry
345 Ret	to enter **Check** number
⬅	to save entry
⬅	to return to **PAYABLE** submenu

You have now entered the payment against the outstanding invoice.

■ *Practice Exercise*

Enter the following purchase and payment for the indicated vendor.

Purchase		Payment	
Vendor#:	2	Vendor #:	2
Invoice #:	124	Invoice #:	124
Date:	12-18-87	Date:	12-30-87
Amount:	$140.00	Amount:	$30.00
		Check #:	411

Displaying Reports

Once you have entered the historical balances into the Bedford Accounting System you may want to look at the information contained in the accounts **PAYABLE** module. The Bedford Accounting System allows you to either display the information on the screen (soft copy) or to print the detail on a printer (hard copy). Being able to view quickly transaction entries on the screen saves time and reduces printing costs. Remember, however, that you must maintain an audit trail in hard copy form in case the computer information is accidentally destroyed.

Now let's look at the display options in the accounts **PAYABLE** module. Press

⬅	to return to accounts **PAYABLE** submenu. (cursor beside **History**)
⬇	to choose **Display**
➡	to activate **Display**

Your screen will now look like Figure 7.9.

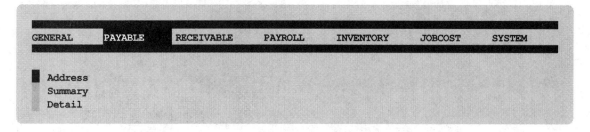

Figure 7.9 Display submenu

You can now choose between displaying the **Address**, **Summary** or **Detail**. Let's look at each of these in turn.

■ *Address Display*

The **Address** item displays the company name, account number and address. This feature allows you to get an address quickly if you want to write to a particular vendor. To display the address, press

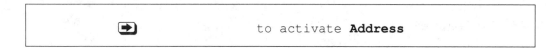

Your screen will display, in columnar form, the information about each vendor on file in numerical order (Figure 7.10).

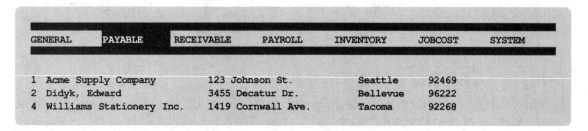

Figure 7.10 Listing of vendor addresses

If you have many vendors you can view a screenful at a time by using the up or down arrow keys.

You can return to the display menu by depressing the ESCape key.

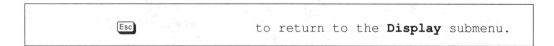

- ### *Summary Display*

Besides the address information we can also display information about each vendor or all vendors in either summary or detail form. The **Detail** option gives us a listing of all transactions currently on the system for each vendor that have not been purged. (Earlier in this chapter we discussed purging the information once an invoice was paid. If we chose **Yes** to purge, when an invoice is paid for, the invoice and payment will disappear from the account. If we chose **No** then the detail would remain on file.)

The **Summary** option will provide a summary of the transaction data and show only one total for each vendor. That total will be broken down into how many days it has been since the invoice was rendered.

Whether you choose the **Detail** or **Summary** option depends on what use you want to make of the data. The **Summary** information can be helpful when planning for cash requirements for the business in the near future. For this purpose you are more interested in the total amount and when this amount will be paid, rather than in the specific items that are payable. On the other hand, if you want to pay for specific invoices, or if you want to find out if a particular invoice has been paid or not, you would want to look at the **Detail** listing.

To display these options, press

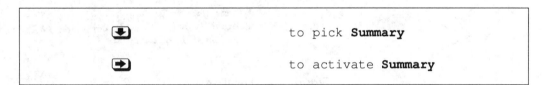

Figure 7.11 Summary information display

Your screen will now resemble Figure 7.11. Note that the aging of these accounts is 0-30, 31-60 and 61+. This aging is the default set up by the system. The default aging periods can be changed to suit the user's needs (See Aging Defaults in this Chapter).

The total of the accounts payable should agree to the control account — accounts payable in the general ledger. The system will not allow you to convert the **PAYABLE** module to READY until these two totals agree.

- **Detail Display**

To display detail of the entry, press

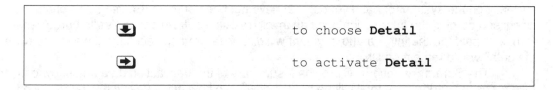

When you choose the **Detail** option, you must tell the Bedford Accounting System if you want to see just one account or all of the accounts. When you activate this option, your screen will look like Figure 7.12.

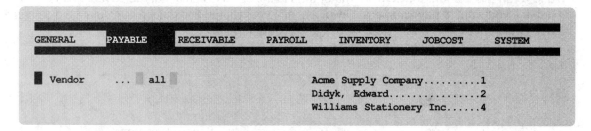

Figure 7.12 Detail screen

On the right side of the screen are listed the companies from which you can choose to view transactions in detail. If you wish to see one specific account, just enter the customer number. If you wish to see the detail of all of the accounts then hold down the SHIFT key and press the ENTER or RETURN key. [SHIFT][ENTER] This indicates to the system that you want to see a complete listing of entries.

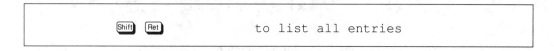

The detail listing of all entries resembles Figure 7.13.

GENERAL	PAYABLE	RECEIVABLE	PAYROLL	INVENTORY	JOBCOST	SYSTEM	
			total	0-30	31-60		61+

```
1 Acme Supply Company
        123     12-15-87 Invoice      123.44      123.44         -            -
        345     12-16-87 Payment       23.44-       23.44-        -            -
        456     12-31-87 Invoice       50.00        50.00         -            -
                                      _____      _____     _____      _____
                                       150.00       150.00        -            -

2 Didyk, Edward
        124     12-18-87 Invoice      140.00       140.00         -            -
        411     12-30-87 Payment       30.00-       30.00-        -            -
                                      _____      _____     _____      _____
                                       110.00       110.00        -            -
```

Figure 7.13 Full listing of detail for all vendors

The entries under detail listing are broken into the same time frames as the summary listing, 0-30 days, 31-60 and 61+. The detail information includes the invoice or check number, the date of the transaction, and the type of transaction — invoice or payment. As mentioned previously, this information allows you to get specific information for each vendor.

When you have finished with the display, press

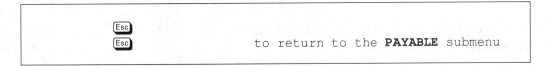

Esc
Esc   to return to the **PAYABLE** submenu

Printing Reports

Displaying reports on the monitor is fine for quick viewing of the data. However, in most cases you want a permanent record, or hard copy. Printing reports is similar to displaying them. With the accounts **PAYABLE** submenu on the screen, place your cursor beside the word **Print** and proceed as follows:

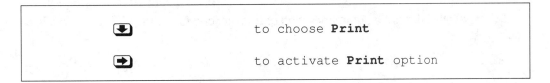

⬇   to choose **Print**

➡   to activate **Print** option

The print menu will now appear as shown in Figure 7.14. The **Print** menu is identical to the **Display** menu except that it contains one additional item — **Label**.

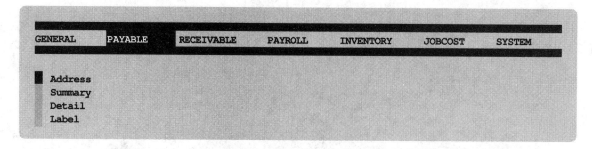

Figure 7.14 The Bedford Print menu

NOTE: Make sure that your printer is turned on, that there is paper in the printer, that the print head is at the top of the page, and that the printer is online, so that data can flow from the computer to the printer. This must be done each time you wish to print something.

Now choose the address listing. With your cursor on **Address** in the **Print** menu press

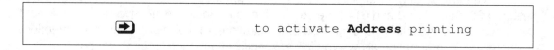

to activate **Address** printing

Your printer will now print out an address listing of vendors as shown in Figure 7.15.

Fast Delivery Inc. FOR INSTRUCTIONAL USE ONLY
VENDOR Address Jan 1,1988

1	Acme Supply Company	123 Johnson St.	Seattle	Wa.	92469	206-669-1331
2	Didyk, Edward	3455 Decatur Dr.	Bellevue	Wa.	96222	206-679-1144
4	Williams Stationery Inc.	1419 Cornwall Ave.	Tacoma	Wa.	92268	206-644-9121

VENDORS on file: 3

Figure 7.15 A printout listing vendor addresses

Now let's print out a summary listing of transactions for vendors. The printout is shown in Figure 7.16.

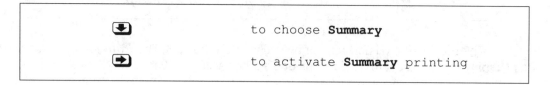

to choose **Summary**

to activate **Summary** printing

Fast Delivery Inc. FOR INSTRUCTIONAL USE ONLY
VENDOR Summary Jan 1,1988

		total	current	31-60	61-90	91+
1	Acme Supply Company	150.00	150.00	-	-	-
2	Didyk, Edward	110.00	110.00	-	-	-
		260.00	260.00	-	-	-

Figure 7.16 A printout of the summary listing for vendors

To get a detail listing of the transactions for vendors choose the **Detail** item from the menu. The printout is shown in Figure 7.17.

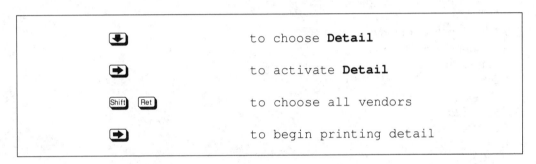

Fast Delivery Inc. FOR INSTRUCTIONAL USE ONLY   Page 1
VENDOR Detail Jan 1,1988

				total	current	31-60	61-90	91+
1	Acme Supply Company	123	12-15-87 Invoice	123.44	123.44	-	-	-
		345	12-16-87 Payment	23.44-	23.44-	-	-	-
		456	12-31-87 Invoice	50.00	50.00	-	-	-
				150.00	150.00	-	-	-
2	Didyk, Edward	124	12-18-87 Invoice	140.00	140.00	-	-	-
		411	12-30-87 Payment	30.00-	30.00-	-	-	-
				110.00	110.00	-	-	-
				260.00	260.00	-	-	-

Figure 7.17 A printout showing detail of transactions for vendors

The item, **Label**, in the **Print** menu, is included so you can prepare address labels for each vendor if a common mailing is necessary. The labels will print on single column label stock. To print the labels press

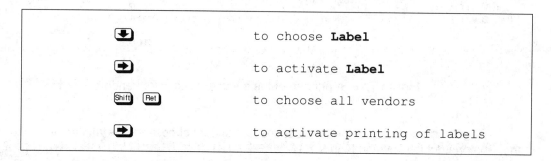

⬇	to choose **Label**
➡	to activate **Label**
Shift Ret	to choose all vendors
➡	to activate printing of labels

Acme Supply Company
123 Johnson St.
Seattle, Wa.
92469

Didyk, Edward
3455 Decatur Dr.
Bellevue, Wa.
96222

Williams Stationery Inc.
1419 Cornwall Ave.
Tacoma, Wa.
92268

Figure 7.18 A printout of address labels from the vendor **Print** menu

To return to the Bedford main menubar, press

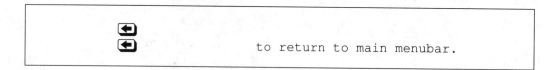

⬅ ⬅	to return to main menubar.

Changing to Ready Mode

Now that we have entered our opening balances, we have completed the conversion process from a manual to a computerized accounts payable system. But before we can enter current data into the accounts payable system we have to go through one more procedure. We have to change the accounts **PAYABLE** module to READY from NOT READY. Remember, once you change to the READY mode, you cannot return to the NOT READY mode. Since you will not be able to change the historical data once the module is in READY mode, be absolutely sure that the data you entered is correct.

However, the Bedford Accounting System will not allow you to change a module to the READY mode until

a. the general ledger is in ready mode and
b. the subledger is in balance with the control account in the general ledger.

If the general ledger is in the NOT READY mode, the program will tell you so. You will then have to go back to the **GENERAL** ledger module and make it READY.

If a subledger is not in balance with the control account, a message will be displayed similar to the one shown in Figure 7.19.

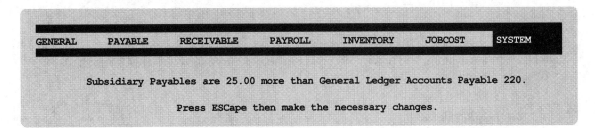

| GENERAL | PAYABLE | RECEIVABLE | PAYROLL | INVENTORY | JOBCOST | SYSTEM |

Subsidiary Payables are 25.00 more than General Ledger Accounts Payable 220.

Press ESCape then make the necessary changes.

Figure 7.19 An example of the message displayed by Bedford if the subledger is not in balance with the respective general ledger control account.

If this message appears you have to correct the imbalance before you can make the accounts **PAYABLE** module READY.

Since we are in balance, we are ready to make the necessary change. Press

```
⬅⬅            to move cursor highlight to SYSTEM.
⬇             to activate SYSTEM module
⬇
⬇
⬇             to choose Default
➡             to activate Default
➡             to activate Module
⬇             to choose Payable
➡             to activate Payable
```

Your screen will now display the default accounts payable settings as shown in Figure 7.20.

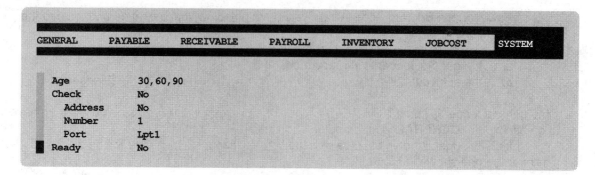

Figure 7.20 Accounts payable default settings

We now have three options to consider: the aging dates, whether or not we wish to print checks with the system, and finally, the option to change from the NOT READY to the READY mode.

▪ *Account Aging Defaults*

Aging of accounts is currently set at 30, 60 and 90 days as mentioned earlier. This indicates the date on which you were invoiced by a vendor, when you paid, and how much you paid. It clearly indicates the invoices that you still have to pay and to whom they are still owing. If these intervals are not what you want, you can change them. For example, you may want to know what is payable in 15, 30 and 45 days. All reports and displays thereafter will take these new intervals into account.

▪ *Printing Checks*

The second option allows you to print checks for payables if you change the **No** to **Yes**. If you wish to print checks, you can purchase specially printed Bedford accounts payable/payroll checks as shown in Figure 7.21 with your company name and address imprinted.

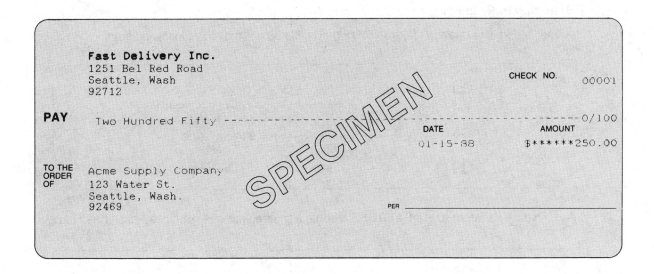

Figure 7.21 Bedford Accounting System accounts payable checks

If you decide to print checks you must also answer the following questions.

Address **Yes** means that you want the address of your company to be printed on the check; **No** will leave it off.

Number This indicates the beginning check number that will be printed on the first check. If we choose the number 59, the program will assign consecutive check numbers starting with the number 59.

Port This is the printer port to which our printer is connected. A printer with a parallel interface will be connected to **Lpt1**, the default port. A serial printer will probably be connected to the **Com1** port. If you are unsure, then check your computer reference book, or look on the back of the computer to determine which port your printer is hooked up to.

• *Changing to Ready Mode*

The final action is to change to the READY mode. To do so, press the following keys:

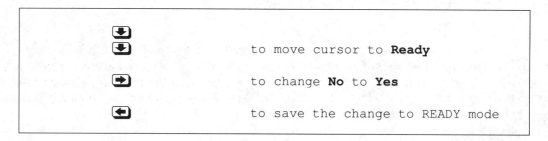

⬇️
⬇️   to move cursor to **Ready**

➡️   to change **No** to **Yes**

⬅️   to save the change to READY mode

Now let's return to the **PAYABLE** module and check to see what this action has changed.

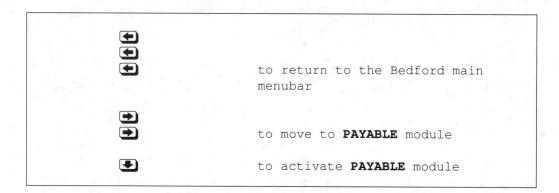

⬅️
⬅️
⬅️   to return to the Bedford main
            menubar

➡️
➡️   to move to **PAYABLE** module

⬇️   to activate **PAYABLE** module

You will notice in Figure 7.22 that the menu has changed. The menu item **History** is now changed to **Journal**. It is through the **Journal** menu item that we will record all journal entries to the system.

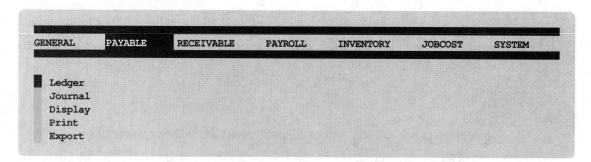

Figure 7.22 Accounts PAYABLE submenu after changing the to READY. History menu item has changed to Journal

ENTERING ACCOUNTS PAYABLE JOURNAL ENTRIES

All accounts payable entries are made through a series of journal entries similar to the journal entries that you made in the **GENERAL** ledger module. The accounts payable ledger accepts two types of journal entries.

a. Purchases   Dr. Asset or Expense Account
                        Cr. Accounts Payable

b. Payments   Dr. Accounts Payable
                        Cr. Cash

You may remember from the discussion earlier in this chapter that subledgers have common accounts in their journal entries. For example, in accounts payable, each purchase entry will have a common credit entry to accounts payable. This helps to speed up transaction entry since you only have to enter the debit side of the entry. The program will add up the debits that you entered and automatically credit accounts payable.

Entering Purchases

Let's make the following entry of a purchase from Acme Supply Company.

January 1, 1988   Dr. Freight Expense   123.00
                         Dr. General Expense   666.00
                              Cr. Accounts Payable   789.00
                 (to record billing from Acme Supply Company, Invoice #111)

You access the purchase entry screen through the **Journal** submenu. Press

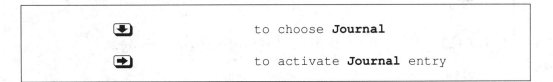

The **Purchase/Payment** menu will appear as in Figure 7.23.

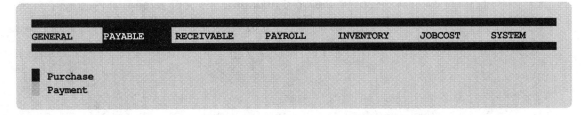

Figure 7.23 Journal submenu for entering purchases or payments

You are now asked if you wish to enter a purchase or a payment. Since you want to enter a purchase you press the right arrow key, as the cursor highlight is already on **Purchase**.

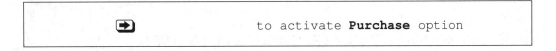

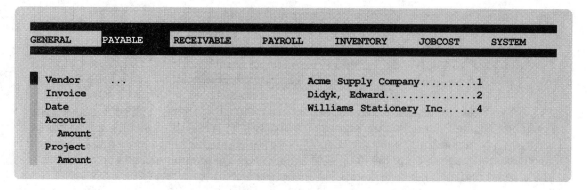

Figure 7.24 Purchase information entry screen

The purchase entry screen will now appear as in Figure 7.24. The cursor is flashing next to the first dot beside the word **Vendor**, waiting for you to enter the number of the vendor from whom you made the purchase. On the right side, the program lists the vendors currently on the system in alphabetical order. Enter the number of the vendor from the list. If there were many vendors you would use the up or down arrow key to see the remaining vendors and their numbers.

1 Ret	to choose **Vendor** number 1. The dots will be replaced by the company name.
111 Ret	to enter vendor **Invoice** #111
010188	to enter **Date** of the invoice, January 1, 1988

Your cursor will now be beside the word **Account**, and your screen will display a listing of the general ledger accounts as in Figure 7.25.

```
GENERAL    PAYABLE    RECEIVABLE    PAYROLL    INVENTORY    JOBCOST    SYSTEM


   Vendor      Acme Supply Company        CURRENT ASSETS.............100
   Invoice     111                        Petty Cash................104
   Date        01-01-88                   First Interstate- General..106
   Account     ...                        Bank B - Receivable.......108
     Amount                               Bank C - Payroll..........110
   Project                                Cash: Total...............112
     Amount                               Accounts Receivable.......120
                                          Advances Receivable.......124
                                          Inventory.................126
                                          Prepaid Insurance.........135
                                          TOTAL CURRENT ASSETS......139
                                          FIXED ASSETS..............150
                                          Building..................154
                                          Accm Depn - Building......156
                                          Automotive................164
                                          Accm Depn - Automotive.....166
                                          Subtotal..................170
                                          Land......................172
                                          TOTAL FIXED ASSETS........175
```

Figure 7.25 Partial listing of general ledger accounts to which purchase will be distributed

The program is asking you to enter the account to which the debit part of the entry will go. Usually, this is to an asset or expense account, but, in some instances, may be to liabilities, owner's equity or revenues. In any case, the accounts with the square boxes to the right of the account number (not shown in Figure 7.25) are the only ones to which entries may be posted. If you do not see the account you wish to post an entry to, use the up and down arrows to locate it.

We wish to enter the account 520, which is three screens down from the top. Press

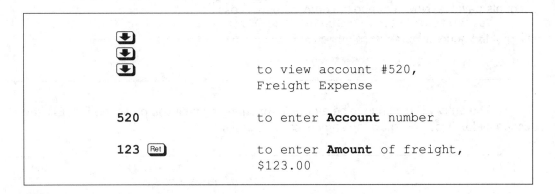

Your cursor will automatically return to the **Account** option, bypassing **Project**. If you had defined one or more projects or departments in the **JOBCOST** module you would be allowed to enter an amount here which would be allocated to a project or department. Only revenue and expense amounts can be allocated in this manner. We will explain this in detail in Chapter 11. Let's complete this entry. Press

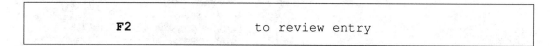

502	to enter general expense account number
666 [Ret]	to enter **Amount** of $666.00

At any time during the entry of a vendor invoice you can review what you have done by depressing the F2 function key, indicated in the upper right hand corner of your screen. Press

F2	to review entry

Your screen will now resemble Figure 7.26.

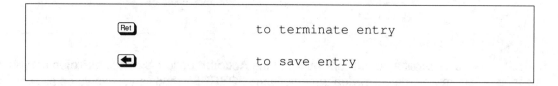

Figure 7.26 Viewing how a journal entry is distributed among accounts.

The program has already added the amounts together and made the credit entry to accounts payable. Now return to the entry screen. Press

F2	to return to entry screen

The entry will continue to be available for changing until you press the ENTER key in the account field. Once you know the entry is correct, press

[Ret]	to terminate entry
[←]	to save entry

Once the entry has been permanently accepted by the program, the vendor balance will be updated in the accounts **PAYABLE** module and the control account — accounts payable, will be updated in the general ledger. Nothing else needs to be done with this entry. Let's look at the data entered just to make sure. Press

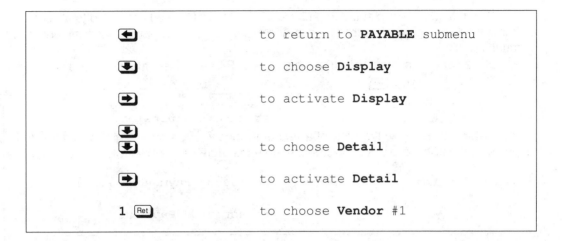

You can see by Figure 7.27 that the items you just entered are reported under the vendor detail screen.

GENERAL	PAYABLE	RECEIVABLE	PAYROLL	INVENTORY	JOBCOST	SYSTEM	
			total	0-30	31-60		61+
1 Acme Supply Company							
123	12-15-87	Invoice	123.44	123.44	-		-
345	12-16-87	Payment	23.44-	23.44-	-		-
456	12-31-87	Invoice	50.00	50.00	-		-
111	01-01-88	Invoice	789.00	789.00	-		-
			939.00	939.00	-		-

Figure 7.27 Vendor detail screen for reviewing entries

When you are finished viewing this screen, press

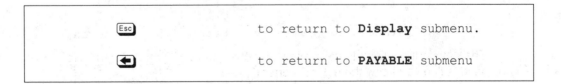

Entering Payments

Besides entering purchases into the system, you must also enter payments made on each outstanding invoice.

Let's record a payment of $689.00 on the invoice that you just entered. This is shown by the following journal entry.

```
Dr. Accounts Payable        689.00
        Cr. Cash                        689.00
```

Remember, this is a standard entry again and therefore you only need to allocate the payment to the proper invoice, the Bedford Accounting System will know that this credit is to the account, Bank.

To enter the payment, begin at the accounts **PAYABLE** submenu and press

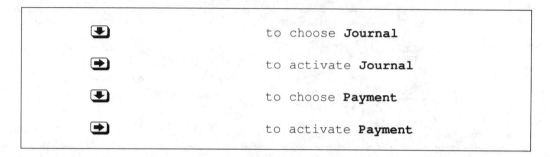

The payment entry screen will now appear as in Figure 7.28.

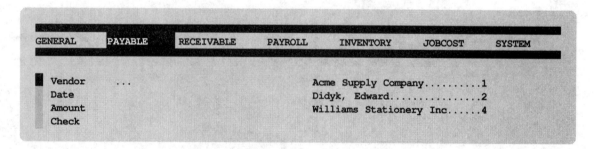

Figure 7.28 Payments input screen

Let's enter the following:

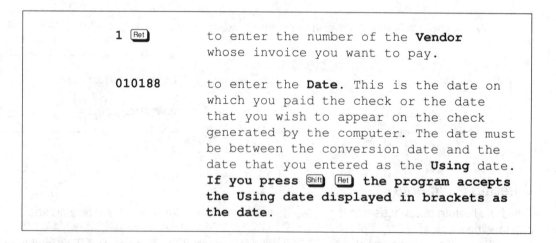

Your cursor will now appear beside **Amount** and your screen will resemble Figure 7.29. On the right side of the screen, you will see the outstanding invoice numbers and the balance owing. If the **Purge** option for a vendor has been set to **No**, you may also see some zero balances. A small arrow will also point toward the first invoice with a balance.

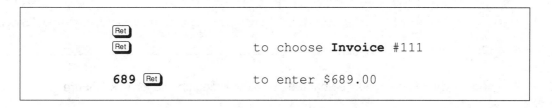

| GENERAL | PAYABLE | RECEIVABLE | PAYROLL | INVENTORY | JOBCOST | SYSTEM |
| | | | | | | purge |

Vendor	Acme Supply Company	► 123...........100.00
Date	01-01-88	456............50.00
Amount	.... 100.00	111..........789.00
Cheque		

Figure 7.29 Screen display showing outstanding invoices. A payment
may be allocated to one or more of the displayed invoices.

Our first task is to pick the invoice we wish to pay. By pressing the ENTER key twice, you can skip the first and second invoice and move on to the third, which is the one we wish to pay. Notice that the amount of the invoice selected appears in shaded parentheses beside the word **Amount**. If you wish to pay the whole amount of the invoice, then press [SHIFT][ENTER]. This will automatically select the outstanding amount. Since we only want to pay $689.00, we would press

Ret
Ret   to choose **Invoice** #111

689 Ret   to enter $689.00

This will allocate the $689.00 to **Invoice** #111. Toward the bottom of the screen you will see a running total of the invoices paid. If more invoices were displayed you could choose to pay another invoice. When you have cycled through all of the vendor's outstanding invoices shown on the right by pressing the ENTER key, the cursor jumps to the **Check** entry. You must now enter a check number. If you are not using the print check option as defined in the **SYSTEM Default**, you would enter the check number with which you will pay the bill. If you are using the check printing option, you would load the checks into the printer and press RIGHT ARROW. This will start the check printing routine.

1100 Ret   to enter the **Check** #1100

◄─   to accept entry

◄─   to return to **PAYABLE** submenu

In either case, after you have printed the check the Bedford Accounting System will update the vendor's account for the payment and proceed to enter the journal entry into the general ledger by debiting accounts payable and crediting cash.

Reconciling the Accounts Payable Ledger with the General Ledger

Now that you have entered an invoice and a payment, let's go back once more and check to see if the integration feature has really worked.

Choose the **Print** option from the accounts payable module and print a **Detail** listing of all vendors. Press

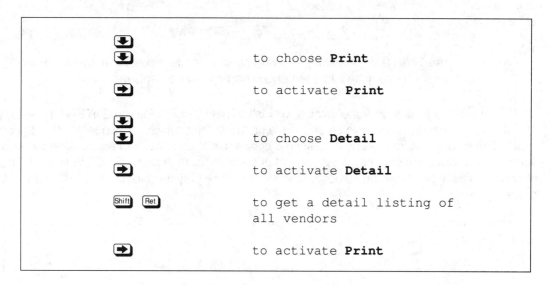

⬇ ⬇	to choose **Print**
➡	to activate **Print**
⬇ ⬇	to choose **Detail**
➡	to activate **Detail**
Shift Ret	to get a detail listing of all vendors
➡	to activate **Print**

The detail listing will now be printed out. Your listing should look like Figure 7.30.

Fast Delivery Inc. FOR INSTRUCTIONAL USE ONLY   Page 1
VENDOR Detail Jan 1,1988

					total	current	31-60	61-90	91+
1	Acme Supply Company	123	12-15-87	Invoice	123.44	123.44	-	-	-
		345	12-16-87	Payment	23.44-	23.44-	-	-	-
		456	12-31-87	Invoice	50.00	50.00	-	-	-
		111	01-01-88	Invoice	789.00	789.00	-	-	-
		1100	01-01-88	Payment	689.00-	689.00-	-	-	-
					250.00	250.00	-	-	-
2	Didyk, Edward	124	12-18-87	Invoice	140.00	140.00	-	-	-
		411	12-30-87	Payment	30.00-	30.00-	-	-	-
					110.00	110.00	-	-	-
					360.00	360.00	-	-	-

Figure 7.30 Printed detail listing of all vendors

You should now compare the total amount shown in the printed detail listing with the balance in the accounts payable account in the general ledger. To do so you want to look at the trial balance in the general ledger. Press

[←] [←]	to get out of the accounts **PAYABLE** module to the Bedford main menubar
[←]	to move cursor highlight to **GENERAL**
[↓]	to activate **GENERAL** ledger module
[↓] [↓]	to choose **Display**
[→]	to activate **Display**
[↓] [↓] [↓]	to choose **Trial** balance
[→]	to activate **Trial** balance
[Shift] [Ret]	to display the trial balance

Look for the accounts payable balance in the trial balance (Figure 7.31). Compare the balance to the printed detail listing. If you have made all the correct entries, they should agree. With this quick check you can make sure that the system is updating the accounts properly.

GENERAL	PAYABLE	RECEIVABLE	PAYROLL	INVENTORY	JOBCOST	SYSTEM	
						debits	credits
104 Petty Cash					300.00	-
106 First Interstate - General				1,429.33	-
108 Bank B - Receivable				0.00	-
110 Bank C - Payroll				0.00	-
120 Accounts Receivable				555.00	-
124 Advances Receivable				0.00	-
126 Inventory				100.00	-
135 Prepaid Insurance				55.67	-
154 Building				15,000.00	-
156 Accm Depn - Building				-	2,500.00
164 Automotive				28,000.00	-
166 Accum Depn - Automotive				-	5,500.00
172 Land				18,000.00	-
220 Accounts Payable				-	360.00
231 FIT Payable				-	0.00
232 SIT Payable				-	0.00
233 FICA Payable				-	0.00
234 FUTA Payable				-	0.00
235 SUTA Payable				-	0.00
236 SDI Payable				-	0.00
237 Local Tax Payable				-	0.00
240 Deduction A Payable				-	0.00
242 Deduction B Payable				-	0.00

244	Deduction C Payable	-	0.00
260	Sales Tax Payable	-	1,019.66
266	Short Term Debt	-	2,000.00
275	Mortgage Payable	-	22,500.00
302	Class A Common	-	5,000.00
303	Class B Common	-	2,000.00
356	Retained Earnings	-	23,474.34
402	General Revenue	-	0.00
406	General Delivery	-	0.00
407	Special Delivery	-	0.00
410	Freight Revenue	-	0.00
426	Insurance Income	-	0.00
427	Interest Income	-	0.00
502	General Expense	791.00	-
506	Truck Rental	0.00	-
507	Fuel	0.00	-
508	Insurance	0.00	-
509	Truck Repairs	0.00	-
510	Permits	0.00	-
520	Freight Expense	123.00	-
530	Wages	0.00	-
531	FICA Expense	0.00	-
532	FUTA Expense	0.00	-
533	SUTA Expense	0.00	-
534	SDI Expense	0.00	-
536	Employee Benefits	0.00	-
538	Warehouse Rent	0.00	-
561	Accounting	0.00	-
562	Advertising	0.00	-
563	Telephone	0.00	-
		64,354.00	64,354.00

Figure 7.31 Trial balance for Fast Delivery Inc. The balance in the printed detail listing should agree with the accounts receivable balance shown in the trial balance of the general ledger.

When you have finished, press

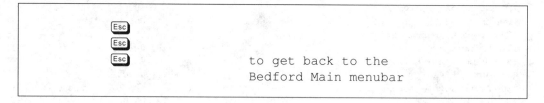

Esc
Esc
Esc   to get back to the
                       Bedford Main menubar

EXPORTING THE FILES

As with other modules in the Bedford Accounting System, you can also export all printable reports to a spreadsheet such as Lotus 1-2-3 or any spreadsheet program that can read Lotus 1-2-3 data files, such as SuperCalc. This allows you to have a closer look at the data and manipulate it in various ways.

The export procedure is identical in each of the modules. Rather than go through it again at this point, go to Chapter 6 and follow the procedures outlined there.

MAINTAINING AN AUDIT TRAIL

As in the general ledger, it is important to set up an audit trail for all accounting entries made. This means preparing a printed list of all the transactions entered — all journal entries made in each session.

Print out the journal entries from the print menu of the **GENERAL** module. Store the listing in a binder marked **PURCHASES AND DISBURSEMENTS.** If you ever want to review the entries made during any session, they are available. It is also a backup in the event that the computer should crash or the data disk is destroyed.

FINISHING THE SESSION

You have now completed the accounts payable tutorial. You should finish this session to save your data to disk. After activating the **Finish** command you will be returned to the disk operating system.

To finish this session, press

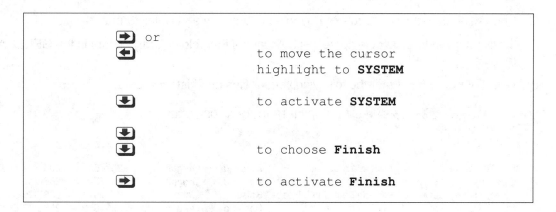

You should always end each session with the **Finish** command. When beginning a new chapter in this tutorial start the Bedford Accounting Program as described earlier in this chapter.

BACKING UP YOUR DATA FILES

You should also make a backup of the data disk at this time, so you have a duplicate in case anything should go wrong with your main data disk. Follow the procedures in Chapters 4 and 5 regarding making backups.

BEDFORD PRACTICE SET

AMERICANA HOME DECORATING AND SERVICE COMPANY

Part II — Accounts Payable

OBJECTIVE

After completing this practice set for accounts payable, you should be able to:

1. Create vendor files.

2. Enter Historical data to accounts.

3. Enter necessary defaults and integration accounts.

4. Set the System to Ready.

5. Enter transactions for: purchases on credit; purchase returns on credit; purchase discounts on credit; all check payments.

6. Print Aging Schedule of Accounts Payable in Summary and Detail format.

7. Verify total vendors payable agrees with Accounts Payable control account in the GENERAL module.

INSTRUCTION: 1.   Enter the following vendor files and historical data.

Americana Decorating Sales & Service Inc. FOR INSTRUCTIONAL USE ONLY
  VENDOR Address Jul 31,1988

1	Bell Telephone	567 Main St	Portland	Oregon	88765	206-687-4567
2	Blue Cross	5436 1st Street	Portland	Oregon	89675	206-657-8986
3	Boise Paint & Paper	2345 Great South Road	Boise	Idaho	78678	208-675-3456
4	Carter, Gary	567 Jefferson St.	Portland	Oregon	89345	206-687-5678
5	Gehrig, Lou	7865 Washington Street	Portland	Oregon	89098	206-687-9476
6	Interior Supply	234 Kennedy Street	Portland	Oregon	83749-7654	503-254-7987
7	Internal Revenue Service	456 Federal Way	Portland	Oregon	84567-8654	503-254-3456
8	Merrill Lynch	9087 Stockbroker Street	Portland	Oregon	83456-7253	503-245-6378
9	Munforte Paint & Paper	7865 Rue St. Antoinette	New Orleans	Louisiana	62364-5789	504-723-4321
10	Northwestern Hydro Co.	7896 Lincoln Avenue	Portland	Oregon	89764-5324	503-245-9876
11	Robinson, Jackie	8967 Liberty Highway	Portland	Oregon	89768-5435	505-678-7654
12	Ruth, Babe	897 Homer Street	Portland	Oregon	89765-0099	503-787-6543
13	Seattle Paint & Paper	8 Waterfront Drive	Seattle	Washington	98122-6754	206-789-7654
14	State of Oregon	789 Tax Street	Portland	Oregon	89078-6543	503-254-6907
15	Sunnybrooke Paint & Paper	897 Green Gable	Lanai City	Hawaii	96763-6789	808-565-3456
16	Tacoma Rainbow Co.	6754 Eastern Avenue	Tacoma	Washington	98423-5678	206-384-5676
17	Texaco Oil Co.	7890 Crude Street	Portland	Oregon	89786-7854	503-786-7567
18	Wahington, George	3456 Apple Tree Lane	Portland	Oregon	89786-7544	503-254-6019
19	Wilson Stationery Co.	8907 Broadway	Portland	Oregon	89345-2312	503-254-7890
20	Zebra Color Stripes	9087 Reagon St.	Portland	Oregon	89675-4321	503-254-0987

VENDORS on file: 20

Americana Decorating Sales & Service Inc. FOR INSTRUCTIONAL USE ONLY   Page 1
   VENDOR Detail Jul 31,1988

					total	current	31-60	61-90	91+
6	Interior Supply	P234	07-08-88	Invoice	12,650.42	12,650.42	-	-	-
		Dm45	07-25-88	Invoice	736.45-	736.45-	-	-	-
					11,913.97	11,913.97	-	-	-
					11,913.97	11,913.97	-	-	-

INSTRUCTION: 2. Enter the integration accounts required for your General Ledger chart of accounts.

INSTRUCTION: 3. Set the SYSTEM>Default>Module>Payable>:

Age   30,60,90
Cheque   Yes
  Address   Yes
  Number   366
  Port   Lpt1
Ready   Yes

INSTRUCTION: 4. Enter the following transactions in the GENERAL and PAYABLE modules for the month of August.

August 1. Received on account from Barbie Gibbons, $13,173.96. R147.

1. Borrowed short term loan from Bank of America, $15,000.00. DN.

1. Paid on account to Interior Supply, $11,913.97, covering invoice P234 for $12,650.42 less Dm45 for $736.45. Ch366.

Note: As you process checks on-line you cannot put the Check symbol Ch at the front of document number. This will be the same when you process invoices in PART III.

1. Purchased merchandise on account from Tacoma Rainbow Co.: paint, $4,357.89; wallpaper, $4,325.78; fabric, $3,789.08; plus freight expense for $647.89; total, $13,120.64. P235

8. Sold merchandise on account to Jim Park: paint, $2,314.50; wallpaper, $1,324.50; fabric, $5,678.32; plus sales tax for $652.21; total, $9,969.53. S408.

8. Purchased merchandise on account from Boise Paint & Paper Co.: paint, $2,315.78; wallpaper, $4,532.89; fabric, $7,098.57; plus freight expense for $345.35; total, $14,292.59. P236

8. Received on account from J. Gonzalez, $10,382.99, covering invoice S406 for $11,375.11 less sales discount: paint, $324.67; wallpaper, $234.67; fabric, $432.78. R148.

8. Returned merchandise to Tacoma Rainbow Co.: paint $279.06; wallpaper; $432.78; fabric, $543.24; total, $1,255.08. Dm46.

8. Sold merchandise on account to S. Smith: paint, $1,768.90; wallpaper $2,315.78; fabric, $6,523.89; decorating service, $7,645.90; plus sales tax of $742.60; total, $18,997.07. S409.

15. Record the withholding taxes payable as debt owing to vendor Internal Revenue Service: Federal Income Tax $2,431.22; Federal Insurance; $1,851.16, total $4,282.38. M77.

   Note: You must enter all liabilities as a purchase to a vendor account so you can then run check payments.

15. Paid withholding taxes to Internal Revenue Service, $4,282.38. Ch367.

15. Record State Income Tax payable, $944.03. M78

   Note: You must record the debt owed to vendor State regulatory body so you can then process check using PAYABLE module.

15. Paid State Income Tax, $944.03. Ch368.

15. Record telephone expense as debt owing to vendor Bell Telephone, $154.78. P237.

15. Paid Bell Telephone Co. for telephone expense, $154.78. Ch369.

15. Record fuel expense as debt owing to vendor Texaco Oil Co., $74.89. P238.

15. Paid Texaco Oil Co. for fuel expense, $74.89. Ch370.

16. Record bank transfer from General to Payroll account, $3,697.40. M79.

16. Record middle of month cash advance given employee vendor Gary Carter, $660.00. M80. Note: Since you are processing a check to the employee you must first record the cash owing to vendor Gary Carter so as to make a second entry of a check payment.

16. Paid middle of month advance to Gary Carter, $660.00. Ch371.

16. Record cash advance to employee vendor Lou Gehrig, $720.00. M81.

16. Paid cash advance to Lou Gehrig, $720.00. Ch372.

16. Record cash advance to employee vendor Jackie Robinson, $750.00. M82.

16. Paid cash advance to Jackie Robinson, $750.00. Ch373.

16. Record cash advance to employee vendor Babe Ruth, $690.00. M83.

16. Paid cash advance to Babe Ruth, $690.00. Ch374.

16. Record cash advance to employee vendor George Washington, $877.40. M84

16. Paid cash advance to George Washington, $877.40. Ch375.

16. Sold merchandise and service to Rebecca Mumford: paint, $876.34; wallpaper, $1,254.89; fabric, $4,789.45; decorating service; $4,578.23; plus sales tax of $804.92; total, $12,303.83. S410

16. Paid on account to Tacoma Rainbow Co., $11,865.56, covering invoice P235 for $13,120.64 less Dm46 for $1,255.08. Ch376.

16. Purchased merchandise on account from Zebra Color Stripes: paint, $3,452.78; wallpaper, $2,345.67; fabric, $5,467.36; total, $11,265.81. P239.

16. Borrowed short term loan from Bank of America, $20,000.00. DN.

16. Recorded company pension owed to vendor Merrill Lynch, $616.23. M85.

16. Paid Merrill Lynch for company pension, $616.23 Ch377.

16. Record medical plan owed to vendor Blue Cross, $270.00. M86.

16. Paid Blue Cross for medical plan, $270.00. Ch378.

16. Record State sales tax payable, $1,546.42. M87.

16. Paid State sales tax payable, $1,546.42. Ch379.

22. Granted credit to S. Smith for merchandise returns: paint, $143.67; wallpaper, $215.67; fabric, $354.90; plus sales tax of $50.00; total, $764.24. Cm57.

22. Record purchase discounts realized for early payment to Boise Paint & Paper : paint, $234.23; wallpaper, $234.78; fabric, $345.78; total, $814.79. Dm47.

22. Paid Boise Paint & Paper , $13,477.80, covering invoice P236 for $14,292.59 less Dm47 for $814.79. Ch380.

22. Received on account from R. Crawford, $11,710.27, covering invoice S410 for $12,303.83 less sales discounts: paint, $231.42; wallpaper, $124.56; fabric, $237.58. R149.

31. Record bank transfer from General to Payroll account , $3,440.21. M88.

31. Record month end payroll owing to employee vendor Gary Carter, $573.02, covering: Salary Expense, $2,200.00 less: Federal Income Tax, $471.35; Federal Insurance, $165..22; State Income Tax, $1700.41; Company Pension, $110.00; Medical, $50.00; Advances Receivable, $660.00. M89.

31. Paid month end payroll to Gary Carter, $573.02. Ch381.

31. Record month end payroll owing to employee vendor Lou Gehrig, $744.66, covering: Salary Expense, $2,400.00 less: Federal Income Tax, $407.02; Federal Insurance, $180.24; State Income Tax, $178.08; Company Pension, $120.00; Medical, $50.00; Advances Receivable, $720.00. M90.

31. Paid month end payroll to Lou Gehrig, $744.66. Ch382.

31. Record month end payroll owing to employee vendor Jackie Robinson, $578.93, covering: Salary Expense, $2,500.00 less: Federal Income Tax, $597.16; Federal Insurance, $187.75 State Income Tax, $201.16; Company Pension, $125.00; Medical, $60.00; Advances Receivable, $750.00. M91.

31. Paid month end payroll to Jackie Robinson, $578.93. Ch383.

31. Record month end payroll owing to employee vendor Babe Ruth, $696.42, covering: Salary Expense, $2,300.00 less: Federal Income Tax, $401.77; Federal Insurance, $172.73; State Income Tax, $169.08; Company Pension, $115.00; Medical, $55.00; Advances Receivable, $690.00. M92.

31. Paid month end payroll to Babe Ruth, $696.42. Ch384.

31 Record month end payroll owing to employee vendor George Washington, $847.18, covering: Salary Expense, $2,924.67 less: Federal Income Tax, $553.92; Federal Insurance, $219.64; State Income Tax, $225.30; Company Pension, $146.23; Medical, $55.00; Advances Receivable, $877.40. M93.

31. Paid month end payroll to George Washington, $847.18. Ch385.

31. Recorded employer's payroll FICA Expense, $925.58. M94.

31. Recorded Bank Reconciliation adjustments: Short Term Loan Payment, $543.80; Mortgage Payment, $345.78; Interest Expense, $1,256.45; Bank Charges Expense, $45.67; Interest Income, $125.67; net total bank debit, $2,066.03. M95.

31. Recorded adjusting entry for insurance expense incurred, $400.00.

31. Recorded adjusting entry for office supplies expense incurred, $115.23.

31. Recorded adjusting entry for estimated depreciation expense incurred: Building, $1,750.00; Automotive, $185.00.

31. Recorded ending inventory change from end of last period, increasing: paint, $6,734.90; wallpaper, $7,123.68; fabric, $7,890.45; total, $21,749.03. Note: Modify the description of account Ending Inventory 07-31-88 to Inventory Change Aug. 1-31 before entering transaction.

INSTRUCTION: 6. Print Aging Schedule of Accounts Payable in Summary and Detail form for all accounts.
Verify that the total of all vendor's account balances agrees with the Accounts Payable control account.
Print General Journal entries from 08-01-88 to 08-31-88.
Print Income Statement for 08-01-88 to 08-31-88.
Modify the description of Inventory Change Aug. 1-31 to Ending Inventory 08-31-88.
Print Income Statement for 01-01-88 to 08-31-88.
Print Balance Sheet for 08-31-88.

Chapter 8
ACCOUNTS RECEIVABLE

Chapter 8
ACCOUNTS RECEIVABLE

PREVIEW

In Chapter 8 you will learn about accounts receivable and how to use the Bedford accounts RECEIVABLE module. Getting ready to convert from a manual to a computerized accounts payable system requires a customer listing, as well as a listing of outstanding invoices.

As in the previous accounts PAYABLE module, the conversion process for accounts RECEIVABLE starts with adding customers to the system. After customer information is entered you will display and print customer files, and then enter historical customer data. After changing the module from NOT READY to the READY mode, you will enter a few journal transactions into the system.

Before finishing with this chapter you will check to see that the transactions entered have actually been transferred to the general ledger. Finally you will be reminded about the importance of an audit trail and backing up current data files.

OBJECTIVES

After reading this chapter you should be able to explain:

1. The meaning of open item accounting and how it applies to accounts receivable;

2. The customer records required and the procedure to be followed before you can begin to convert from a manual to the computerized accounts receivable system;

3. How to enter information about a customer into the system, how to modify existing information, and how to delete a customer from the system if necessary;

4. How to enter the opening balances for customer purchases and payments;

5. How to display detail and summary information about data entered;

6. How to print reports of various types;

7. How to change the accounts receivable module to READY mode, and how to set the various options presented on that menu;

8. How to enter accounts receivable transactions into the system;

9. Why an audit trail is necessary and how to create one.

After having worked through the accounts PAYABLE module you should have an easier time with the accounts RECEIVABLE module. This module is used for tracking the credit sales of a business organization and recording customer payments. The module allows you to prepare a report called an **aged trial balance**. The aged trial balance is different from the general ledger trial balance in that it indicates the customers that owe the company money, how much each customer owes, and the time that has elapsed since the sale was made. This will give the owner or manager some idea of the total amount outstanding, and which customers have not paid their bills on time.

The accounts RECEIVABLE module also provides a listing of the customers with their addresses and telephone numbers. This listing helps the credit manager contact customers who are delinquent with their payments or who have exceeded their credit limit.

ACCOUNTS RECEIVABLE SOURCE DOCUMENTS

In the accounts payable chapter we used certain source documents that tracked the purchases and payments of Fast Delivery Inc. In accounts receivable, we use similar source documents to keep track of the customers' purchases and subsequent payments for those purchases.

First, accounts receivable must allow us to record sales information which we get from the *sales invoice.* A general journal entry to record sales is as follows:

        Dr. Account Receivable   xxx
            Cr. [Various Sales Accounts]   xxx

There is always a debit entry to accounts receivable. The credit entry could be distributed to one or more revenue accounts.

Second, the accounts receivable module allows us to record customer payments — the amount, the invoice against which a payment is being made and the name of the customer. The general journal entry for cash receipts is:

        Dr. Cash   xxx
            Cr. Accounts Receivable   xxx

OPEN ITEM ACCOUNTING

As with the accounts PAYABLE module, the Bedford Accounting System uses the open item method of accounting for accounts receivable as opposed to the balance forward method. As you may recall from the previous chapter, the open item method keeps track of all individual invoices as well as the payments made on those invoices. This method allows you to identify how much is owing from a specific customer, and which invoices are unpaid or owing. Once the invoices are fully paid you have the option of retaining this information in the system or clearing it out. If you clear it out of the system, or Purge it, the information is lost forever except for the printed copy that you retained. In most instances that is what you want to do after a certain period of time has elapsed.

The open item method of accounting for invoices provides you with particular kinds of information.

▪ *Interest on Late Payments*

The open item method allows you to calculate interest charges on overdue accounts receivable.

If you charge interest on a customer's overdue balance, it would be entered into the accounts receivable module as an invoice and the customer would pay it along with the regular payment. You would record the interest charge with a credit to interest income.

▪ *Bad Debts*

The open item method also identifies invoices that are overdue so that you can make a judgement as to whether or not you think they will be collectible. To record such an invoice you would put through a negative invoice, with the debit going to bad debt expense.

- *Prepayments*

There are times when your customer wants to make a prepayment for goods or services that will be received at some future date. To record this transaction you would enter it as a negative invoice, using the check number as the invoice number.

The ability to identify specific invoices is the key to good internal control. For this reason the open item method is superior to the balance forward method, which only accounts for the total owing and not for specific invoices. The open item method would be difficult to implement under a manual accounting system, but the computerized Bedford Accounting System makes it possible.

COMPUTERIZING ACCOUNTS RECEIVABLE

As with the accounts **PAYABLE** module, before you can begin to convert your manual accounts receivable system to the Bedford Accounting System you must organize your existing data. Let's look at what is involved in organizing data.

Organizing Customer Records

As with accounts payable, there are three steps to organizing your customer records:

1. prepare a customer listing;

2. list the outstanding invoices;

3. ensure that the total amount of outstanding invoices agrees with the balance in the control account, accounts payable, in the general ledger.

- *Prepare a Customer Listing*

Prepare a complete listing of customers who can purchase goods from you on credit. You need their name, street address, city, state, zip code and telephone number. The Bedford Accounting System automatically assigns customer account numbers for you. It will then sort the customers into an alphabetical listing for easy access.

- *List Outstanding Invoices*

Make a listing of all unpaid invoices for each customer up to the time of conversion. The listing should include the date of the invoice, the invoice number and the amount owing. Any partial payments made by customers against these invoices must also be listed. For example, you may have the following situation:

number	date	item	amount
XYZ Freight Co.			
12345	12-15-87	invoice	123.45
123	12-16-87	partial payment	-23.45
Total			100.00
Westwind Securities Inc.			
12346	12-30-87	invoice	455.00
Total			455.00
Total Accounts Receivable (to agree to control)			555.00

▪ *Agree to Control Account*

Total all outstanding amounts and make sure this total agrees with the amount showing in the accounts receivable account in the existing general ledger or your trial balance. You must start with the listing equal to your control account otherwise the program will not allow you to change the **RECEIVABLE** module to READY mode.

Beginning the Accounts Receivable Conversion

Once you have the above information you are ready to begin computerizing your accounts receivable function. Start the Bedford Accounting System program by typing

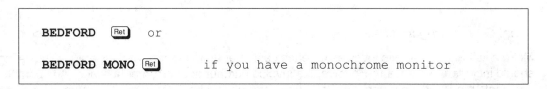

After a few seconds, the opening menu will appear, as shown in Figure 8.1A.

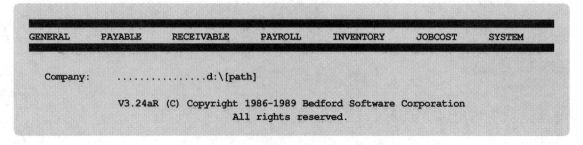

Figure 8.1A Bedford opening screen

Enter the location of the data files either in Drive B, or if you have a hard disk, in Drive C. If you are using Drive B for your data files be sure that you have a floppy disk in that drive with data files in the subdirectory FASTDEL.

B:\FASTDEL
C:\FASTDEL

011588   to enter a new **Using** date. The using
                      date should normally be the date that
                      you are entering information for or the
                      current date that you are working on.
                      In this case we are changing the using
                      date because we assume two weeks have
                      gone by. Once a using date has been
                      entered, you will not be able to return
                      to a previous date. You will be able to
                      enter information for a prior date (up
                      to the beginning of a fiscal year), but
                      you cannot enter data for a date subse-
                      quent to the using date. For these
                      reasons, it is important that you
                      ensure the using date is correct before
                      you enter it.
                      If the new **Using** date is more than one
                      week since the last using date, the
                      Bedford Accounting System will notify
                      you with a system message. (See Figure
                      8.1B.) You will have to press Ret again
                      in order to continue. (See Figure
                      8.1C.)

GENERAL	PAYABLE	RECEIVABLE	PAYROLL	INVENTORY	JOBCOST	SYSTEM

Company: C:\FASTDEL   ▶ 01-01-88
Using: ......mmddyy   01-01-88
                                                                          ▶ 12-31-88
                                                                          ▶ 01-01-89

CAUTION: This date is more than one week past the previous using date. If you
          proceed, you will be unable to move the using date back.

*** press RETURN to proceed or ESCape to reconsider ***

Figure 8.1B Message indicating that the new using date is
more than one week past the previous using date.

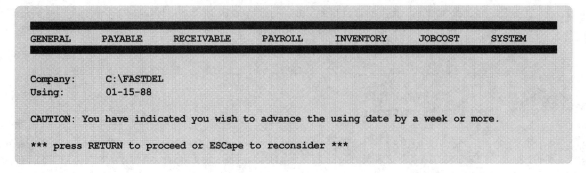

| GENERAL | PAYABLE | RECEIVABLE | PAYROLL | INVENTORY | JOBCOST | SYSTEM |

Company: C:\FASTDEL
Using: 01-15-88

CAUTION: You have indicated you wish to advance the using date by a week or more.

*** press RETURN to proceed or ESCape to reconsider ***

Figure 8.1C Second message indicating the advance of the using date

After you press the ENTER key again, the main menubar of the Bedford Accounting System will appear on the screen.

Your cursor should now highlight the word **GENERAL** on the main menubar. Press

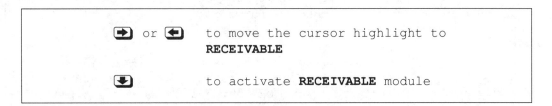

➡ or ⬅	to move the cursor highlight to **RECEIVABLE**
⬇	to activate **RECEIVABLE** module

Your screen will now display the accounts **RECEIVABLE** submenu as shown in Figure 8.2.

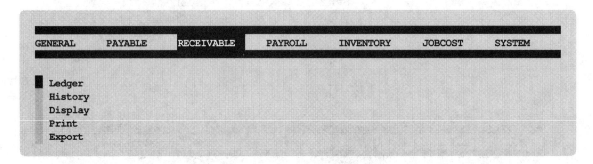

| GENERAL | PAYABLE | RECEIVABLE | PAYROLL | INVENTORY | JOBCOST | SYSTEM |

Ledger
History
Display
Print
Export

Figure 8.2 Accounts RECEIVABLE submenu

At this point you have no customers in the accounts **RECEIVABLE** module so you can only activate the ledger portion from this menu. To enter customer information, press

| ➡ | to activate **Ledger** |

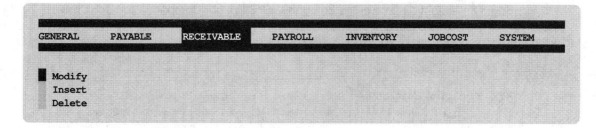

Figure 8.3 Accounts RECEIVABLE Ledger submenu

You now have another menu as shown in Figure 8.3 from which you can either insert or delete an account or modify information about a customer. Since we have no customers in the module at the present time, we can only activate the **Insert** command. Press

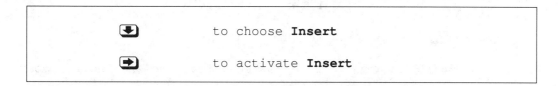

to choose **Insert**

to activate **Insert**

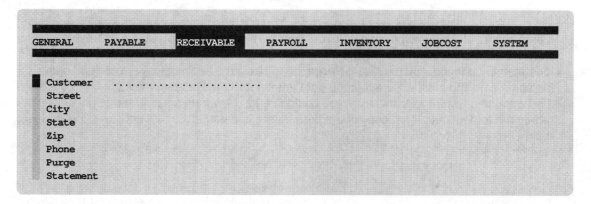

Figure 8.4 Accounts RECEIVABLE customer information input screen

You can now enter customer account information to begin the accounts receivable conversion.

- *Entering Customers into the Accounts Receivable Module*

Using the customer listing that we compiled earlier we will now add some customers to the accounts **RECEIVABLE** module. Let's enter the following customer:

Customer Name	XYZ Freight Company
Street Address	466 Water St.
City	Seattle
State	Wa.
Zip Code	98423
Phone Number	206-556-8545

Begin entering the name of the company, XYZ Freight Company. You don't have to hold the SHIFT key down to capitalize the first letter, X, of the company name. However, the Y and Z will not be capitalized unless you depress the SHIFT key.

XYZ Freight Company `Ret` to enter the name of the
Customer. If you make a mistake, simply
use the `BS` key to erase the errors and
retype the correct letters.

466 Water St. `Ret` to enter the **Street** address

Seattle `Ret` to enter the **City**

Wa. `Ret` to enter the **State**

98423 `Ret` to enter the **Zip** code

2065568545 to enter the area code and **Phone** number

Your cursor will now be next to **Purge**. You can choose to retain the invoice and payments history of the customer or not. If you want to retain the history you would enter **No** to **Purge**. Because a customer's payment history may be important for extending future credit and for statement printing, you may want **Purge** set to **No** in the accounts receivable subledger. At the same time you must ensure that the data does not fill the Random Access Memory associated with the payment information or you couldn't enter new transaction data. In any case, remember to print out a hard copy of the data before you purge. We will choose to purge the data.

Y to choose **Yes** for **Purge**

Once you make that selection the cursor will move to the word **Statement**. Entering a **Yes** in this space will automatically prepare a printed statement when you request it later. A **No** answer will not print the statement.

Keep in mind that this is a default choice only. When you get to the point of printing statements, you will be given the choice of printing statements for all customers or only for a specific customer. If you choose all customers, then the statements will be printed automatically for each customer whose default has been set to Yes. If you ask for a specific customer, then the program will ignore the default setting for that customer and print a statement. Let's change the default to **Yes** so that we get a printed statement later.

Y to choose **Yes** for printing **Statements**

Once you have entered all of the customer data and indicated your choices for the various options and defaults, you can edit any of the customer data that you have entered. Use the arrow key to move to any field. Keep in mind that you can always change customer information by using the **Modify** command later. Nevertheless, you should always make sure that customer information is entered correctly in the first place.

When complete your screen should resemble Figure 8.5.

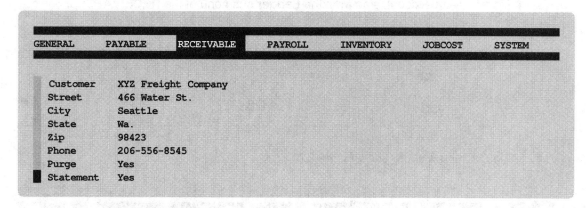

| GENERAL | PAYABLE | RECEIVABLE | PAYROLL | INVENTORY | JOBCOST | SYSTEM |

```
Customer    XYZ Freight Company
Street      466 Water St.
City        Seattle
State       Wa.
Zip         98423
Phone       206-556-8545
Purge       Yes
Statement   Yes
```

Figure 8.5 Customer information entered

After you are satisfied that the entry is complete, press

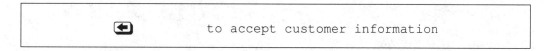

to accept customer information

Note: If you press the ESCape key at this point the program will not accept the data you have entered. The ESCape key in this case is handy to erase information about a customer that you realize is wrong while entering. After pressing the ESCape key you will have to enter the information again.

Once the program has accepted the vendor information that you entered above, the program will automatically assign the number "1" to this customer, since it is the first one in the system. The program does not allow you to enter customer account numbers selectively.

▪ Practice Exercise

Enter the following customers into the system using the following information:

Customer	Westwind Securities Inc.	Weston, Lathrop & Co.	Rainier Bank
Address	4466 Grant Street	2399 Ellensburg Ave.	1111 W. 43rd
City	Seattle	Federal Way	Bellevue
State	Wa.	Wa.	Wa.
Zip Code	98222	97416	94163
Phone Number	206-674-1256	206-435-2111	206-667-1212
Purge	Y	Y	Y
Statement	Y	Y	Y

▪ *Modifying Customer Information*

There are times when we wish to change the information about a customer in the system. For example, we may want to change the customer's name or phone number, or change the purging option to Yes when we no longer need it.

To modify an account, start from the **Ledger** submenu of the **RECEIVABLE** module. Press

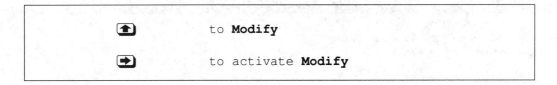

Your screen will now show Figure 8.6.

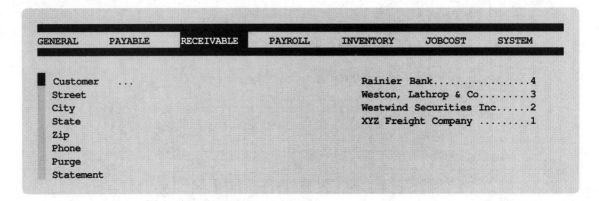

Figure 8.6 Modifying customer information

Notice that the input screen for modifying customer information looks identical to the **Insert** screen. At the right of the screen is a list of the customers that you just entered. To **Modify** customer #2, Westwind Securities Inc., type

The display beside customer will change to show the company name and the rest of the information about the company will appear beside their respective headings. Now let's change the telephone number to 206-645-4866:

⬇	to choose **Phone**
➡	to activate **Phone**
2066454866	to insert new phone number
⬅	to accept modifications made

▪ *Deleting Customers*

Although the Bedford Accounting System can accommodate up to 999 customers in the accounts **RECEIVABLE** module, there may be times when a particular customer should be deleted from the list. The Bedford Accounting System will only allow you to delete customers that have no current balances in them. If you attempt to delete one with an active balance, the program will inform you with a message on the screen, and not allow you to proceed with the deletion. This prevents you from deleting an account with an active balance, which would throw you out of balance with your control account in the general ledger.

You should still be in the **Ledger** submenu. To delete a customer, press

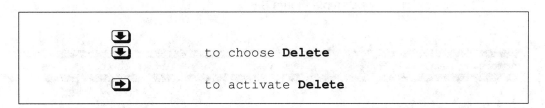

⬇ ⬇	to choose **Delete**
➡	to activate **Delete**

To delete a customer, you would enter the customer number from the list on the right side of the screen and press ENTER. You would then have one more chance to change your mind. Pressing ENTER would delete the customer from the system . Since you do not wish to delete an account, press

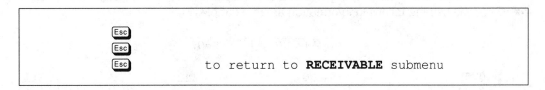

Esc Esc Esc	to return to **RECEIVABLE** submenu

▪ *Entering the Opening Balances*

When you first entered the customers into the accounts **RECEIVABLE** module you did not include balances outstanding. You have to now enter the outstanding invoices and partial payments for each customer. Leaving one out will cause the listing to go out of balance.

To enter the opening balances, begin with the **RECEIVABLE** submenu. Notice that the second item in the menu is **History** (See Figure 8.7). The opening (historical) balances can only be entered while the system is in the NOT READY mode. Once you change to the READY mode you will no longer be able to change the historical balances.

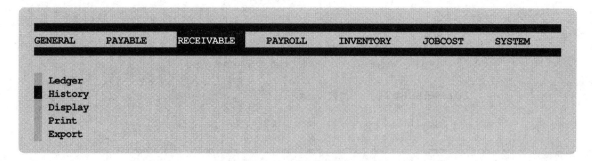

Figure 8.7   The accounts receivable submenu showing that the item History is about to be activated

Press

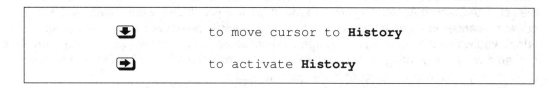

Your screen will now resemble Figure 8.8.

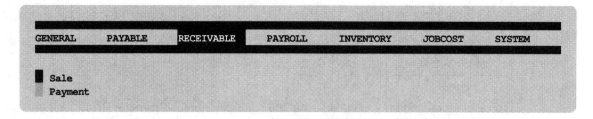

Figure 8.8 Accounts receivable history submenu for entering sale or payment information

You can now enter opening invoices under **Sale** and any partial payments under **Payment**. We will use the following information as an example.

XYZ Freight Company

number	date	item	amount
12345	12-15-87	invoice	123.45
123	12-15-87	payment	-23.45
		total	$ 100.00

▪ *Entering Sales*

To enter the opening sales invoice for XYZ Freight Company, place your cursor beside the word **Sale** and press

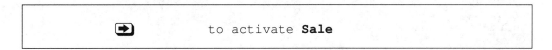

Your screen should now resemble 8.9.

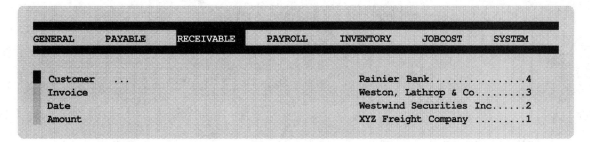

Figure 8.9   The sale menu item activated — choosing a customer for which historical sales information is to be entered

Now enter the following information

1 `Ret`	to enter the **Customer** XYZ Freight Company
12345 `Ret`	to enter **Invoice** #12345
121587	to enter the **Date.** Notice that the date that you must enter is between the opening date and the year end date as displayed on the right hand side of the screen.
123.45 `Ret`	to enter the **Amount** of the sale

Your screen should now resemble Figure 8.10. The information about the customer sale has been entered.

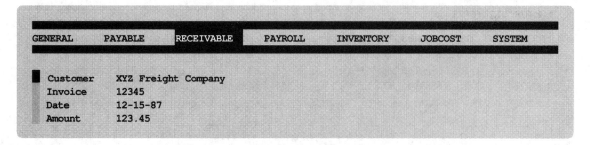

Figure 8.10 Sale information entered for customer

To get the program to accept the information press

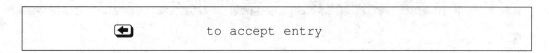

to accept entry

- *Entering Payments*

Entering full or partial payments is done in the same manner as entering invoices, except you choose **Payment** from the **History** submenu instead of Sale. You should be in the **History** submenu shown in Figure 8.8. Press

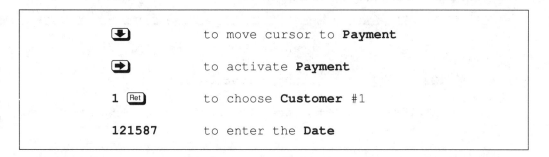

to move cursor to **Payment**

to activate **Payment**

1 Ret   to choose **Customer** #1

121587   to enter the **Date**

A list of outstanding invoices will appear on the right hand side of the screen with an arrow pointing to the first (and in this instance only) invoice. You must always allocate a payment to an invoice. You can select one of the listed invoices on the right hand side of the screen by pressing the ENTER key until the arrow points to the invoice you want. In our case, there is only one invoice so we will allocate the payment to it. If we were entering a customer prepayment, we would have to enter it as a negative invoice (See Figure 8.11).

Once you have the correct invoice amount showing beside the amount in brackets, type:

23.45 Ret   to enter **Amount** of payment

123 Ret   to enter the **Check** number

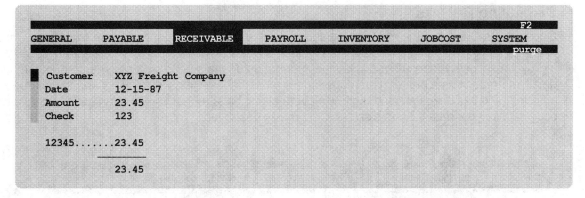

Figure 8.11 History payment information entered for a customer

Notice the notation F2 in the upper right hand corner of the screen. Until you have accepted the entry it will stay on the screen reminding you that you can view the entry and the distribution to the various accounts by simply pressing the F2 function key (See Figure 8.12).

F2	to view journal entry

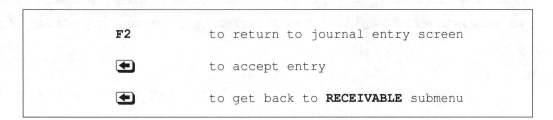

Figure 8.12 Pressing the F2 function key allows you to see
the details of the payment journal entry (J5)

F2	to return to journal entry screen
⬅	to accept entry
⬅	to get back to **RECEIVABLE** submenu

You have now entered the outstanding invoice.

■ *Practice Exercise*

Enter another sale for the following customer:

Customer	#2
Invoice	# 12346
Date	12-30-87
Amount	$455.00

Displaying Reports

Once you have entered the historical balances into the Bedford Accounting System you may want to look at the information contained in the accounts **RECEIVABLE** module. The Bedford Accounting System allows you to either display the information on the screen (soft copy) or to print the detail information on a printer (hard copy). In many instances, simply displaying it on the screen is sufficient and can save time and money. Nevertheless, be sure that you keep an audit trail in hard copy in case your data files on disk are accidentally destroyed.

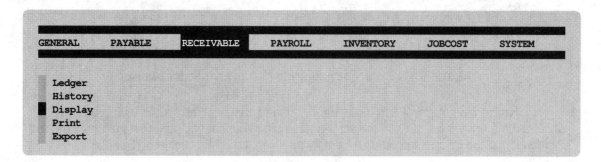

Figure 8.13 Accounts RECEIVABLE submenu

Now let's look at the Display option in the accounts **RECEIVABLE** module. Start with the **RECEIVABLE** submenu as shown in Figure 8.13, and press

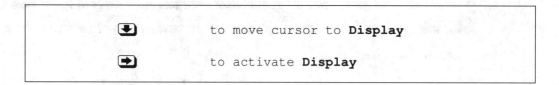

Your screen will now look like Figure 8.14.

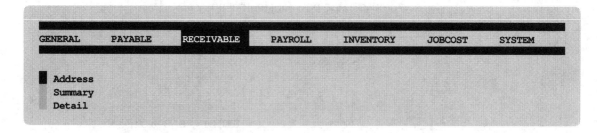

Figure 8.14 Display options submenu

- *Address Display*

Notice we have a choice of displaying **Address, Summary** or **Detail**. Let's look at each of these in turn.

The **Address** menu item displays the company account number, name and address for quick correspondence. To display customer addresses, press

---

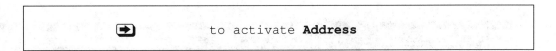

Your screen will display in columnar form, the address information about each company on file in numerical order as shown in Figure 8.15.

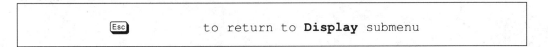

GENERAL	PAYABLE	RECEIVABLE	PAYROLL	INVENTORY	JOBCOST	SYSTEM

4	Rainier Bank	1111 W. 43rd	Bellevue	94163
3	Weston, Lathrop & Co.	2399 Ellensburg Ave.	Federal Way	97416
2	Westwind Securities Inc.	4466 Grant Street	Seattle	98222
1	XYZ Freight Company	466 Water St.	Seattle	98423

Figure 8.15 Company information displayed through Address option

Since we have only four customers entered, we can display all of them on one screen. If you have many customers you can view a screenful at a time by using the up or down arrow key.

When you are finished looking at the customer screen, press the ESCape key to return to the display submenu.

[Esc]   to return to **Display** submenu

■ *Summary Display*

The **Summary** option summarizes all of the data and shows only one total for the customer. The total is then broken down into how many days it has been since the invoice was rendered.

To display the summary press

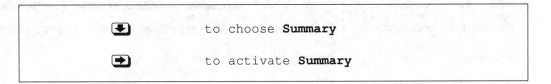

↓   to choose **Summary**

→   to activate **Summary**

Your screen will now resemble Figure 8.16.

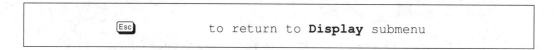

GENERAL	PAYABLE	RECEIVABLE	PAYROLL	INVENTORY	JOBCOST	SYSTEM
			total	0-30	31-60	61+
2 Westwind Securities Inc.			455.00	455.00	—	—
1 XYZ Freight Company			100.00	—	100.00	—
			555.00	455.00	100.00	—

Figure 8.16 Customer summary of purchases and payment information

When you are finished looking at the summary information screen, press the ESCape key to return to the display submenu.

[Esc] to return to **Display** submenu

■ *Detail Display*

The **Detail** display option will give you a listing of all current customer transactions. Press

[↓] to choose **Detail**

[→] to activate **Detail**

If you select the detail option you must also tell the Bedford Accounting System if you want to see just one account or all the accounts. When you activate this option, your screen will appear as shown in Figure 8.17.

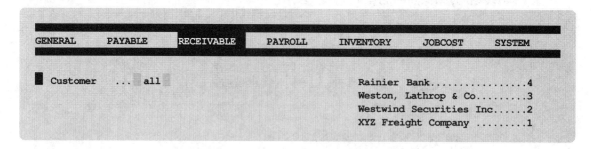

GENERAL	PAYABLE	RECEIVABLE	PAYROLL	INVENTORY	JOBCOST	SYSTEM

■ Customer ... all

Rainier Bank...............4
Weston, Lathrop & Co........3
Westwind Securities Inc......2
XYZ Freight Company 1

Figure 8.17 Choosing customer(s) for detail display of purchase and payment information

We can choose from the companies listed along the right side of the screen. If you wish to see one specific account, just enter the customer number. If you wish to see the detail of all the accounts, press the SHIFT and ENTER key at the same time. This signals to the program that you want to see a full listing.

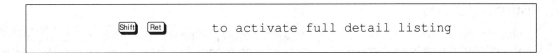

The detail listing for all customers resembles Figure 8.18.

GENERAL	PAYABLE	RECEIVABLE	PAYROLL	INVENTORY	JOBCOST	SYSTEM
			total	0-30	31-60	61+
2 Westwind Securities Inc.						
12346	12-30-87	Invoice	455.00	455.00	—	—
1 XYZ Freight Company						
12345	12-15-87	Invoice	123.45	—	123.45	—
123	12-15-87	Payment	23.45-	—	23.45-	—
			100.00	—	100.00	—

Figure 8.18 Customer detail information

The detail is broken into the same time frames as the summary listing, but includes the invoice or check number, the date of the transaction and the type of transaction, either invoice or payment. As mentioned previously, this information can provide us with answers about any customer's account.

Notice that the amount owing is broken down into the number of days since the sale date, 0-30, 31-60 and 61+ days. These are called the **aging dates** which can be set in the **SYSTEM** module. Depending on your collection policy, you can use this report to tell whether or not a customer is current with payments. For example, if your policy is NET 30, meaning the entire amount of the invoice is to be paid in 30 days, then a customer having an amount in 31-60 or 61+ tells you that this customer is slow in paying the bills. You may want to send a bill collector or at least call the customer with a reminder that a payment is due. You may also use this information to prevent the customer from getting further credit extended until a payment is forthcoming or to withhold credit privileges altogether.

Whether you should get a detail or a summary listing depends on the use you make of the information. The **Summary** information is useful for cash budgeting. It provides information about the total cash inflow that can be expected over specific periods in the near future. On the other hand, the **Detail** display for each customer provides information about specific invoices that are outstanding, which is not too useful for cash budgeting.

When you have finished viewing these displays, return to the **RECEIVABLE** submenu by pressing

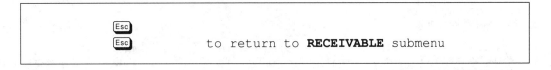

Printing Reports

Displaying reports on the monitor is fine for quick viewing of the data. In most cases however, you want a printed report for a permanent record. Printing reports is similar to displaying them. With your monitor displaying the accounts **RECEIVABLE** submenu, press

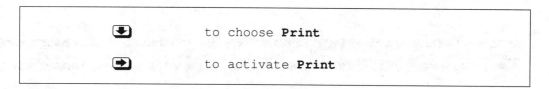

The **Print** submenu will now appear as shown in Figure 8.19.

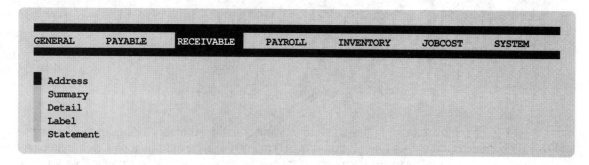

Figure 8.19 Accounts receivable print submenu

The **Print** submenu is identical to the **Display** submenu except for the printing of labels. Let's look at each of the options in more detail.

> NOTE: Make sure your printer is turned on, that there is paper in the printer, that the print head is at the top of the paper and the online button is activated, allowing data to flow from the computer to the printer. This should be checked each time you wish to print something.

Now choose the address listing. With your cursor on **Address**, press

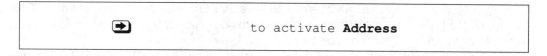

Your printer will now print out an address listing as shown in Figure 8.20A.

Fast Delivery Inc. FOR INSTRUCTIONAL USE ONLY
CUSTOMER Address Jan 15, 1988

4	Rainier Bank	1111 W. 43rd	Bellevue	Wa.	94163	206-667-1212
3	Weston, Lathrop & Co.	2399 Ellensburg Ave.	Federal Way	Wa.	97416	206-435-2111
2	Westwind Securities Inc.	4466 Grant Street	Seattle	Wa.	98222	206-645-4866
1	XYZ Freight Company	466 Water St.	Seattle	Wa.	98423	206-556-8545

CUSTOMERS on file: 4

Figure 8.20A Printout of customer address listing

To get a print out of the **Summary** listing press

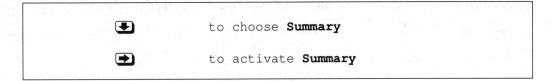

A printout of the **Summary** listing is shown in Figure 8.20B.

Fast Delivery Inc. FOR INSTRUCTIONAL USE ONLY
CUSTOMER Summary Jan 15,1988

		total	current	31-60	61-90	91+
2	Westwind Securities Inc.	455.00	455.00	-	-	-
1	XYZ Freight Company	100.00	-	100.00	-	-
		555.00	455.00	100.00	-	-

Figure 8.20B Print-out of customer summary listing

Similarly, to get a printout of the **Detail** listing press

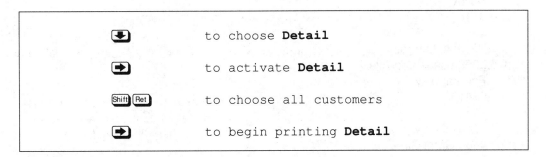

The **Detail** listing is shown in Figure 8.20C.

Fast Delivery Inc. FOR INSTRUCTIONAL USE ONLY   Page 1
CUSTOMER Detail Jan 15,1988

				total	current	31-60	61-90	91+
2	Westwind Securities Inc.	12346	12-30-87 Invoice	455.00	455.00	-	-	-
1	XYZ Freight Company	12345	12-15-87 Invoice	123.45	-	123.45	-	-
		123	12-15-87 Payment	23.45-	-	23.45-	-	-
				100.00	-	100.00	-	-
				555.00	455.00	100.00	-	-

Figure 8.20C Print-out of customer detail listing

The **Label** option is specifically included to allow you to prepare address labels for each customer in the event that you want to contact them through a mass mailing. The labels are designed to print on single column labels. (See Figure 8.20D). To print labels press

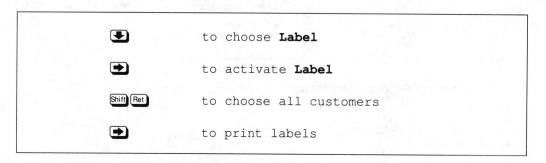

After the labels have been printed, you will have to advance the paper in your printer to the top of the page before making your next printout. Press the on-line button. That disengages your computer from your printer. Then press the form feed button. Your printhead should now advance to the top of the next page. Press the on-line button again to re-establish the printer-computer connection.

Rainier Bank
1111 W 43rd
Bellevue, Wa.
94163

Weston, Lathrop & Co.
2399 Ellensburg Ave.
Federal Way, Wa.
97416

Westwind Securities Inc.
4466 Grant Street
Seattle, Wa.
98222

XYZ Freight Company
466 Water St.
Seattle, Wa.
98423

Figure 8.20D Print-out of customer address labels

Printing Statements

Now print out the statements for the customers on hand. Figure 8.20E shows a printout of a statement. Be sure that your printer is ready before proceeding.

Press

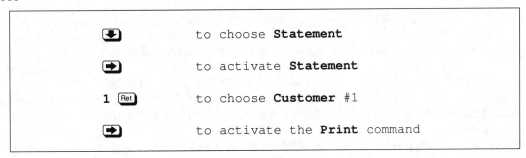

⬇	to choose **Statement**
➡	to activate **Statement**
1 Ret	to choose **Customer** #1
➡	to activate the **Print** command

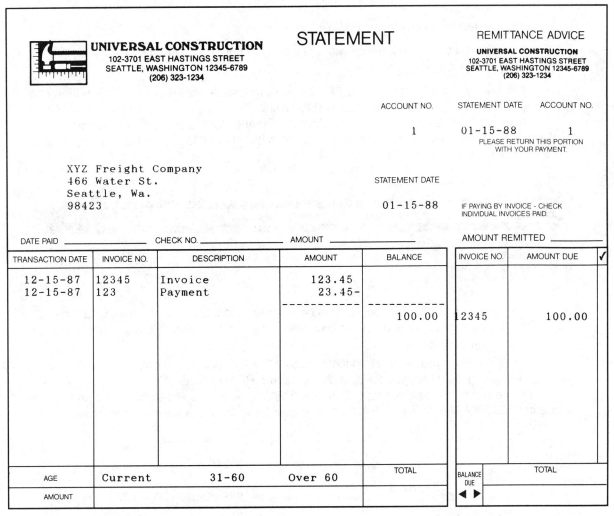

Figure 8.20E Customer statement printed on a custom Bedford statement

After the statement has printed, press

⬅ ⬅	to return to the Bedford main menubar

Changing to Ready Mode

Now that we have entered our customers and the historical balances, we have completed the conversion process from a manual to a computerized accounts receivable system. We are now ready to enter current transactions into the accounts **RECEIVABLE** module.

Before we can do that however, we must go through the procedure of changing the accounts **RECEIVABLE** module from the NOT READY mode to the READY mode. Remember, once you change to the READY mode, you cannot return to the NOT READY mode. This means you will not be able to change the historical data that you entered. Therefore be absolutely sure that the data you entered is correct.

As a safety precaution the Bedford Accounting System will not allow you to change the module to the READY mode until two conditions are met:

a. the general ledger is in READY mode and

b. the subledger is in balance with the control account — accounts receivable, in the general ledger.

If the general ledger is not in READY mode, a message will tell you so. You will have to go into the **GENERAL** module and make it READY first.

If an out of balance message is displayed, it means that the accounts receivable subledger is not in balance with the control account in the general ledger. An example of such a message is shown in Figure 8.21.

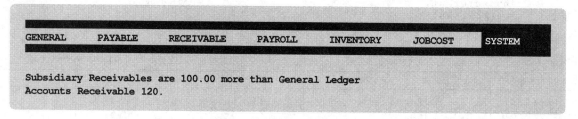

```
GENERAL      PAYABLE      RECEIVABLE      PAYROLL      INVENTORY      JOBCOST      SYSTEM

Subsidiary Receivables are 100.00 more than General Ledger
Accounts Receivable 120.
```

Figure 8.21   Example of an out of balance message indicating that the accounts receivable subledger is out of balance with the control account in the general ledger

If this happens you must return to the accounts **RECEIVABLE** module and make the necessary adjustment. Then go back and change to the READY mode.

Since we do not have an out of balance problem we can go ahead and make the accounts **RECEIVABLE** module READY. You should be at the Bedford main menubar.

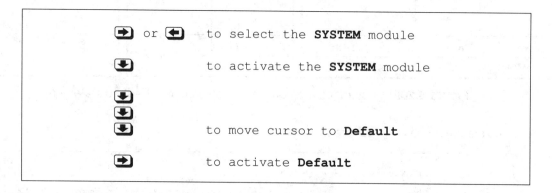

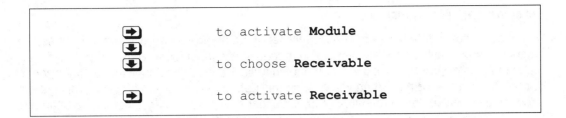

Your screen will now display the default accounts **RECEIVABLE** module settings as shown in Figure 8.22.

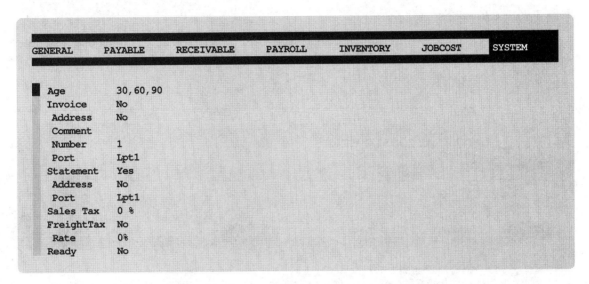

Figure 8.22 Accounts RECEIVABLE module default settings

There are eight options in the accounts receivable default settings. Let's change to the READY mode first before we discuss the other default settings. Press

⬆   to choose **Ready**

➡   to change **No** to **Yes**

⬅   to make the change permanent

➡   to activate **Receivable** again

Now let's look at the other options that we can set. Refer to the menu listed on the screen.

▪ *Account Aging Defaults*

The account aging default setting is currently set at 30, 60 and 90 days. Although this setting is standard, there may be good reasons to change this setting, at least temporarily, if you want to get some idea of your cash inflow over a particular time period. You may want to know what is due in 15, 30 and 45 days. When you change this default option, all reports and displays will show the information for these dates. You can change these dates anytime and as often as you like so you could get some idea of your cash inflow for different account aging dates. The account aging function clearly indicates those customers who are delinquent in their payments so that collection proceedings can be stepped up.

▪ *Printing Invoices*

The second option is the ability to print an invoice. If you wish to do so you must use a standard Bedford sales invoice (Figure 8.23) available in stationery stores or directly from a printing company.

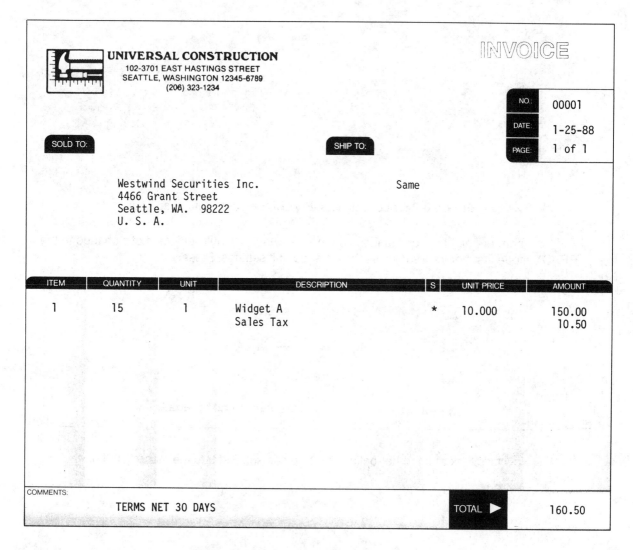

Figure 8.23 Standard Bedford sales invoice

If you change the default to **Yes**, the system will print sales invoices. You must then provide information about additional options as follows:

Address **Yes** means that you want the address of the company to be printed on the check; **No** will leave it off.

Comment A space on the invoice allows you to print a comment. In this area, you can put a standard comment that will appear on the bottom of all invoices such as "All invoices due in 30 days" or "Merry Christmas and Happy New Year."

Number If you want to print invoices you must indicate what the first invoice number will be.

Port This is the printer port that the program will send all the data to. If you have a parallel printer, it will in all likelihood be on the default port **Lpt1**. If your printer is connected to a serial port, this will probably be the **Com1** port. You will have to check your computer reference manual, or look on the back of the computer to determine which port your printer is hooked up to.

▪ Printing Statements

Another option is whether or not you want statements printed. Under the print option of the accounts **RECEIVABLE** module you can specify that you want to send a statement to any or all of your customers. This is only possible however, if the default option in the **SYSTEM** module is set to **Yes** for printing statements for the entire customer base. If you enter a **No** instead as a default in the **SYSTEM** module, you will not be able to print statements for any customer no matter what you have chosen in each account in the **RECEIVABLE** module.

A statement is different from an invoice. An invoice provides information about a particular sale, whereas a statement is a summary of all sales and payments made for a period of time. Normally you would want this default set to **Yes**. A standard Bedford statement is shown in Figure 8.20E.

If we set the print invoice default to **Yes** we must give the system two more pieces of information:

Address Answering **Yes** will cause the company address to be printed on all company statements. If your company does not have preprinted forms with the company logo, you would choose **Yes**.

Port This refers to the printer port as discussed above.

We will leave the printing of statements set to **No** for now.

▪ Setting SalesTax and FreightTax Criteria

The next set of options asks you to set applicable sales tax and whether or not tax is charged on freight. **SalesTax** refers to the rate of state sales tax charged on regular sales. If there is a local tax in addition to state tax, then you add the two together and enter the total amount. If your company does not charge state sales tax, this would be set to 0 percent.

FreightTax is set to **No** by default. If you choose **Yes**, state tax will be calculated on the total amount including the freight charge.

We will not make any changes for these items at this time. Let's return to the accounts **RECEIVABLE** module. Press

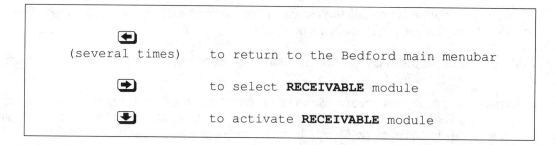

You will now see Figure 8.24. Notice that the menu has changed.

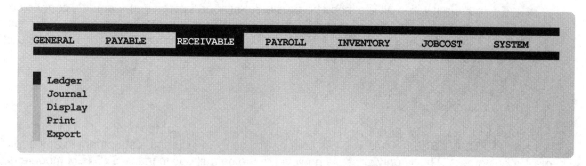

Figure 8.24 Accounts receivable submenu with module in READY mode —
the menu item History has now changed to Journal

The menu item **History** has changed to **Journal**. The **Journal** is the menu item that will be used to record all journal entries to the system.

ENTERING ACCOUNTS RECEIVABLE JOURNAL ENTRIES

All accounts receivable transactions are entered through a series of journal entries, much like the journal entries we made in the accounts PAYABLE module in the previous chapter. The accounts RECEIVABLE ledger will be used to enter two kinds of entries.

a. Sales   Dr. Accounts Receivable or Cash
                     Cr. Sales Revenue

b. Payments   Dr. Cash
                     Cr. Accounts Receivable

Let's use the following entry as an example.

January 15, 1987	Dr. Accounts Receivable	256.00	
	Cr. General Delivery		256.00
	(to record a sale to XYZ Freight Company, invoice #522)		

As mentioned before, subledgers have common accounts to which debits or credits can be posted as one total. For accounts receivable, each customer purchase entry will have a credit to sales or general revenue and a debit to accounts receivable. Because the debit entry is always to accounts receivable, we can have the program keep track of debits and enter the total debit amount automatically after we complete the transaction entry.

Entering Sales

To enter a sale transaction, press

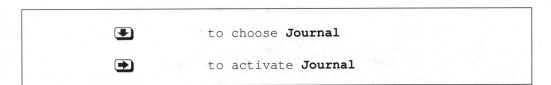

The **Journal** submenu will appear as in Figure 8.25. The program then asks you to indicate whether the entry is a sale or a payment. Since we want to record a sale we leave the cursor highlight next to **Sale** and press

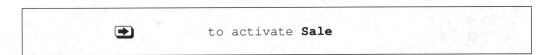

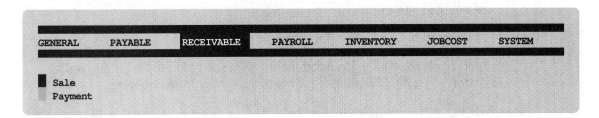

Figure 8.26 Customer sale entry menu

The sale entry input screen will now appear as in Figure 8.26. The cursor highlight is beside the word **Customer**. On the right hand side, the program lists the customers currently on our system in alphabetical order.

Enter the number of the customer from the list. If you had many customers you might have to use the down or up arrow keys to see the remaining customers and their numbers.

Now enter the invoice number. This is the number that appears on the customers invoice.

> **522** [Ret]   to enter **Invoice** #522

Now enter the date of the transaction, January 12, 1988

> **011288**   to enter **Date**

Your cursor will now be beside **Account**. To display a listing of the general ledger accounts as shown in Figure 8.27 you have to press the down arrow key twice.

```
GENERAL     PAYABLE     RECEIVABLE     PAYROLL     INVENTORY     JOBCOST     SYSTEM


  Customer    XYZ Freight Company              TOTAL CURRENT LIABILITIES..269
  Invoice     522                              LONG TERM DEBT............271
  Date        01-12-88                         Mortgage Payable..........275
■ Account      ...                             TOTAL LONG TERM DEBT.......280
  Amount                                       SHARE CAPITAL.............301
  Project                                      Class A Common............302
  Amount                                       Class B Common............303
                                               TOTAL SHARES..............310
                                               EARNINGS..................350
                                               Retained Earnings.........356
                                               Current Earnings..........360
                                               TOTAL EARNINGS............369
                                               REVENUE...................400
                                               General Revenue...........402
                                               General Delivery..........406
                                               Special Delivery..........407
                                               TOTAL SERVICE REVENUE.....410
                                               OTHER REVENUE.............419
                                               Freight Revenue...........420
```

Figure 8.27 Display of GENERAL ledger accounts to which sale is distributed

The program is waiting for you to enter the account to which the credit part of the entry will go. Usually, this is to general revenue or sales, but in some cases can be to liabilities, owner's equity or revenues. Note that the accounts with the little boxes to the right of the account number are the only ones to which you can post amounts, so you must pick one of these accounts. If you do not see the account you wish to post to, use the up and down arrow keys to list other screens.

We wish to enter the account number for General Delivery.

⬇
⬇   to move to screen that shows the General
                           Delivery account

406   to enter **Account** #406

256 `Ret`   to enter **Amount** of invoice, $256.00

Your cursor will automatically return to the **Account** option, bypassing **Project**. As mentioned in the previous chapter, if you had defined one or more projects or departments in the **JOBCOST** module you could allocate this freight expense to a project or department.

At any time during the entry of an invoice from a customer, you can review your entry by pressing the F2 function key. It is shown at the top right hand corner of the screen. Let's see what we have done so far. Press

F2   to review entry

Your screen will now resemble Figure 8.28.

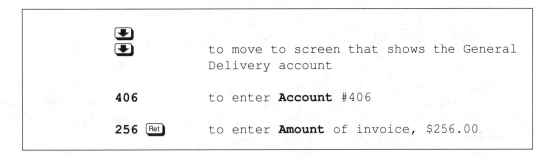

							F2
GENERAL	PAYABLE	RECEIVABLE	PAYROLL	INVENTORY	JOBCOST	SYSTEM	
J5				debits	credits		
120	Accounts Receivable			256.00			
406	General Delivery				256.00		
				256.00	256.00		

Figure 8.28 Reviewing a journal entry using the F2 function key

The program has already added the amounts together and made the credit entry to accounts receivable. Now return to the entry screen.

F2   to return to entry screen

As long as the cursor is still in the account field you can change the entry. Once you know the entry is correct, press

`Ret`   to terminate entry

At this point you could cancel the entire entry by pressing the ESCape key. You would then have to reenter the transaction. Since the entry is correct press

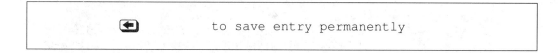

Once you have accepted the entry, the customer balance will be updated in the accounts **RECEIVABLE** module and the control account will be updated in the general ledger. Let's look at the customer data to make sure.

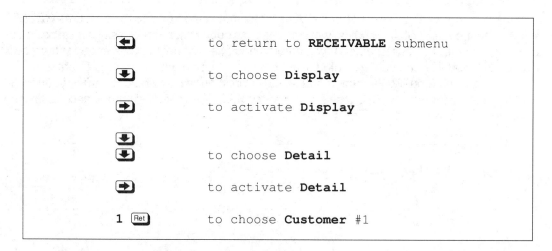

You can see in Figure 8.29 that the items you just entered are reported in the detail llisting.

GENERAL	PAYABLE	RECEIVABLE	PAYROLL	INVENTORY	JOBCOST	SYSTEM
			total	0-30	31-60	61+

1 XYZ Freight Company

			total	0-30	31-60	61+
12345	12-15-87	Invoice	123.45	—	123.45	—
123	12-15-87	Payment	23.45-	—	23.45-	—
522	01-12-88	Invoice	256.00	256.00	—	—
			356.00	256.00	100.00	—

Figure 8.29 Detail display of customer purchases and payments

When you have finished viewing this screen, press

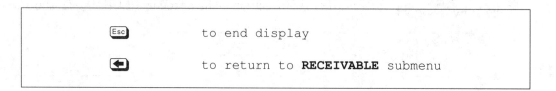

■ *Practice Exercise*

Enter the following sales for Fast Delivery Inc.

Customer #	3	4	3	2
Invoice #	523	524	525	526
Date	01/07/88	01/08/88	01/12/88	01/14/88
Account name	Special	General	Special	General
Amount	$1501.00	$1624.00	$3146.00	$310.00

Entering Customer Payments

The second type of accounts receivable transaction that is entered into the accounts **RECEIV-ABLE** module, is the payment of invoices or cash receipts. Payments by customers made between the conversion date and the using date are recorded as paid and allocated to the specific invoice outstanding.

Let's record a $169 payment by XYZ Freight Company made on January 15, 1988. $100 is to be paid on invoice #12345 and $69 on invoice #522. The required journal entry is as follows:

    Dr. Cash   169.00
        Cr. Accounts Receivable   169.00

Remember, this is a standard accounts receivable entry so we only have to allocate the payment to the proper invoice.

To enter the payment, begin at the accounts **RECEIVABLE** submenu and press

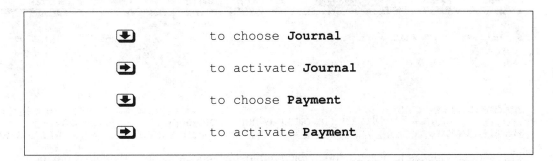

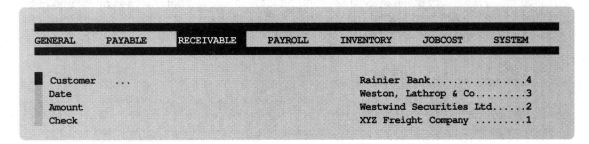

Figure 8.30 The customer payment entry screen of the accounts RECEIVABLE submenu

The payment entry screen will appear as in Figure 8.30. You can now enter the following information:

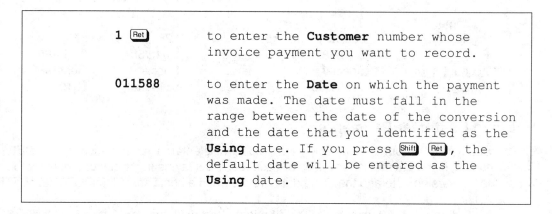

Your cursor will now appear beside **Amount** and your screen will resemble Figure 8.31. On the right side of the screen, you will see the customer's outstanding invoice numbers and the respective balances. If the **Purge** option for a customer has been set to **No**, there may also be some zero balances showing. You will also notice a small arrow pointing toward the first invoice with a balance.

GENERAL	PAYABLE	RECEIVABLE	PAYROLL	INVENTORY	JOBCOST	SYSTEM

purge

Customer	XYZ Freight Company		▸12345...........100.00	
Date	01-15-88		522.............256.00	
Amount	..........100.00			
Check				

Figure 8.31 Allocating invoice payments against outstanding invoices

Our first task is to pick out the invoice against which we want to allocate a payment. Notice that the amount of the invoice selected appears in shaded parentheses at the end of the dotted line in the **Amount** field. If you wish to pay the entire amount of the invoice, holding the SHIFT key down and pressing ENTER will automatically enter the outstanding amount. In our case, we wish to pay invoice #12345 in full. Press

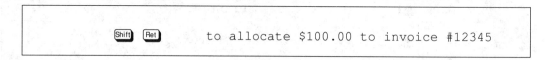

This will allocate the $100.00 to invoice #12345. At the bottom of the screen, you will see a running total of the payments for this customer. Your cursor will remain next to **Amount**, so that you can allocate another payment against an invoice.

```
69 [Ret]          to allocate $69.00 to invoice #522.
                  Note that the figure in Amount is the
                  sum of all invoice payments made;
                  in this instance $169.00.

146 [Ret]         to enter Check number

F2                to review entry

F2                to return to entry screen

[←]               to save entry
```

The Bedford Accounting System will update the customer's account for the payment and the general ledger by crediting accounts receivable and debiting cash. Since the invoice #12345 was paid in full, and purge is on, the record of the transaction is removed. The balance is now zero.

▪ Practice Exercise

Enter the following cash receipts from customers:

Customer	3	2
Invoice	523	526
Date	01/15/88	01/15/88
Amount	$475.00	$310.00
Check #	2192	47

Reconciling the Accounts Receivable Ledger with the General Ledger

Now that you have entered an invoice and a payment, let's go back once more and check to see if the integration is intact.

```
[←]               to return to RECEIVABLE submenu
                  with cursor on Journal

[↓]
[↓]               to choose Print option

[→]               to activate Print

[↓]
[↓]               to choose Detail
```

➡️		to activate **Detail**
[Shift] [Ret]		to choose all customers
➡️		to activate **Print**

Your listing should look like Figure 8.32.

Fast Delivery Inc. FOR INSTRUCTIONAL USE ONLY
CUSTOMER Detail Jan 15,1988   Page 1

					total	current	31-60	61-90	91+
4	Rainier Bank	524		01-08-88 Invoice	1,624.00	1,624.00	-	-	-
3	Weston, Lathrop & Co.	523		01-07-88 Invoice	1,501.00	1,501.00	-	-	-
		2192		01-12-88 Payment	475.00-	475.00-	-	-	-
		525		01-12-88 Invoice	3,146.00	3,146.00	-	-	-
					4,172.00	4,172.00	-	-	-
2	Westwind Securities Inc.	12346		12-30-87 Invoice	455.00	455.00	-	-	-
1	XYZ Freight Company	522		01-12-88 Invoice	256.00	256.00	-	-	-
		146		01-15-88 Payment	69.00-	69.00-	-	-	-
					187.00	187.00	-	-	-
					6,438.00	6,438.00	-	-	-

Figure 8.32 Customer printout of detail listing

Now press

[Esc] [Esc]		to get out of the accounts **RECEIVABLE** module to main menubar
⬅️		to choose the **GENERAL** module.
⬇️		to activate **GENERAL** module
⬇️		to move to **Display**
➡️		to activate **Display**
⬇️		to choose **Trial** balance
➡️		to activate **Trial** balance
[Shift] [Ret]		to accept current date for the display

Look in the trial balance until you see the accounts receivable balance. This balance should be equal to the balance in the detail listing received from the printout. We know then that the system is updating properly.

GENERAL	PAYABLE	RECEIVABLE	PAYROLL	INVENTORY	JOBCOST	SYSTEM
					debits	credits
104	Petty Cash				300.00	—
106	First Interstate - General				2,383.33	—
108	Bank B - Receivable				0.00	—
110	Bank C - Payroll				0.00	—
120	Accounts Receivable				6,438.00	—
124	Advances Receivable				0.00	—
126	Inventory				100.00	—
135	Prepaid Insurance				55.67	—
154	Building				15,000.00	—
156	Accm Depn - Building				—	2,500.00
164	Automotive				28,000.00	—
166	Accm Depn - Automotive				—	5,500.00
172	Land				18,000.00	—
220	Accounts Payable				—	360.00
231	FIT Payable				—	0.00
232	SIT Payable				—	0.00
233	FICA Payable				—	0.00
234	FUTA Payable				—	0.00
235	SUTA Payable				—	0.00
236	SDI Payable				—	0.00
237	Local Tax Payable				—	0.00
240	Deduction A Payable				—	0.00
242	Deduction B Payable				—	0.00
244	Deduction C Payable				—	0.00
260	Sales Tax Payable				—	1,019.66
266	Short Term Debt				—	2,000.00
275	Mortgage Payable				—	22,500.00
302	Class A Common				—	5,000.00
303	Class B Common				—	2,000.00
356	Retained Earnings				—	23,474.34
402	General Revenue				—	0.00
406	General Delivery				—	2,190.00
407	Special Delivery				—	4,647.00
420	Freight Revenue				—	0.00
426	Insurance Income				—	0.00
427	Interest Income				—	0.00
502	General Expense				791.00	—
506	Truck Rental				0.00	—
507	Fuel				0.00	—
508	Insurance				0.00	—
509	Truck Repairs				0.00	—
510	Permits				0.00	—
520	Freight Expense				123.00	—

530	Wages	0.00	—
531	FICA Expense	0.00	—
532	FUTA Expense	0.00	—
533	SUTA Expense	0.00	—
534	SDI Expense	0.00	—
536	Employee Benefits	0.00	—
538	Warehouse Rent	0.00	—
561	Accounting	0.00	—
562	Advertising	0.00	—
563	Telephone	0.00	—
		71,191.00	71,191.00

Figure 8.33 Trial balance in the general ledger showing the control account, accounts receivable and that total debits is equal to total credits

When you have finished viewing the trial balance, press

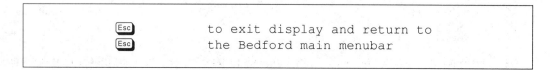

```
[Esc]            to exit display and return to
[Esc]            the Bedford main menubar
```

EXPORTING THE FILES

As with the accounts **PAYABLE** module, all accounts receivable reports can be exported to a LOTUS spreadsheet file or to a text file that can be used by a word processor for generating a report. The four files that can be created are labelled ADDRESS.EXT, SUMMARY.EXT, DETAIL.EXT or LABEL.EXT where EXT is the extension appropriate to your Lotus 1-2-3 or any spreadsheet program that can read Lotus 1-2-3 data files such as SuperCalc. This allows you to have a closer look at the data and manipulate it in various ways. The exported files are located in the subdirectory that you have identified in the **SYSTEM** module.

The export procedure is identical in each of the modules. Rather than go through it again at this point, go to Chapter 6 and follow the procedures outlined there.

MAINTAINING AN AUDIT TRAIL

As in the general ledger, it is important to maintain an audit trail for all accounting entries made. This means preparing a printed list of all the transactions entered — all journal entries made in each session.

Print out the journal entries from the **GENERAL** print menu. Store the listing in a binder marked **SALES AND RECEIPTS**. If you ever want to review the entries made during any session they are available. It is also a backup in the event that the computer should crash or the data disk is destroyed.

FINISHING THE SESSION

You have now completed the accounts receivable tutorial. You should finish this session to save your data to disk. After activating the **Finish** command you will be returned to the disk operating system.

To finish this session, press

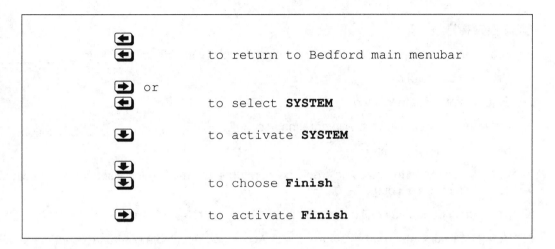

In the following chapters you should always end each session with the **Finish** command. When beginning each chapter in this tutorial start the Bedford Accounting Program as described earlier in this chapter.

BACKING UP YOUR DATA FILES

You should always make a backup of the data files on your computer system to guard against loss of files or hardware failure. Follow the procedures outlined in Chapter 4 for making backups.

BEDFORD PRACTICE SET
AMERICANA HOME DECORATING AND SERVICE COMPANY

Part III — Accounts Receivable

OBJECTIVE

After completing this practice set for accounts receivable, you should be able to:

1. Create customer files.

2. Enter historical data to accounts.

3. Enter necessary defaults and integration accounts.

4. Set the SYSTEM to Ready.

5. Enter transactions for: sales on credit; sales returns on credit; sales discounts on credit; all cash receipts on account.

6. Print Aging Schedule of all customers in Summary and Detail format.

7. Verify total customer accounts agrees with Accounts Receivable control account in the GENERAL module.

INSTRUCTION: 1.   Enter the following customer files and historical data.

Americana Decorating Sales & Service Inc. FOR INSTRUCTIONAL USE ONLY
CUSTOMER Address Aug 31,1988

1	Campbell, Carolyn	3456 Bush Street	Portland	Oregon	87613-2423	503-254-1526
2	Flintstone, Fred	7856 Quarry Avenue	Portland	Oregon	84273-6453	503-686-5432
3	Gretzky, Wayne	8906 Kings Street	Portland	Oregon	84532-6754	503-999-9999
4	MacDonald, Ronald	5678 Golden Arch Avenue	Portland	Oregon	87652-3415	503-786-5433
5	Monroe, Marilyn	567 Hollywood Avenue	Portland	Oregon	87690-6543	503-454-6789
6	North, Ollie	6745 Papershredder Lane	Portland	Oregon	87654-2382	503-787-6543
7	Park, Jim	8976 Trailblazer Rd.	Portland	Oregon	87098-4563	503-456-7876
8	Redford, Robert	4563 Oscar Rd.	Portland	Oregon	87690-8765	503-425-3675
9	Smith, S.	8765 Winterhawks Lane	Portland	Oregon	87651-0975	503-567-4899
10	Thomas, Marlo	45820 Kay Street	Portland	Oregon	86746-2823	503-478-5902
11	Tyler, Toby	4567 Disney Street	Portland	Oregon	86756-3521	503-758-6738
12	Voyageur, Guy	5678 Paris Street	Portland	Oregon	87634-5432	503-245-7569
13	Wai, Kay	8976 Orient Street	Portland	Oregon	87656-7897	503-675-4398
14	Winston, Mary	7896 Salem Avenue	Portland	Oregon	87690-9872	503-879-7563
15	Zeller, Fuzzy	4567 Augusta Lane	Portland	Oregon	89098-6756	503-457-6890

CUSTOMERS on file: 15

Americana Decorating Sales & Service Inc. FOR INSTRUCTIONAL USE ONLY   Page 1
CUSTOMER Detail Aug 31,1988

					total	current	31-60	61-90	91+
1	Campbell, Carolyn	S407	07-18-88	Invoice	8,499.58	-	8,499.58	-	-
7	Park, Jim	S408	08-08-88	Invoice	9,969.53	9,969.53		-	-
9	Smith, S.	S409	08-08-88	Invoice	18,997.07	18,997.07	-	-	-
		Cm57	08-22-88	Invoice	764.24-	764.24-	-	-	-
					18,232.83	18,232.83	-	-	-
14	Winston, Mary	S405	07-06-88	Invoice	8,239.32	-	8,239.32	-	-
		Cm56	07-24-88	Invoice	352.46-	-	352.46-	-	-
					7,886.86	-	7,886.86	-	-
					44,588.80	28,202.36	16,386.44	-	-

INSTRUCTION: 2.   Enter the integration accounts required for your General Ledger chart of
                      accounts.

INSTRUCTION: 3.   Set the SYSTEM>Default>Module>Receivable:

                      Age   30,60,90
                      Invoice   Yes
                        Address   Yes
                        Comment   If You Liked Our Service Please Tell a Friend!
                        Number   411
                        Port   Lpt1
                      Statement   Yes
                        Address   Yes
                        Port   Lpt1
                      Sales Tax   7%
                      Freight Tax No
                      Rate   0%
                      Ready   Yes

INSTRUCTION: 4.   Enter the following transactions in the GENERAL, PAYABLE, and
                      RECEIVABLE modules for month of September.

Sept.   1.   Received on account from Mary Winston, $7,886.86, covering invoice S405 for
                  $8,239.32 less Cm56 for $352.46. R150.

1. Sold merchandise and service on account to Ollie North: S411.

Item	Quantity	Unit	Detail	Price	Amount
1	80	Gallon	Ceiling Flat Latex	$16.00	$1,280.00
10	150	Roll	Waldec	16.00	2,400.00
13	100	Sq/Yd	Lace	40.00	4,000.00
			Freight		75.00
			SST @ 7%		537.60
					$8,292.60

1. Sold merchandise and service on account to Fuzzy Zeller: S412.

Item	Quantity	Unit	Detail	Price	Amount
4	70	Gallon	Satin Latex	$18.00	$1,260.00
8	15	Roll	Jack & Jill	12.00	180.00
15	80	Sq/Yd	Velvet	50.00	4,000.00
			Freight		80.00
			SST @ 7%		380.80
					$5,900.80

8. Purchased merchandise on account from Munforte Paint & Paper: paint, $2,435.78; wallpaper, $1,342.56; fabric, $3,426.65; total, $7,204.99. P240.

8. Returned merchandise on account to Zebra Color Stripes: paint, $324.78; wallpaper, 324.89; fabric; 654.89; total, $1,304.56. Dm48.

8. Sold merchandise on account to Fred Flinstone: S413.

Item	Quantity	Unit	Detail	Price	Amount
2	80	Gallon	Eggshell Latex	$22.00	$1,760.00
6	70	Roll	Colorol	8.00	560.00
14	60	Sq/Yd	Cotton	20.00	1,200.00
			Freight		90.00
			SST @ 7%		246.40
					$3,856.40

8. Granted credit on account to Carolyn Campbell for sales discounts: paint, $78.89; wallpaper; $154.67; fabric; $234.78; total, $468.34. Cm58.

Note: Take the RECEIVABLE module off-line for generating invoices before entering this transaction.

8. Received on account from Carolyn Campbell, $8,031.24, covering invoice S407 for $8,499.58 less Cm58 for $468.34. R151.

8. Granted credit on account to Jim Park for sales returns: S414

Note: Enter this transaction with the system on-line so you can process a document to the customer. Under accounting principals you would call this a credit memo but you cannot enter letters for invoice number in the Receivable default. TO IDENTIFY THIS NEGATIVE SALES INVOICE ENTER "CUSTOMER RETURN" IN THE SHIP TO FIELD.

Item	Quantity	Unit	Detail	Price	Amount
5	10-	Gallon	Semi-Gloss Latex	$24.00	$ 240.00-
9	5-	Roll	Select	14.00	70.00-
12	20-	Sq/Yd	Cotton/Polyester	30.00	600.00-
			SST @ 7%		63.70-
					$ 973.00-

8. Received on account from Jim Park, $8,995.83, covering invoice S408 for $9,969.53 less S414 for $973.70. R152.

15. Record the withholding taxes payable as debt owing to vendor Internal Revenue Service: Federal Income Tax, $2,431.22; Federal Insurance; $1,851.16, total $4,282.38. M96.

Note: You must enter all liabilities as a purchase to a vendor account so you can then run check payments.

15. Paid withholding taxes to Internal Revenue Service, $4,282.38. Ch386.

15. Record State Income Tax payable, $944.03. M97.

Note: You must record the debt owed to vendor State regulatory body so you can then process check using PAYABLE module.

15. Paid State regulatory body for State Income Tax, $944.03. Ch387.

15. Record telephone expense as debt owing to vendor Bell Telephone, $134.78. P241.

15. Paid Bell Telephone Co. for telephone expense, $134.78. Ch388.

15. Record fuel expense as debt owing to vendor Texaco Oil Co., $87.56. P242.

15. Paid Texaco Oil Co. for fuel expense, $87.56. Ch389.

15. Record utilities expense to vendor Northwestern Hydro Co., $235.78. P243.

15. Paid Northwestern Hydro Co. for utilities expense, $235.78. Ch390.

16. Record bank transfer from General to Payroll account, $3,697.40. M98.

16. Record middle of month cash advance given employee vendor Gary Carter, $660.00. M99.

Note: Since you are processing a check to the employee you must first record the cash owing to vendor Gary Carter so as to make a second entry of a check payment.

16. Paid middle of month advance to Gary Carter, $660.00. Ch391.

16. Record cash advance to employee vendor Lou Gehrig, $720.00. M100.

16. Paid cash advance to Lou Gehrig, $720.00. Ch392.

16. Record cash advance to employee vendor Jackie Robinson, $750.00. M101.

16. Paid cash advance to Jackie Robinson, $750.00. Ch393.

16. Record cash advance to employee vendor Babe Ruth, $690.00. M102.

16. Paid cash advance to Babe Ruth, $690.00. Ch394.

16. Record cash advance to employee vendor George Washington, $877.40. M103.

16. Paid cash advance to George Washington, $877.40. Ch395.

16. Paid part of principal owing to Bank of America, $10,000.00. M104.

   Note: *Bank debited our account so no check was processed.*

16. Sold merchandise and service on account to S. Smith: S415.

Item	Quantity	Unit	Detail	Price	Amount
4	60	Gallon	Ceiling Flat Latex	$16.00	$ 960.00
7	50	Roll	Dimensional Living	10.00	500.00
13	15	Sq/Yd	Lace	40.00	600.00
			Freight		60.00
			SST @ 7%		144.20
					$2,264.20

16. Recorded company pension owed to vendor Merrill Lynch Co. $616.23. M105.

16. Paid Merrill Lynch Co. for company pension, $616.23. Ch396

16. Record medical plan owed to vendor Blue Cross, $270.00. M106.

16. Paid Blue Cross for medical plan, $270.00. Ch397.

16. Record sales tax owed vendor State regulatory body, $2,149.73 M107.

16. Paid State regulatory body for sales tax, $2,149.73. Ch398.

30. Record bank transfer from General to Payroll account, $3,440.21. M108.

30. Record month end payroll owing to employee vendor Gary Carter, $573.02, covering: Salary Expense, $2,200.00 less: Federal Income Tax, $471.35; Federal Insurance, $165.22; State Income Tax, $170.41; Company Pension, $110.00; Medical, $50.00; Advances Receivable, $660.00. M109.

30. Paid month end payroll to Gary Carter, $573.02. Ch399.

30. Record month end payroll owing to employee vendor Lou Gehrig, $744.66, covering: Salary Expense, $2,400.00 less: Federal Income Tax, $407.02; Federal Insurance, $180.24; State Income Tax, $178.08; Company Pension, $120.00; Medical, $50.00; Advances Receivable, $720.00. M110.

30. Paid month end payroll to Lou Gehrig, $744.66. Ch400.

30. Record month end payroll owing to employee vendor Jackie Robinson, $578.93, covering: Salary Expense, $2,500.00 less: Federal Income Tax, $597.16; Federal Insurance, $187.75 State Income Tax, $201.16; Company Pension, $125.00; Medical, $60.00; Advances Receivable, $750.00. M111.

30. Paid month end payroll to Jackie Robinson, $578.93. Ch401.

30. Record month end payroll owing to employee vendor Babe Ruth, $696.42, covering: Salary Expense, $2,300.00 less: Federal Income Tax, $401.77; Federal Insurance, $172.73; State Income Tax, $169.08; Company Pension, $115.00; Medical, $55.00; Advances Receivable, $690.00. M112.

30. Paid month end payroll to Babe Ruth, $696.42. Ch402.

30. Record month end payroll owing to employee vendor George Washington, $847.18, covering: Salary Expense, $2,924.67 less: Federal Income Tax, $553.92; Federal Insurance, $219.64; State Income Tax, $225.30; Company Pension, $146.23; Medical, $55.00; Advances Receivable, $877.40. M113.

30. Paid month end payroll to George Washington, $847.18. Ch403.

30. Recorded employer's payroll FICA Expense, $925.58. M114.

30. Recorded Bank Reconciliation adjustments: Short Term Loan Payment, $543.80; Mortgage Payment, $345.78; Interest Expense, $1,125.34; Bank Charges Expense, $24.35; Interest Income, $103.45; net total bank debit, $1,935.82. M115.

30. Recorded adjusting entry for insurance expense incurred, $400.00.

30. Recorded adjusting entry for office supplies expense incurred, $115.23.

30. Recorded adjusting entry for estimated depreciation expense incurred: Building, $1,750.00; Automotive, $185.00.

30. Recorded adjusting entry for inventory change from end of last period, decreasing: paint, $1,234.34; wallpaper, $789.23; fabric, $1,100.99; total, $3,124.56.

Note: Modify the description of account Ending Inventory 08-31-88 to Inventory Change Sept. 1-30.

INSTRUCTION: 5. Print Aging Schedule of Accounts Receivable in Summary and Detail form for all accounts.
Verify that the total of all customer's account balances agrees with the Accounts Receivable control account.
Print Aging Schedule of Accounts Payable in Summary and Detail form for all accounts.
Verify that the total of all vendor's account balances agrees with the Accounts Payable control account.
Print General Journal entries from 09-01-88 to 09-30-88.
Print Income Statement for 09-01-88 to 09-30-88.
Modify the description of Inventory Change Sept 1-30 to Ending Inventory 09-30-88.
Print Income Statement for 01-01-88 to 09-30-88.
Print Balance Sheet for 09-30-88.

Chapter 9
PAYROLL

Chapter 9
PAYROLL

PREVIEW

In this chapter you will get a thorough understanding of payroll, how to calculate it and the various employee deductions that have to be taken. After this initial introduction to payroll you will follow similar steps as in the previous two modules, accounts payable and accounts receivable — to convert from a manual to a computerized payroll system. You will then enter some employees into the **PAYROLL** module and calculate their pay. In the last part of the chapter you will learn how to correct payroll information that was inadvertently entered incorrectly.

OBJECTIVES

After reading this chapter you should be able to explain:

1. What the payroll accounting module does;

2. How an employee's gross earnings are determined, and the various deductions that have to be taken;

3. The money you have to remit to the government each month and the various deductions that are often handled by the employer on behalf of the employee;

4. The various employment costs born by the employer;

5. The maintenance of employee records to generate earnings statements for individual filing at the end of the year;

6. How to get ready to convert form a manual payroll system to the Bedford accounting payroll module;

7. The basic employee information that must be entered into the payroll module prior to conversion;

8. How to modify employee information once entered;

9. Entering historical employee data;

10. How to display the information on the screen once it is entered;

11. How to print a variety of reports;

12. How to enter employee pay data after making the system READY;

13. How to display and print detail and summary reports of data entered into the payroll module;

14. How to correct payroll data once entered;

15. Why and how to develop an audit trail.

All states require that each employer adhere to the Federal and State Income Tax Acts in whose jurisdiction the employee works, regardless of the head office of the company itself. For this reason, and because of the importance of maintaining accurate payroll transactions, the payroll module is one of the most important modules in an accounting system. Each of the states has a different set of rules and rates for various withholding taxes. **Withholding taxes** are taxes and payments that are deducted by the employer and include Federal Income Tax, State Income Tax, Federal Insurance Contributions and State Disability Insurance. The employer must then remit these payments to the Internal Revenue Service on behalf of the employee. Needless to say it is a complicated and difficult task for managers with employees in more than one state to keep up to date on these rules and rates.

The **PAYROLL** module is designed to

1.   keep track of each individual employee with regard to all aspects of payroll;
2.   calculate payroll and withholding taxes;
3.   report to the employee as to his net pay calculations;
4.   report to the employee as to the amount of the remittance to be paid to the Internal Revenue Service;
5.   prepare year end reports such as W-4s and payroll summaries.

The **PAYROLL** module is not designed to

1.   tell you which benefits are taxable and which are not taxable;
2.   show you how to fill in government forms;
3.   tell you when to remit funds to the Internal Revenue Service and other governmental bodies.

Before you attempt to do your company payroll using the Bedford **PAYROLL** module for active employees it is important that you become familiar with the regulations required by the State and Federal Government with respect to the state that you live in or have employees working in. You can do this by obtaining and reading the following documents:

1.   Circular "E", Employer's Tax Guide;
2.   State Tax Guide for each State.

PAYROLL ACCOUNTING

Payroll accounting is done at the end of each pay period. Pay periods are determined by how often employees are paid during the year as follows:

	times per year	pay period
a.	1	annual
b.	10	monthly (for teachers)
c.	12	monthly
d.	13	every four weeks
e.	22	
f.	24	bi-monthly
g.	26	bi-weekly
h.	52	weekly

Preparing a company payroll requires the following steps:

1. determining the gross earnings for each employee for the pay period;
2. determining the deductions that each employee is subject to;
3. calculating the net pay for the employee;
4. calculating the remittance to the relevant authorities;
5. creating the journal entries;
6. preparing the checks for each employee;
7. remitting the withholding funds calculated under part 4.

It is important to note that, in this process, the employer is required by law to keep two sets of records for payroll — one for his own use and one for each employee. The record of each employee is then disclosed at the end of each calendar year to the Internal Revenue Service and to the employee through the filing of forms for each employee which include a "941" (Employer's Quarterly Federal Income Tax Return), "940" (Employer's Annual Federal Unemployment Tax Return), and a "W-2", (Wage and Tax Statement). The latter two are annual forms. These forms are used by the employee to prepare his/her personal tax return.

Determining Employee Gross Earnings Per Pay Period

The gross earnings of an employee for the pay period represents the total amount of compensation that is received. This can be a single amount as in the case of a salaried person, or as a total sum of a number of amounts such as hourly, overtime and commission person.

The most common components of gross earnings are as follow:

Regular pay	xxx
Overtime pay	xxx
Salary	xxx
Commission and tips	xxx
Taxable benefits	xxx
Vacation pay paid	xxx
Total Gross Earnings	xxx

▪ *Regular Pay*

Regular pay is the amount paid per hour to an employee. For example, an employee may earn $12.00 per hour for a job 8 hours a day, 5 days a week. At the end of a two week period, this person has worked 80 hours (10 working days, 8 hours per day). To find the total regular pay you multiply the number of hours worked by the hourly rate:

80 hours x $12.00 per hour = $960.00 (regular pay)

In all states as well as for all federal employees, there is a restriction as to the number of regular hours that an employee can work in a given pay period. This is set out in the labor code for the state or for the federal government. A phone call to the Department of Labor office will give you the information. Any hours in excess of the regular hours are overtime hours.

▪ Overtime Pay

An employee working in excess of the regular hours allowed will be entitled to overtime pay. Overtime pay rates are set up in the employee record and are usually the regular pay multiplied by 1.5 or "time and a half". For our employee above with a $12.00 per hour regular pay rate, the overtime rate would therefore be $18.00 ($12.00 x 1.5). This amount is set up in each individual's employee record (See Defaults for payroll).

Once the number of hours have been determined for the employee, overtime pay is calculated on the same basis that regular pay is calculated - multiplying the overtime hours times the overtime rate.

$$4 \text{ overtime hours x } \$18.00 = \$72.00$$

▪ Salary

Many employees are paid a fixed amount each month — salary — regardless of the total hours or days worked. The amount of salary is most often stated as an annual amount, such as $18,000 per annum. To enter this employee's monthly salary you must first determine the pay period and then divide the annual amount by the number of pay periods. For example, if our employee is paid on a monthly basis or 12 times per year, the amount we would enter under the salary portion is:

$$\$18,000/12 = \$1,500 \text{ per month.}$$

It is possible for an employee to receive a salary, yet also receive an amount of regular or overtime pay. In this case, you would have to keep track of each type of pay and record them separately into the program.

▪ Commission and Tips

A commission is usually based on the amount sold by an employee or based on some other performance criteria. It is calculated by applying a rate of commission to a dollar value of performance (such as sales) or an amount of performance (such as piece-work). Commission amounts change each month and therefore must be calculated each time a payroll is prepared. The Bedford Accounting System requires that the commission amount be entered as a total amount. For example, if a sales person sold $20,000 worth of advertising during the month and has a commission rate of 20%, the amount that would be entered under commission would be:

$$\$20,000 \text{ x } 20\% = \$4,000$$

Tips are earned by an employee in the performance of the job and are usually paid by customers rather than an employer. The Internal Revenue Service states that tips do not have to be reported unless they exceed $20.00 a month. If tips do exceed $20 per month, the employee must keep track and report the amount on a monthly basis to the employer. If income from tips for one month exceeds the $20.00 maximum, however, all income must be reported, not just income over $20.00.

If an employee receives taxable amounts of tips, the employer must show the tip income as a separate item on the pay advice and include it in gross income when calculating withholding taxes.

▪ *Taxable Benefits*

Taxable benefits are non-cash items that the employee receives from the employer. For tax purposes, these benefits are included in income from employment and therefore form part of taxable income and are subject to withholding tax.

These taxable benefits must be calculated by the employer and entered as one lump sum into the Bedford Accounting System. An example of a taxable benefit would be an automobile supplied by the employer, or the employer's portion of payments to a state medical plan.

▪ *Vacation Pay Paid*

Every employee is entitled to a minimum number of days off per year with pay. Part time employees receive a percentage of their total pay as vacation pay. The basic rate is established by state and federal legislation. In unionized firms the minimum is set down in the collective agreement, but it must be at least as high as specified by federal and state legislation. An employee can elect to have their vacation pay treated in one of two ways;

    a. paid out with each pay check, or
    b. paid out at some later time when the employee takes time off for vacation.

The treatment of each method requires different accounting entries.

    a. Vacation pay paid out with each paycheck.

        If the employee elects to have it paid out with each paycheck, then you would multiply the gross earnings for the period and multiply it by the vacation pay rate applicable to that employee. If the salaried individual above was entitled to two weeks vacation per year, or 4% per year which is equivalent, then the vacation pay would equal:

        $18,000/12 = $1,500 per month x 4% = $60.00 (holiday pay)

        This amount would then form a component part of the gross earnings each month.

    b. Vacation pay retained and paid out at some later date.

        If the employee elects to have the vacation pay retained for some later date, then you must make an entry into the general ledger to recognize that an expense was incurred even though the money was not paid out. The amount of vacation pay will be the same as calculated above ($60.00). The accounting entry will be as follows:

            Dr. Vacation expense $60.00
                Cr. Vacation pay payable $60.00

        This amount will then accumulate until the employee takes vacation or has it paid out for some other reason. When it is paid out, the total amount will be included in the gross pay for that particular period. The journal entry made will be a debit to vacation pay payable to clear out the amount expensed each month.

Determining Employee Deductions

Once you have calculated the gross amount of pay for each employee, then you must determine deductions that must be withheld from the employee pay. There are two types of deductions: **Statutory deductions,** which are those that the employer is required by law to deduct, and **Other deductions,** those that are determined by the employee or by some labor agreement between the employer and the employees.

The statutory deductions are

> Federal Income Tax (FIT)
> State Income Tax (SIT)
> Federal Insurance Contributions (FICA)
> State Unemployment Tax (SUTA)
> State Disability Insurance (SDI)

These amounts must be withheld from each employee who qualifies for the deductions, and remitted, along with the employer's portion to the Internal Revenue Service, within a given time period. Late payments will result in fines and penalties as these amounts are not the property of the employer but of the employee in the trust of the employer.

▪ *Federal Income Tax (FIT)*

Employers are required to deduct federal income tax, FIT, from an employee's paycheck each pay period. The employer must in turn remit it to the IRS at specified intervals. The amount of FIT deducted from each employee varies. It is dependent upon the following:

1. the gross earnings of the employee
2. the number of pay periods per year
3. the employee's marital status
4. the federal allowances claimed by the employee.

The gross earnings, as indicated previously, is the sum of all wages and benefits earned by the employee in the period, while the number of pay periods is simply determined by how often in a calendar year the paychecks are made up, usually 12, 24, 26 or 52 times.

To determine the latter two items – the employee's marital status and the federal allowances claimed – the employee must submit a W-4, an employee's withholding allowance certificate. This form is filled out by the employee at the beginning of employment or when there is a change in personal allowances such as marriage, birth of a child, etc. If the employee is single, with earnings less than $1,050 annually (for 1988), no FIT is deducted. This exemption amount rises to $3,050 for a married couple.

The FIT for an employee earning $1,500 per month and single with two federal withholding allowances based on 12 payroll periods per year (every two weeks) would be calculated as follows:

Gross pay	$1,500.00
Less: Federal allowances 2 x 1,950 = 3,900.00 per year	
3,900.00/12 (# of pay periods)	325.00
Gross earnings subject to FIT	1,175.00
Federal Income Tax (from tax table)	195.00

▪ State Income Tax (SIT)

Most states require state income tax, SIT, to be deducted, as well as FIT, from the employees check each month. Some states use a formula similar to FIT while others have developed their own method for calculating the tax.

The SIT deduction depends on the particular state in which the employee lives and works, the gross earnings and the number of pay periods per year. Some of the following may also be used to determine SIT:

1) FIT deducted;
2) marital status of employee;
3) number of federal withholding allowances claimed;
4) number of state withholding allowances claimed;
5) number of additional withholding allowances claimed;
6) number of dependents.

Several states calculate SIT on the total gross earnings, however, most states require a minimum amount of earnings before SIT will be deducted at all.

Using tables provided by the particular state, you would usually calculate SIT as follows:

Earnings subject to SIT (after allowances)	$1,350.00
State Income Tax (as per tax table)	$31.60

When the paycheck is produced, this amount will be withheld from the employee and remitted to the state tax authority.

▪ Federal Insurance Contributions Act (FICA)

FICA is a non-voluntary insurance plan to which all Americans must contribute, except for ministers, certain religious groups and federal employees. An individual's required contribution is based on gross earnings while the accumulated gross earnings for the year is less than a maximum amount ($45,000 in 1988). These earnings are then multiplied by the applicable rate to arrive at the necessary contribution. The 1988 rate was 7.51%, making the maximum annual contribution $3,379.50 ($45,000 x 7.51%) per employee.

Assuming an individual had a salary of $18,000 per annum and the current pay period is monthly, the amount contributed to FICA, assuming the employee had not reached the maximum payment for the year, would be as follows:

Gross Pay	$18,000/12 periods	=	$ 1,500.00
FICA rate			7.51%
Premium			$ 112.65

Once calculated, this amount is added to the amount withheld from the employee in the previous periods during the calendar year. If the resulting figure is less than or equal to the annual limit, the amount calculated is deducted from the employee's gross income. If the amount calculated for the current month plus the total for the year-to-date is greater than the annual limit, then the amount deducted for the current month from gross income is the amount that would bring the annual limit to the maximum.

The following three examples show the amount that would be deducted from an employee's gross pay for the current period if the annual limit is $3,379.50 and the current premium is calculated at $112.65:

Amount deducted to date:	$2,600.00	$3,309.00	$3,379.00
Withholding equals lesser of:			
Current amount	112.65	112.65	112.65
and amount necessary to bring total to $3,379.50	779.50	90.50	0.00
Current withholding	112.65	90.50	0.00

The amount withheld from employees for FICA must be remitted to the IRS as required. The employer's portion will also be included in the remittance. (See Remitting Withholding Taxes.)

▪ State Unemployment Tax Act (SUTA)

As with FICA, each state requires employees and employers to contribute to SUTA. The joint contributions are for the benefit of workers who are temporarily unemployed. While looking for another job, an employee can draw from this fund based on previous earnings and contributions.

An employee's contribution for state unemployment insurance is based on

a.   gross earnings of the employee;
b.   the regulations of the state in which the employee works;
c.   whether the employee has reached the maximum deduction for the year.

The amount thus calculated is then multiplied by the premium rate in effect for the current year. In 1989, this rate was .625%. A person earning $18,000 per annum based on a monthly pay period would have the following amount withheld for State Unemployment Insurance:

Lesser of:

1. $\frac{\$18,000}{12}$ = $1,500 x .625% = $ 9.38

2.   Maximum annual amount:
          12,000 x .625%   75.00

The employer must keep track of the total amount contributed to ensure the employee does not contribute over $75.00 annually.

▪ State Disability Insurance (SDI)

A few states require SDI in addition to the foregoing deductions. This amount is calculated by applying a percentage rate as specified by each state to the gross earnings. There is a maximum amount each employee must contribute so the employer must track the amount contributed on an annual basis. SDI payable is based on

a) gross earnings;
b) the state in which the employee is working;
c) maximum annual contributions not being exceeded.

Assuming gross earnings are again $1,500 per month and the maximum has not yet been reached, then SDI would be calculated as follows:

$1,500 x .5% $7.50

This amount will then be deducted from the employee and remitted to the appropriate state agency responsible for disability insurance (see Remitting Withholding Taxes).

▪ Local Tax

In many cities, counties, and other jurisdictions throughout the country, employers are required to deduct and remit local taxes in addition to the federal and state taxes. This calculation is usually based on a percentage amount which is then applied to either the gross earnings, the amount of federal income tax paid, or the amount of state income tax paid, depending on the local law.
Based on our employee making $1,500.00 per month and a 1% local tax, the amount would be calculated as follows:

$1,500.00 x 1% $15.00

This amount is deducted from the employee's check and remitted to the local government.
Once the amounts that have to be withheld are determined, the employee's payroll will be journalized as follows:

Dr. Salaries Expense	1,500.00	
Cr. FIT (Federal Income Tax) payable		195.00
Cr. SIT (State Income Tax) payable		31.60
Cr. FICA (Federal Insurance) payable		112.65
Cr. SUTA (State Insurance) payable		9.38
Cr. SDI (Disability) payable		7.50
Cr. Local tax payable		15.00
Cr. Bank (check to employee)		1,128.87

In the above example, the employee would receive a paycheck for $1,128.87 representing the net amount of pay after withholding the mandatory amounts.

▪ *Remitting Withholding Taxes*

An employer is required to remit employee tax deductions along with the employer portion of premiums for each of the plans at regular intervals to the Internal Revenue Service, State Revenue Service and local governments.

For FICA, the employer must match the employee's contribution. In the above journal entry, we see that the employee must pay $112.65 in premiums. This means that the amount that the employer must remit in total is $225.30; $112.65 withheld from the employee and $112.65 on behalf of the company.

In the case of FUTA, SUTA and SDI, the employer calculates the contribution on behalf of each employee by applying the applicable rate prescribed by the state or the federal government by the amount of earnings applicable to the plan.

FUTA (Federal Unemployment Tax Act) contributions must be paid by the employer for every employee, but no contribution is required by the individual employee. The FUTA percentage is applied to no more than $7,000.00 of each employee's gross earnings.

Assuming the rates were .8%, .8% and 1.1% respectively, the calculation for the plans would be as follows:

FUTA	$1,500.00	x	.8%	=	12.00
SUTA	1,500.00	x	.8%	=	12.00
SDI	1,500.00	x	1.1%	=	16.50

These amounts are also subject to the maximum annual limits upon which employee deductions for these amounts are based.

There is no additional employer contribution for income taxes payable by the employee.

In the previous journal entry we have only recorded the employee's portion of income tax withheld. We must make another entry to record the employer portions for the various withholding plans.

Dr. FICA expense (employer)	112.65	
Dr. FUTA expense (employer)	12.00	
Dr. SUTA expense (employer)	12.00	
Dr. SDI expense (employer)	16.50	
Cr. FICA payable		112.65
Cr. FUTA payable		12.00
Cr. SUTA payable		12.00
Cr. SDI payable		16.50

However, there is no need to make two separate entries. We could combine the two entries into one as follows:

Dr. Salaries expense	1,500.00
Dr. FICA expense (employer)	112.65
Dr. FUTA expense (employer)	12.00
Dr. SUTA expense (employer)	12.00
Dr. SDI expense (employer)	16.50
Cr. FIT payable	195.00
Cr. SIT payable	31.60
Cr. FICA payable	225.30
Cr. FUTA payable	12.00
Cr. SUTA payable	21.38
Cr. SDI payable	24.00
Cr. Local tax	15.00
Cr. Net payable to employee	1,128.87

▪ Other Deductions

There may be other deductions taken by the employer on either the behalf of the union or the employee. Some common deductions in this category are

1. Union dues
2. Medical plans
3. Dental plans
4. Registered pension plans

Some of these deductions may be partially paid for by the employer. For example, many employees have part or all of their medical premium paid by the employer. The amount that the employee is responsible for would be withheld and remitted by the employer to the company providing the medical coverage. In the case of union dues and registered pension plans the employee usually pays the entire amount.

Let's assume that the employee has a medical plan which costs $42.00 per month, with the employer paying one-half of the cost. In addition, the employee contributes $27.00 per month to union dues. The net pay calculation for this employee would be as follows:

Salary		1,500.00
less:		
FIT	195.00	
SIT	31.60	
FICA	112.65	
SUTA	9.38	
SDI	7.50	
Local tax	15.00	
Union Dues	27.00	
Medical (1/2 by employee)	21.00	
Net pay		
		1,080.87

Now we must also change our journal entry to reflect the withholding of these amounts and the payable associated. To do this we would enter the lines listed in bold face to our journal entry. Notice that the amount of "net payable to employee" has changed to reflect the amount we have withheld for the employee portions of medical, and union dues. Also note that we have added a line for medical expense to reflect the employer's portion of the medical costs.

Dr. Salaries expense	1,500.00
Dr. FICA expense (employer)	112.65
Dr. FUTA expense (employer)	12.00
Dr. SUTA expense (employer)	12.00
Dr. SDI expense (employer)	16.50
Dr. Medical expense (employer)	**21.00**
Cr. FIT payable	195.00
Cr. SIT payable	31.60
Cr. FICA payable	225.30
Cr. FUTA payable	12.00
Cr. SUTA payable	21.38
Cr. SDI payable	24.00
Cr. Local tax	15.00
Cr. Due to medical plan	42.00
Cr. Union dues payable	**27.00**
Cr. Net payable to employee	1,080.87

MAINTAINING EMPLOYEE RECORDS

As mentioned earlier, the employer must keep track of the payroll transactions for the company. In addition, the employer must also keep a record of all payroll transactions by employee — the employee payroll record. This information is necessary to allow the employer to prepare reports to the different governmental bodies.

The first report is called a W-2, which is filed for each employee at the end of the calendar year. It reports to the government the amount of earnings that the employee had in the year and the amount withheld for the various deductions that were remitted on behalf of that employee. A typical W-2 is shown in Figure 9.1.

Figure 9.1 W-2 statement

In addition to this annual report, employers must report quarter-to-date and year-to-date totals for employees within the organization.

COMPUTERIZING THE PAYROLL

Although brief, the previous discussion should clarify the accounting entries required for a person in charge of company payroll. We can now prepare for converting a manual payroll system to the computerized Bedford payroll system. The best time to convert is at the beginning of a calendar year. At that time the historical records for the current year are at zero and therefore no reconciliation of employee records need be done before conversion. If you want to convert during the calendar year you would have to input all employee records contained in your manual system into the Bedford Accounting System.

Organizing Employee Records

As was the case with the other modules, you have to prepare the employee data before actually beginning the payroll conversion process. First, you should:

1. Prepare a list of all employees and their personal information;
2. Calculate the year-to-date totals (if you are not converting at the beginning of a calendar year);
3. Ensure that the control accounts of advances, receivable and vacation pay in the general ledger, agree to your year-to-date listings.

■ *Prepare an Employee Listing*

The first thing we have to do before we can actually use the payroll module is prepare an employee listing of all the employees currently on staff, as well as the employees who worked in the firm during the present calendar year. This is necessary so that we can balance the amounts remitted to the various government agencies during the year.

The listing must include the following for each employee:

a. Personal Information
1. Employee name
2. Street address
3. City
4. State
5. Zip code
6. Phone number
7. Social security number
8. Birth date
9. State of taxation
10. Pay periods per year
11. Marital status
12. Number of dependents
13. Number of federal allowances (from Federal W-4 form)
14. Number of state allowances (from state form)

b. Variable employee information
      1. Regular wage rate (in dollars per hour)
      2. Overtime wage rate (in dollars per hour)
      3. Regular salary (in dollars per pay period)

▪ *Calculate Quarter— and Year-to-Date Totals*

Quarter and year-to-date totals include the following:

a. Quarter and year to date totals for:
      1. Regular wages
      2. Overtime wages
      3. Salary
      4. Tips
      5. Commission
      6. Taxable benefits
      7. Vacation pay paid out
      8. FIT
      9. SIT
    10. FICA
    11. SUTA
    12. SDI
    13. Local tax
    14. Union dues
    15. Medical plan
    16. Dental plan
    17. FICA - employer portion
    18. FUTA - employer portion
    19. SUTA - employer portion
    20. SDI - employer portion

b. Any advances paid to the employee as of the conversion date.

Before the **PAYROLL** module can be used the above information must be entered so that the Bedford Accounting System can calculate each employee's pay. Inaccurate data will produce inaccurate paychecks.

▪ *Agree to Control Account in General Ledger*

After the listing has been made and the year-to-date totals calculated, the final step before converting is to ensure that the total amount owing for employee advances and vacation pay owed agree with the respective control accounts in the existing general ledger. The Bedford Accounting System will not allow you to change the payroll module to READY later until these two totals agree.

Some businesses do not keep track of unpaid vacation pay. If this is the case with your business, it will be necessary for you to enter a journal entry through the general ledger module to record this unpaid expense. You would make the following entry:

        Dr. Vacation pay expense   xxx
           Cr. Vacation pay payable   xxx

Beginning the Payroll Conversion

With the above information before you, you are ready to begin the payroll conversion. Start the Bedford Accounting System by typing:

BEDFORD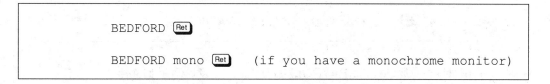

BEDFORD mono [Ret]   (if you have a monochrome monitor)

The start up menu will be displayed on your screen as shown in Figure 9.2.

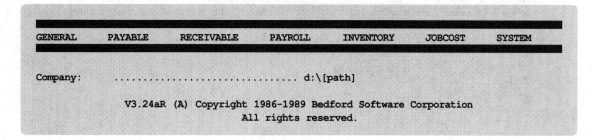

GENERAL	PAYABLE	RECEIVABLE	PAYROLL	INVENTORY	JOBCOST	SYSTEM

Company: .... d:\[path]

V3.24aR (A) Copyright 1986-1989 Bedford Software Corporation
All rights reserved.

Figure 9.2 Bedford startup display

Enter the location of the data files.

B:\FASTDEL	**C:\FASTDEL**
013188	to enter **Using** date. Since this date is more than one week past the previous Using date that you entered when you began the accounts receivable module, you will get a message informing you that you are advancing the **Using** date by more than one week. Press
[Ret]	displays a final message about the new **Using** date
[Ret]	to accept the new date
NOTE:	If you had pressed [Esc] before pressing [Ret] above you could have reentered a new **Using** date.

NOTE: Beginning with this chapter we will only indicate the arrow key that has to be used to reach a particular menu item. For example, if more than one down arrow is required to get to a particular menu item we only show one down arrow. We assume that by now you are sufficiently familiar with the program to get to the proper menu item.

The main menubar of the Bedford Accounting System will now appear. Press

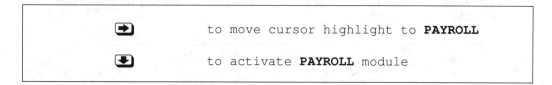

    to move cursor highlight to **PAYROLL**

    to activate **PAYROLL** module

Your screen will now display the **PAYROLL** submenu as shown in Figure 9.3.

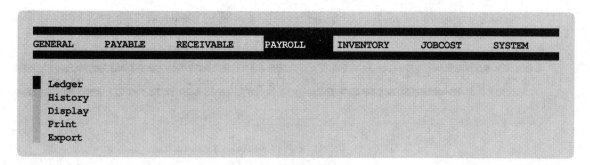

Figure 9.3 Payroll submenu

We are now ready to begin the conversion.

▪ *Entering Employee Information*

First we have to enter the employee information into the payroll module as per our listing. Following is the information for one of our employees.

1.	Employee Name	JONES, GRAHAM
2.	Street Address	123 Ogden Blvd.
3.	City	Bellevue
4.	State	Wa
5.	Zip Code	98455
6.	Phone Number	206-669-4568
7.	Social Security Number	123-45-6782
8.	Birth Date	06-20-51
9.	Table	Washington
10.	Periods	12
11.	Dependents	n/a
12.	Federal Allowances	2
13.	Marital Status	Married
14.	State Allowances	n/a
15.	Status	n/a

With your screen displaying the payroll menu and your cursor next to the word **Ledger**, (See Figure 9.3), press

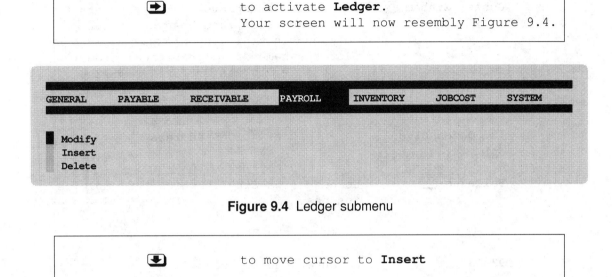

Figure 9.4 Ledger submenu

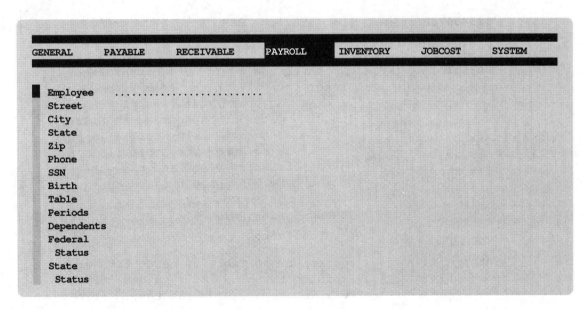

Your screen will now resemble Figure 9.5, which lists all of the above items for which we have to supply the required information for each employee.

Figure 9.5 Employee information input screen

Let's enter the information for our first employee. The cursor is flashing on the first dot beside the word Employee. As you enter this information the first letter will be capitalized automatically. You may have to press the ENTER key to move the cursor to the next item.

Jones, Graham [Ret]   To enter the **Employee** name. Enter the last name first, and then the first name and initial. The program will then list the names in alphabetical order, which makes it easier for us to find the corresponding employee number assigned to the employee.

123 Ogden Blvd.
[Ret]   to enter the street **Address**

Bellevue [Ret]   to enter the **City** in which the employee resides.

Wa. [Ret]   to enter the **State**

98455   to enter the **Zip** code

2066694568   to enter the **Phone** number. It is a good idea to enter the area code with the actual number. If you don't then you will have to press [Ret] to advance the cursor to the next entry.

123456782   to enter the **SSN**, Social Security Number

062051   to enter the employee's **Birth** date. Enter the date in the format (mmddyy) – months, days and year. The program will insert spaces or hyphens as necessary. Notice also that the program will only allow you to enter into this field a date between 01-01-00 and the current Using date. Any date entered outside of this range is considered an error by the program, which will not allow you to enter it.

48 [Ret]   to enter the **Table** of deductions according to which employee deductions will be calculated. The table corresponds to the state that the employee lives in. When you activate this field, a list of the fifty states appears on

	the right hand side of your screen, with a number for each state. Enter the number of the appropriate area. For this exercise we choose "48" for the state of Washington.
12	to enter the pay **Periods** per year. (Refer to the discussion on pay periods earlier in this chapter.)
	At this point, the **Dependents** entry will be skipped as the field is not used in the calculation of payroll for Washington. If it is used by a particular state, then the field would become available for entry.
2 Ret	to enter the amount of **Federal** allowances
2 Ret	to enter the marital **Status**
	After you enter this amount the cursor will jump over the area marked **State** (allowances) and **Status**, which does not apply to employees in the state of Washington. If it applies to your particular state, or to the state in which the employee is working, it will become available for entry.

When all the employee data has been entered, your screen should resemble Figure 9.6. You can use the up and down arrow key to move to the field in which you want to make any changes. Then press the right arrow key to activate that field.

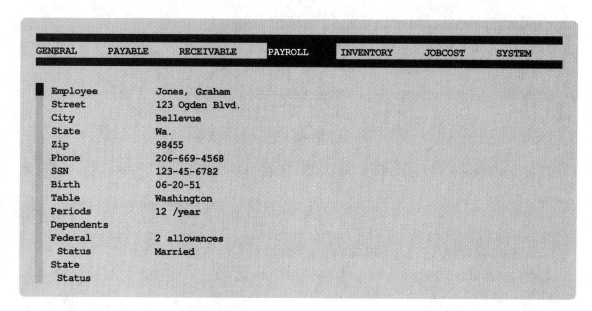

| GENERAL | PAYABLE | RECEIVABLE | PAYROLL | INVENTORY | JOBCOST | SYSTEM |

```
Employee        Jones, Graham
Street          123 Ogden Blvd.
City            Bellevue
State           Wa.
Zip             98455
Phone           206-669-4568
SSN             123-45-6782
Birth           06-20-51
Table           Washington
Periods         12 /year
Dependents
Federal         2 allowances
 Status         Married
State
 Status
```

Figure 9.6 Employee information input screen with all employee information entered

When you are certain that the information is correct, press the left arrow key to accept the data. This creates an employee record.

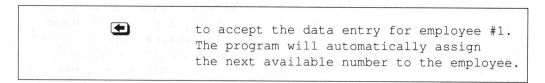

```
        ←         to accept the data entry for employee #1.
                  The program will automatically assign
                  the next available number to the employee.
```

If you want to check that the record in fact exists, press the right arrow key to activate **Insert.** You will now see the name of the first employee displayed on the right side of the screen with a number beside it.

▪ *Practice Exercise*

Enter a second employee using the following information:

1.	Employee Name	Best, Georgina
2.	Street Address	4558 Lange St.
3.	City	Seattle
4.	State	Wa.
5.	Zip Code	98125
6.	Phone Number	206-772-1234
7.	Social Security Number	987-65-2321
8.	Birth Date	01-15-61
9.	Table	Washington
10.	Periods	12
11.	Dependents	n/a
12.	Federal Allowances	2
13.	Marital Status	Married
14.	State Allowances	n/a
15.	Status	n/a

▪ Modifying Employee Information

If, after entering an employee record, you wish to change some of the data, such as the address, phone number, etc. you can use the **Modify** command.

Let's change the phone number of employee #2, to 206-772-1244. To modify an employee record, start from the **Ledger** submenu. Press

⬆	to move to **Modify**
➡	to activate **Modify**

You now have a choice of modifying personal or company information. Since our change is an employee telephone number we will activate the item, **Personal.** Press

➡	to activate **Personal**

Your screen will now look like Figure 9.7. There are two employees listed on the right side of your screen.

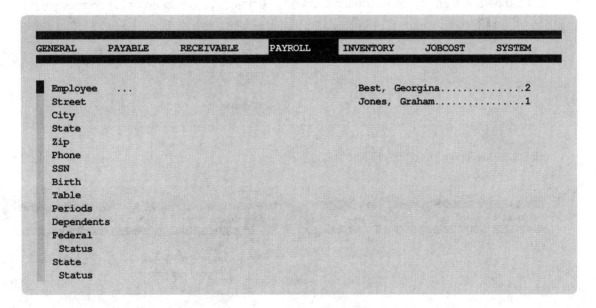

GENERAL	PAYABLE	RECEIVABLE	PAYROLL	INVENTORY	JOBCOST	SYSTEM

```
Employee    ...                          Best, Georgina..............2
Street                                   Jones, Graham...............1
City
State
Zip
Phone
SSN
Birth
Table
Periods
Dependents
Federal
  Status
State
  Status
```

Figure 9.7 The personal employee information screen. You can now choose one of your employees for whom you want to change information.

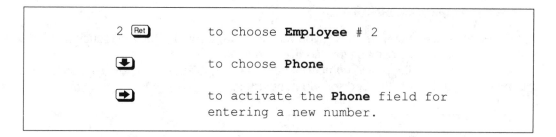

If you enter the number and the area code then the program will automatically close the field for you when you enter the last digit. If you only enter the telephone number and leave out the area code then you will have to press ENTER first.

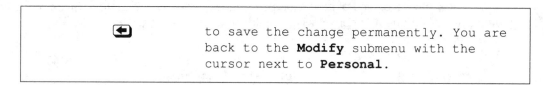

▪ *Entering Company Data*

Once the personal employee information has been entered, you must enter the company data for each employee. Press

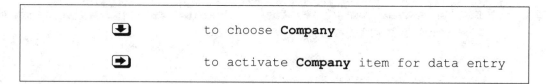

Your screen will now resemble Figure 9.8.

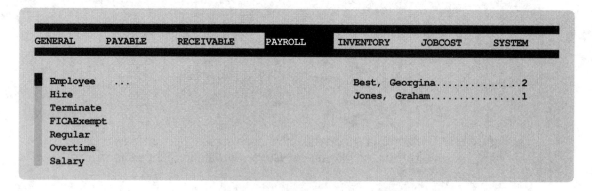

Figure 9.8 Company information input screen activated

1 Ret	to enter the **Employee** number for Jones, Graham. After you press the Ret key, the cursor jumps to the **Hire** field. Then the right arrow to activate the Hire field and enter the date. If you want to enter the default date, just press Shift Ret . Otherwise enter the actual date. Let's enter November 15, 1987 as the hiring date.
111587	to enter **Hiring** date
	You can now enter other information. This employee is not **FICAexempt**, so skip this field. You can change this item to **Yes**, if applicable, by pressing the right arrow key.
⬇	to choose **Salary**
➡	to activate **Salary** item
1800 Ret	to enter monthly salary for Graham Jones

Your screen should now resemble Figure 9.9.

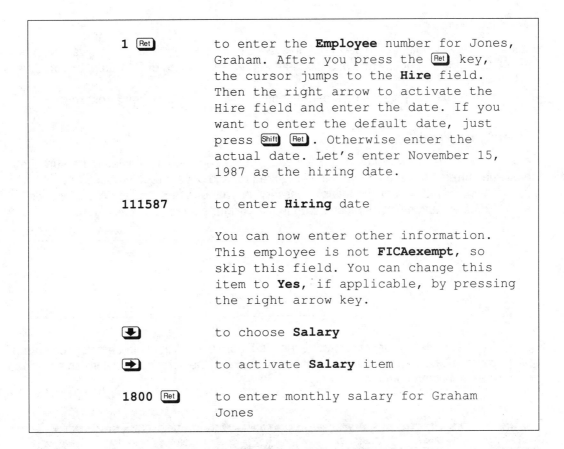

GENERAL	PAYABLE	RECEIVABLE	PAYROLL	INVENTORY	JOBCOST	SYSTEM

Employee	Jones, Graham
Hire	11-15-87
Terminate	
FICAExempt	No
Regular	0.00 /hour
Overtime	0.00 /hour
Salary	1,800.00 /period

Figure 9.9 Company information entered

If all of the entered data is correct, press

⬅	to accept the data permanently

▪ *Practice Exercise*

Enter the company data for the second employee, Best, Georgina. This person was hired on January 5, 1988 at an hourly rate of $ 7.50 and at an overtime rate of $ 11.25 per hour. She is not FICA exempt.

Remember, to save the data permanently you must press the left arrow key.

▪ *Deleting Employees*

If a particular employee no longer works for you, that person should be deleted. Be sure that there is no current annual data that will be required for end of year reports to the government. Otherwise you would destroy the totals necessary for year end reporting for W-2 purposes.

To delete an employee record, start in the **Ledger** submenu. Press

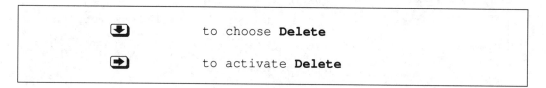

Once activated, your screen will resemble Figure 9.10. A list of the employees currently on the system will be displayed in the right hand column of the screen. To delete an employee, pick the corresponding number.

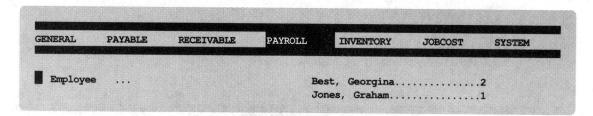

Figure 9.10 Current employees in the system

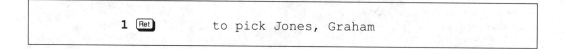

Your screen will now respond with the message shown in Figure 9.11.

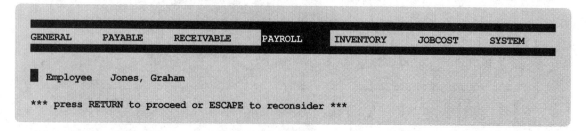

Figure 9.11 Deleting an employee from the system has to be confirmed

Since we do not want to delete this employee, press the ESCape key to cancel the delete function and leave the employee on file.

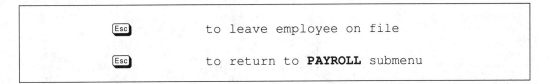

[Esc]	to leave employee on file
[Esc]	to return to **PAYROLL** submenu

You can always delete employees from active records while you are in the NOT READY mode. Once the **PAYROLL** module is in the READY mode, the only employee records that you can delete are records that have no advances paid or vacation pay owed in the record.

▪ Entering Historical Data

The second step in the payroll conversion process, is to enter the year-to-date amounts for the employees. Since this is the end of the first month in the fiscal year, there is as yet no year-to-date or quarter-to-date payroll figure. If this was a month later, then you would have to enter the earnings, deductions and employer contributions for each employee for the month of January through the **History** entry screen.

▪ Printing Payroll Reports

The printing of payroll reports is similar to the printing of reports in the other modules. You should be in the **PAYROLL** submenu. Press

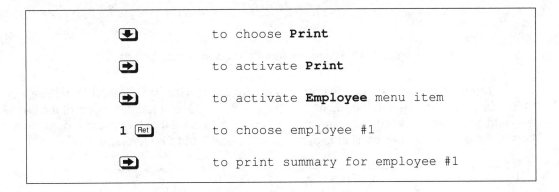

[↓]	to choose **Print**
[→]	to activate **Print**
[→]	to activate **Employee** menu item
1 [Ret]	to choose employee #1
[→]	to print summary for employee #1

1 Jones, Graham   qtd   ytd

Personal	Earnings:		Earnings:	
Street .... 123 Ogden Blvd.	Regular	0.00	Regular	0.00
City .... Bellevue	Overtime...................	0.00	Overtime	0.00
State .... Wa.	Salary	0.00	Salary	0.00
Zip 98455	Tips	0.00	Tips	0.00
Phone 206-669-4568	Commission	0.00	Commission	0.00
SSN 123-45-6782	Benefit	0.00	Benefit	0.00
Birth 06-20-51	Vacation Paid	0.00	Vacation Paid	0.00
Table .... Washington	Gross	0.00	Gross	0.00
Periods .... 12 /year				
Dependents	Deductions:		Deductions:	
Federal .... 2 allowances	FIT	0.00	FIT	0.00
Federal Status .... Married	SIT	0.00	SIT	0.00
State	FICA	0.00	FICA	0.00
State Status	SUTA	0.00	SUTA	0.00
Company:	SDI	0.00	SDI	0.00
Hire 11-15-87	Local	0.00	Local	0.00
Termination	Union	0.00	Union	0.00
FICAExempt .... No	Medical	0.00	Medical	0.00
Regular .... 0.00 /hour	Dental	0.00	Dental	0.00
Overtime .... 0.00 /hour	Withheld	0.00	Withheld	0.00
Salary .... 1,800.00 /period	Net Pay	0.00	Net Pay	0.00
	Expenses:		Expenses:	
	FICA	0.00	FICA	0.00
	FUTA	0.00	FUTA	0.00
	SUTA	0.00	SUTA	0.00
	SDI	0.00	SDI	0.00
	Expense	0.00	Expense	0.00
	Advance Paid	0.00	Advance Paid	0.00

Figure 9.12 Printed output of employee historical data

The printed output shows the data entered for Jones, Graham in report form (See Figure 9.12.). Once the module is in the READY mode, you can also print a detail report of the payroll to date, address labels for each employee in case you wish to correspond with some or all of them, W-2s at the end of the year for all employees, and 941, 940 and SUTA reports.

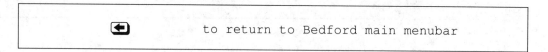

to return to Bedford main menubar

Changing to Ready Mode

Now that you have entered the opening balances, the conversion process to a computerized payroll is complete. But before we can enter current payroll data into the Bedford **PAYROLL** module you must change the module from the NOT READY mode to the READY mode. Remember, once you change to the READY mode, you cannot return to the NOT READY mode to change any historical data that you entered. So be absolutely sure that the data you entered is correct.

Remember, you cannot change to the READY mode until two conditions are met.

a.   the general ledger is in ready mode and
b.   the payroll subledger is in balance with the control accounts in the general ledger.

If the general ledger is NOT READY a message will appear telling you so. You then have to go back to the **GENERAL** module and make it READY first.

If the payroll subledger is not in balance with the general ledger control account(s), a message will be displayed informing you that the ledger is not in balance and that you must rectify this problem before you can proceed.

Since we are in balance, we are ready to change to the READY mode. Press

➡ or ⬅	to move the cursor highlight to **SYSTEM**
⬇	to execute the **SYSTEM** module
⬇	to choose **Default**
➡	to activate **Default**
➡	to activate **Module**
⬇	to choose **Payroll**
➡	to activate **Payroll**

Your screen will now display the default payroll settings as shown in Figure 9.13.

GENERAL	PAYABLE	RECEIVABLE	PAYROLL	INVENTORY	JOBCOST	SYSTEM

```
Automatic      Yes
FederalID      —
StateID
FUTARate       0.8 %
SUTARate       0.8 %
SDIRate        1.5 %
IncomeA        Salary
IncomeB        Commission
DeductionA     Union
DeductionB     Medical
DeductionC     Dental
Check          No
  Address      No
  Number       1
  Port         Lpt1
Ready          No
```

Figure 9.13 Default payroll settings

As you can see we have a few things to consider. But before we look at each of these options lets change to READY mode. Press

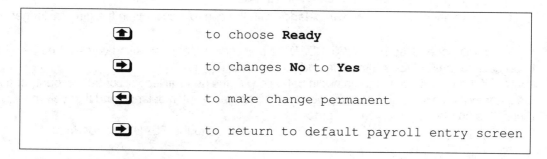

```
    ⬆        to choose Ready

    ➡        to changes No to Yes

    ⬅        to make change permanent

    ➡        to return to default payroll entry screen
```

- *Default options to Consider*

Now let's consider some of the other options. We should change any of the default items required by our company.

Automatic calculation

Automatic is set to **Yes** by default. Choosing the **Yes** option will let the Bedford Accounting System make the calculations for withholding items automatically. If you set this option to **No,** you will have to calculate the various tax deductions and insurance requirements manually on a calculator and enter them into the program here.

You may want to set this item to **No** if a mistake has been made in payroll. By changing this setting to **Manual,** you can reverse any incorrect calculations and enter new ones (See Correcting Payroll later in this chapter).

FederalID

The employer's Internal Revenue Service Identification Number should be entered here.

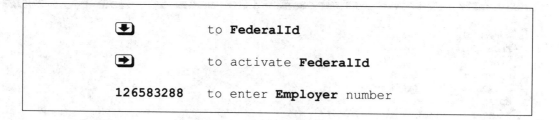

```
    ⬇            to FederalId

    ➡            to activate FederalId

126583288        to enter Employer number
```

StateID

```
875421369        to enter the StateId, your company's
                 identification number issued by the
                 state.
```

FUTA, SUTA and SDI rates

These rates are specified by the various governments for these deductions. They can be changed.

IncomeA and IncomeB

These items can be changed to suit the firm. Normally they would be **Salary** and **Commission** respectively. However, an employer may not have any commissions to pay but may instead pay an override on some sales. You would then change **Income** to **Override.** These amounts are both included in taxable gross.

DeductionA, DeductionB and DeductionC

These items are used to enter deductions after taxes have been calculated. You can change them to whatever is required such as **Union, Medical,** or **Dental.**

Check Printing

If you wish to have the system print a **Check,** or a check facsimile, set this option to **Yes.** If you choose Yes, you must also tell the system whether or not you want the name and address of the company printed on the check. The program will generate its own check numbers from 00001 to 50000. You must indicate the starting check number.

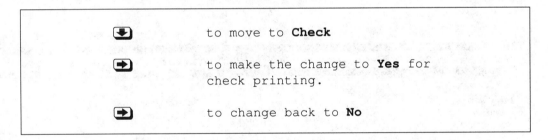

You must also indicate which port on your computer the printer is connected to. As mentioned before this is usually a parallel port, **Lpt1**. If you are unsure, check the back of the computer to see if there is some identifying mark which tells you what port the printer is connected to. Otherwise consult your computer manual.

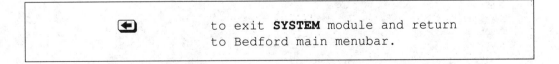

ENTERING PAYROLL JOURNAL ENTRIES

We are now ready to enter current payroll data into the Bedford module. Let's return to the **PAYROLL** module. Press

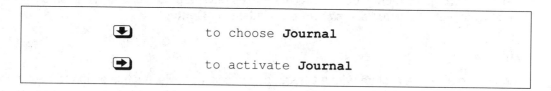

The **PAYROLL** submenu has now changed because the module has been made READY. The menu item **History** has been changed to **Journal.** It is through the **Journal** menu item that we will record all payroll journal entries to the system.

Entering Current Payroll Data

With the **PAYROLL** submenu showing, press

⬇	to choose **Journal**
➡	to activate **Journal**

Let's use our previously entered employee, Graham Jones, and prepare his pay for January. Once the **Journal** menu item is activated your screen will look like the one shown in Figure 9.14.

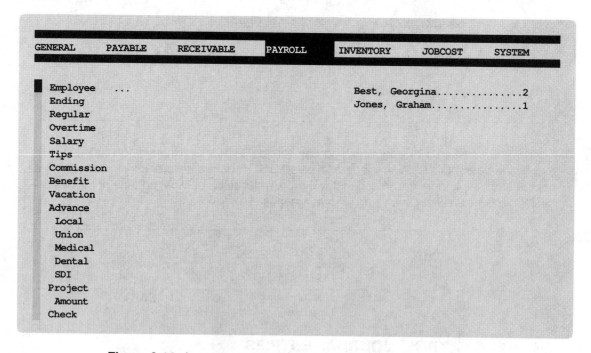

Figure 9.14 Journal entry screen for entering current payroll data

All employees and their assigned numbers are listed at the right hand side of the screen and the items requiring data are listed on the left side.

You want to enter payroll data for Graham Jones, employee #1.

1 Ret	to choose **Employee** #1

The ending date of the pay period is now requested. This date must be between the start date and the using date. Any other date will be rejected.

013188	to enter the **Ending** date of the pay period.

The cursor will now jump to the menu item **Salary**. If we had set an hourly rate for this employee or overtime hours, the cursor would stop there. The program is now asking you for the salary. In brackets beside **Salary** is the monthly salary amount that you entered previously when you modified company information.

Shift Ret	to accept the default amount for **Salary**
0 Ret	to enter the default amount for **Tips**
0 Ret	to enter the amount of **Commission**
0 Ret	to enter taxable **Benefits**
72 Ret	to enter **Vacation** pay owing based on the amount of gross pay. ($72.00 is the amount calculated by multiplying $1,800 by the 4%.) Under normal circumstances the employee would receive his/her total vacation pay upon vacation.
0 Ret	to put 0 in **Advance**. Many salaried employees get a draw at the middle of the month which is not subject to any withholding amounts. If an advance has been paid, a negative amount will be displayed in brackets. You could accept this amount by pressing Shift Ret and the advance, or the amount that would not cause gross pay to be negative, will be entered in this item.
0 Ret	to enter the amount of any **Local** income tax to be withheld from the employee.

0 [Ret]   to enter zero for **Union**

0 [Ret]   to enter zero for **Medical**

0 [Ret]   to enter zero for **Dental**

0 [Ret]   to enter zero for **SDI** (State Disability
                   Insurance)

                   The Bedford Accounting System payroll
                   module will now skip over the **Project**
                   and **Amount** areas of the entry since we
                   have as yet not defined any projects or
                   departments. Otherwise payroll expense
                   could be allocated to various depart-
                   ments or projects as desired. We will
                   discuss projects and departments in
                   Chapter 11.

129 [Ret]   to enter the **Check** number.

If you have entered incorrect amounts you can correct them by using the up and down arrow keys and activating any field with the right arrow key. Because check printing is set to **No** for our example, we must enter the check number manually. If the check printing option is set to **Yes** in the **SYSTEM** module you can print the check by pressing the right arrow key when your cursor is next to **Check.** The program will print a program-generated number on the check. (See Figure 9.15.) You can reprint a check as many times as necessary until you accept the entry with the left arrow key.

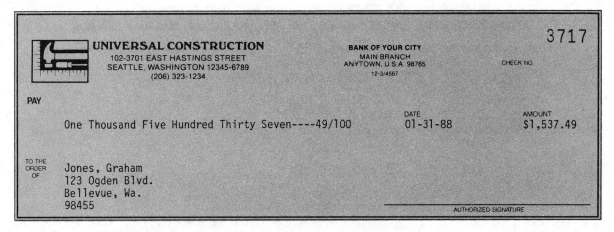

Figure 9.15 Printout of check and payroll information

Before you save the entry you can look at both the journal entry created and the net payroll calculation. Press

[F2]	to see journal entry

The journal entry should be displayed as shown in Figure 9.16.

```
                                                                      F2
GENERAL     PAYABLE      RECEIVABLE      PAYROLL     INVENTORY    JOBCOST     SYSTEM
J13                                                   debits      credits

530  Wages                                          1,872.00
531  FICA Expense                                     140.59
532  FUTA Expense                                      14.98
533  SUTA Expense                                      14.98
231  FIT Payable                                                  193.92
233  FICA Payable                                                 281.18
234  FUTA Payable                                                  14.98
235  SUTA Payable                                                  14.98
106  First Interstate — General                                 1,537.49
                                                    _____    _____
                                                    2,042.55      2,042.55
```

Figure 9.16 Display of payroll journal entry

```
     [F2]              to return to entry
```

To see the net payroll calculation, press

```
     [F3]              to see net payroll calculation
```

Your screen should now resemble Figure 9.17.

```
                                                                      F3
GENERAL     PAYABLE      RECEIVABLE      PAYROLL     INVENTORY    JOBCOST     SYSTEM

Salary.........1,800.00    FIT.............193.92    Gross..........1,872.00
Vacation..........72.00    FICA............140.59    Withheld.........334.51-
             _____                 _____                 _____
Gross..........1,872.00    Withheld........334.51    Net............1,537.49
```

Figure 9.17 Display of net payroll calculation

```
     [F3]              to return to entry
```

Once you are satisfied with the entry, and the check number has been assigned, you can press the left arrow key to accept it. If you don't want the entry recorded permanently, then press the ESCape key.

```
┌──────────────────────────────────────────────────────────┐
│         ⬅         to accept entry                          │
└──────────────────────────────────────────────────────────┘
```

Before the program will accept the payroll journal entry, it makes sure that the date is within the dates used by the deduction tables. If the date of the entry is not within this range, you will see:

Error message — date of entry does not agree with date range of deduction tables

You can accept the entry but you must realize that the calculation is likely to be wrong.

▪ Practice Exercise

For practice, prepare the payroll entry for the employee, Best, Georgina with the following payroll data.

Pay date	January 31, 1988
Regular hours	80
Overtime hours	5
Vacation pay paid	$0.00
Check number	130

Displaying and Printing reports

Once you have entered the information into the payroll module you may want to view it on the monitor or print it out. From the main **PAYROLL** module select **Display** and display the detail information for Graham Jones. The detail should be as shown in Figure 9.18. You can see that the employee record has been updated to include the salary that was just paid to him.

GENERAL	PAYABLE	RECEIVABLE	PAYROLL	INVENTORY	JOBCOST	SYSTEM	
date	pp	gross	fit	fica	sit	suta	sdi	local
01-31-88	12	1,872.00	193.92	140.59	0.00	0.00	0.00	0.00
		1,872.00	193.92	140.59	0.00	0.00	0.00	0.00

Figure 9.18 Detail information showing payroll data for an employee

We can also get quarter-to-date and year-to-date displays for each individual showing earnings, deductions and expenses as shown in Figure 9.19.

```
 GENERAL      PAYABLE      RECEIVABLE      PAYROLL      INVENTORY      JOBCOST      SYSTEM


 Employee .........Jones, Graham

 Regular ...................0.00
 Overtime ..................0.00
 Salary ................1,800.00
 Tips ......................0.00
 Commission ................0.00
 Benefit ...................0.00
 Vacation Paid ............72.00
                      _____
 Gross .................1,872.00

 Advance Paid ..............0.00
```

```
 GENERAL      PAYABLE      RECEIVABLE      PAYROLL      INVENTORY      JOBCOST      SYSTEM


 Employee.........Jones, Graham

 FIT ....................193.92
 SIT ......................0.00
 FICA ...................140.59
 SUTA .....................0.00
 SDI ......................0.00
 Local ....................0.00
 Union ....................0.00
 Medical ..................0.00
 Dental ...................0.00
                      _____
 Withheld ...............334.51
```

```
 GENERAL      PAYABLE      RECEIVABLE      PAYROLL      INVENTORY      JOBCOST      SYSTEM


 Employee .........Jones, Graham

 FICA ...................140.59
 FUTA ....................14.98
 SUTA ....................14.98
 SDI ......................0.00
                      _____
 Expense.................170.55
```

Figure 9.19 Qtd information showing earnings, deductions and expenses for an employee

If you want printed reports you would choose the **Print** item from the **PAYROLL** submenu and activate it by pressing the right arrow key. You would then be able to print out a variety of reports similar to the ones shown in Figure 9.19.

■ *Practice Exercise*

Now print out the following reports from the **Print** menu.

1. Employee summary (Figure 9.20)
2. Detail (Figure 9.21)
3. W-2 form (Figure 9.22)

Fast Delivery Inc. FOR INSTRUCTIONAL USE ONLY   Page 2
EMPLOYEE Summary Jan 31,1988

1 Jones, Graham   qtd   ytd

Personal:	Earnings:		Earnings:	
Street .... 123 Ogden Blvd.	Regular	.... 0.00	Regular	.... 0.00
City .... Bellevue	Overtime	.... 0.00	Overtime	.... 0.00
State .... Wa.	Salary	.... 1,800.00	Salary	.... 1,800.00
Zip 98455	Tips	.... 0.00	Tips	.... 0.00
Phone 206-669-4568	Commission	.... 0.00	Commission	.... 0.00
SSN 123-45-6782	Benefit	.... 0.00	Benefit	.... 0.00
Birth 06-20-51	Vacation Paid	.... 72.00	Vacation Paid	.... 72.00
Table .... Washington	Gross	.... 1,872.00	Gross	.... 1,872.00
Periods .... 12 /year				
Dependents	Deductions:		Deductions:	
Federal .... 2 allowances	FIT	.... 193.92	FIT	.... 193.92
Federal Status .... Married	SIT	.... 0.00	SIT	.... 0.00
State	FICA	.... 140.59	FICA	.... 140.59
State Status	SUTA	.... 0.00	SUTA	.... 0.00
Company:	SDI	.... 0.00	SDI	.... 0.00
Hire 11-15-87	Local	.... 0.00	Local	.... 0.00
Termination	Union	.... 0.00	Union	.... 0.00
FICAExempt .... No	Medical	.... 0.00	Medical	.... 0.00
Regular .... 0.00 /hour	Dental	.... 0.00	Dental	.... 0.00
Overtime .... 0.00 /hour	Withheld	.... 334.51	Withheld	.... 334.51
Salary .... 1,800.00 /period	Net Pay	.... 1,537.49	Net Pay	.... 1,537.49
	Expenses:		Expenses:	
	FICA	.... 140.59	FICA	.... 140.59
	FUTA	.... 14.98	FUTA	.... 14.98
	SUTA	.... 14.98	SUTA	.... 14.98
	SDI	.... 0.00	SDI	.... 0.00
	Expense	.... 170.55	Expense	.... 170.55
	Advance Paid	.... 0.00	Advance Paid	.... 0.00

EMPLOYEES on File: 2

Figure 9.20 Print-out of employee payroll summary information

Fast Delivery Inc. FOR INSTRUCTIONAL USE ONLY
Payroll Register Jan 31,1988

Best, Georgina

date	pp	gross	fit	fica	sit	suta	sdi	local	union	medical	dental
01-31-88	12	656.25	11.56	49.28	-	0.00	-	0.00	-	-	-
		656.25	11.56	49.28	-	0.00	-	0.00	-	-	-

Jones, Graham

date	pp	gross	fit	fica	sit	suta	sdi	local	union	medical	dental
01-31-88	12	1,872.00	193.92	140.59	-	0.00	-	0.00	-	-	-
		1,872.00	193.92	140.59	-	0.00	-	0.00	-	-	-

Do NOT Cut or Separate Forms on This Page

1 Control number	22222	For Paperwork Reduction Act Notice, see back of Copy D. OMB No. 1545-0008	**For Official Use Only ▶**	

2 Employer's name, address, and ZIP code	3 Employer's identification number	4 Employer's state I.D. number
FAST DELIVERY INC. 1251 Bel Red Road Bellevue, Wa. 98625	12-6583288	875421369

5 Statutory employee [X]	Deceased ☐	Pension plan ☐	Legal rep. ☐	942 emp. [X]	Subtotal ☐	Deferred compensation ☐	Void ☐

6 Allocated tips	7 Advance EIC payment

8 Employee's social security number 987-65-2321	9 Federal income tax withheld 193.92	10 Wages, tips, other compensation 1872.00	11 Social security tax withheld 140.59

12 Employee's name (first, middle, last) GRAHAM JONES	13 Social security wages 1872.00	14 Social security tips 0.00

123 Ogden Blvd. Bellevue Wa. 98455	16 (See Instr. for Forms W-2/W-2P)	16a Fringe benefits incl. in Box 10 0.00

	17 State income tax 0.00	18 State wages, tips, etc.	19 Name of state WA.

15 Employee's address and ZIP code	20 Local income tax 0.00	21 Local wages, tips, etc.	22 Name of locality

Form **W-2 Wage and Tax Statement 1988**

Copy A For Social Security Administration   Dept. of the Treasury—IRS

Figure 9.21 Print-out of employee payroll detail information

CORRECTING THE PAYROLL

There may be times when the data entered for a particular employee is wrong. For example, if an employee received a raise during the pay period that you are not aware of, or if the employee asked for new deductions. In this instance you make a reversing entry, and then reenter the new payroll data.

To do so, follow these steps.

1. Move to the **SYSTEM** module.

2. From the **SYSTEM** submenu, choose **Default** and activate, then **Module** and **Payroll.** When in this final entry display, change the item **Automatic** to **No.**

3. Save the new setting and return to main menubar. Then move to the **PAYROLL** module and activate it.

4. Move cursor next to **Journal** and activate it. The payroll entry screen will now be some-what different to allow data entry into the fields that were previously calculated automati-cally by the computer. (See Figure 9.23.) You must now manually enter each of the amounts reported on the incorrect payroll journal, each amount followed by a minus sign so it will be subtracted from the totals in the employee record.

5. Save these negative entries with the left arrow key.

6. Return to the **SYSTEM** module and set **Automatic** to **Yes** again.

7. Return to the **PAYROLL** module and enter the corrected entry.

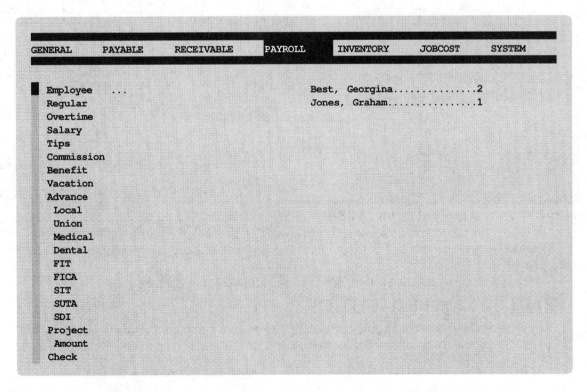

Figure 9.23 Payroll journal entry screen for manually adjusting payroll data.
Automatic calculation has been set to No in the SYSTEM module
for the purpose of reversing entries.

EXPORTING PAYROLL FILES

There are three payroll reports that can be exported — payroll register, employee summary and employee address labels. The exported reports listed will have files names, EMPLOYEE.EXT, DETAIL.EXT, and LABEL.EXT respectively, where EXT refers to the specific file format that you need for your spreadsheet:

The method for exporting the files is the same as discussed in the **RECEIVABLE** and **PAYABLE** modules. Follow the steps at the end of those chapters.

MAINTAINING AN AUDIT TRAIL

As mentioned previously, it is important to establish an audit trail for all accounting entries made. An audit trail is a printed list (hard copy) of all the payroll transactions entered during a particular session.

When you have printed out the journal entries from the print menu, be sure to store the entries in a binder marked **PAYROLL.** You can then use that file to review any of the entries made in the event the computer should crash or the disk is destroyed.

FINISHING THE SESSION

You have now completed the payroll tutorial. You should end this session to save your data to disk. After activating the **Finish** command you will be returned to the disk operating system.

To finish this session, press

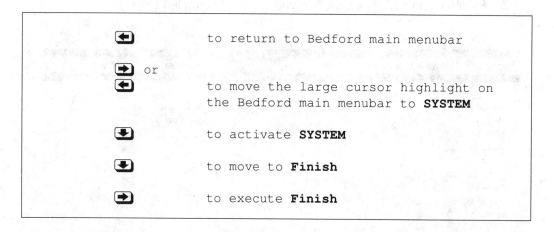

```
⬅        to return to Bedford main menubar

➡  or
⬅        to move the large cursor highlight on
         the Bedford main menubar to SYSTEM

⬇        to activate SYSTEM

⬇        to move to Finish

➡        to execute Finish
```

In the following chapters you should always end each session with the **Finish** command. When beginning each chapter in this tutorial start the Bedford Accounting Program as described earlier in this chapter.

BACKING UP YOUR DATA FILES

You should always make a backup of the data files on your computer system to guard against loss of files or hardware failure. Follow the procedures outlined in Chapter 4 for making backups.

BEDFORD PRACTICE SET
AMERICANA HOME DECORATING AND SERVICE COMPANY

Part IV - Payroll

OBJECTIVE

After completing this practice set for payroll, you should be able to:

1. Create employee files.

2. Enter historical data to accounts.

3. Enter necessary defaults and integration accounts.

4. Set the SYSTEM to READY.

5. Enter transactions for: middle of month advances; end of month payroll.

6. Print individual employee earnings records.

7. Print payroll register of all employees.

8. Verify that total employee accounts agrees with Payroll control accounts in the GENERAL module.

INSTRUCTION: 1. Enter the following employee files and historical data.

Americana Decorating Sales & Service Inc. FOR INSTRUCTIONAL USE ONLY   Page 1
EMPLOYEE Summary Sept. 30,1988

1 Carter, Gary ..

Personal:	Earnings:	qtd	Earnings:	ytd
Street .... 567 Jefferson St.	Regular 0.00		Regular 0.00	
City .... Portland	Overtime 0.00		Overtime 0.00	
State .... Oregon	Salary 0.00		Salary 19,800.00	
Zip 89345	Tips 0.00		Tips 0.00	
Phone 503-687-5678	Commission 0.00		Commission 0.00	
SSN 306-91-2314	Benefit 0.00		Benefit 0.00	
Birth 04-06-54	Vacation Paid 0.00		Vacation Paid 0.00	
Table .... Oregon	Gross 0.00		Gross 19,800.00	
Periods .... 24 /year				
Dependents	Deductions:		Deductions:	
Federal .... 2 allowances	FIT 0.00		FIT 4,242.15	
Federal Status .... Single	SIT 0.00		SIT 1,533.69	
State .... 2 allowances	FICA 0.00		FICA 1,486.98	
State Status .... Single	SUTA 0.00		SUTA 0.00	
Company:	SDI 0.00		SDI 0.00	
Hire	Local 0.00		Local 0.00	
Termination	Union 0.00		Union 990.00	
FICAExempt .... No	Medical 0.00		Medical 450.00	
Regular .... 0.00 /hour	Dental 0.00		Dental 0.00	
Overtime .... 0.00 /hour	Withheld 0.00		Withheld 8,702.82	
Salary .... 2,200.00 /period	Net Pay 0.00		Net Pay 11,097.18	
	Expenses:		Expenses:	
	FICA 0.00		FICA 1,486.98	
	FUTA 0.00		FUTA 56.00	
	SUTA 0.00		SUTA 112.00	
	SDI 0.00		SDI 0.00	
	Expense 0.00		Expense 1,654.98	
	Advance Paid 0.00		Advance Paid 0.00	

Americana Decorating Sales & Service Inc. FOR INSTRUCTIONAL USE ONLY   Page 2
EMPLOYEE Summary Sept. 30,1988

2 Gehrig, Lou ...   qtd   ytd

Personal:	Earnings:		Earnings:	
Street .... 7865 Washington Street	Regular 0.00		Regular 0.00	
City .... Portland	Overtime 0.00		Overtime 0.00	
State .... Oregon	Salary 0.00		Salary 21,600.00	
Zip 89098	Tips 0.00		Tips 0.00	
Phone 503-687-9476	Commission 0.00		Commission 0.00	
SSN 522-46-7890	Benefit 0.00		Benefit 0.00	
Birth 07-04-45	Vacation Paid 0.00		Vacation Paid 0.00	
Table .... Oregon	Gross 0.00		Gross 21,600.00	
Periods .... 24 /year				
Dependents	Deductions:		Deductions:	
Federal .... 3 allowances	FIT 0.00		FIT 3,663.18	
Federal Status .... Married	SIT 0.00		SIT 1,602.72	
State .... 2 allowances	FICA 0.00		FICA 1,622.16	
State Status .... Married	SUTA 0.00		SUTA 0.00	
Company:	SDI 0.00		SDI 0.00	
Hire	Local 0.00		Local 0.00	
Termination	Union 0.00		Union 1,080.00	
FICAExempt .... No	Medical 0.00		Medical 450.00	
Regular .... 0.00 /hour	Dental 0.00		Dental 0.00	
Overtime .... 0.00 /hour	Withheld 0.00		Withheld 8,418.06	
Salary .... 2,400.00 /period	Net Pay 0.00		Net Pay 13,181.94	
	Expenses:		Expenses:	
	FICA 0.00		FICA 1,622.16	
	FUTA 0.00		FUTA 56.00	
	SUTA 0.00		SUTA 112.00	
	SDI 0.00		SDI 0.00	
	Expense 0.00		Expense 1,790.16	
	Advance Paid 0.00		Advance Paid 0.00	

Americana Decorating Sales & Service Inc. FOR INSTRUCTIONAL USE ONLY   Page 3
EMPLOYEE Summary Sept. 30,1988

3 Robinson, Jackie   qtd   ytd

Personal:	Earnings:		Earnings:	
Street .... 8976 Liberty Highway	Regular 0.00		Regular 0.00	
City .... Portland	Overtime 0.00		Overtime 0.00	
State .... Oregon	Salary 0.00		Salary 22,500.00	
Zip 89768-5435	Tips 0.00		Tips 0.00	
Phone 505-678-7654	Commission 0.00		Commission 0.00	
SSN 324-65-7890	Benefit 0.00		Benefit 0.00	
Birth 12-03-60	Vacation Paid 0.00		Vacation Paid 0.00	
Table .... Oregon	Gross 0.00		Gross 22,500.00	
Periods .... 24 /year				
Dependents	Deductions:		Deductions:	
Federal .... 1 allowance	FIT 0.00		FIT 5,374.44	
Federal Status .... Single	SIT 0.00		SIT 1,810.44	
State .... 1 allowance	FICA 0.00		FICA 1,689.75	
State Status .... Single	SUTA 0.00		SUTA 0.00	
Company:	SDI 0.00		SDI 0.00	
Hire	Local 0.00		Local 0.00	
Termination	Union 0.00		Union 1,125.00	
FICAExempt .... No	Medical 0.00		Medical 540.00	
Regular .... 0.00 /hour	Dental 0.00		Dental 0.00	
Overtime .... 0.00 /hour	Withheld 0.00		Withheld 10,539.63	
Salary .... 2,500.00 /period	Net Pay 0.00		Net Pay 11,960.37	

Expenses:		Expenses:	
FICA	0.00	FICA	1,689.75
FUTA	0.00	FUTA	56.00
SUTA	0.00	SUTA	112.00
SDI	0.00	SDI	0.00
Expense	0.00	Expense	1,857.75
Advance Paid	0.00	Advance Paid	0.00

Americana Decorating Sales & Service Inc. FOR INSTRUCTIONAL USE ONLY

EMPLOYEE Summary Sept. 30,1988

4   Ruth, Babe ....   qtd   ytd

Personal:		Earnings:		Earnings:	
Street	897 Homer Street	Regular	0.00	Regular	0.00
City	Portland	Overtime	0.00	Overtime	0.00
State	Oregon	Salary	0.00	Salary	20,700.00
Zip	89765-0099	Tips	0.00	Tips	0.00
Phone	503-787-6543	Commission	0.00	Commission	0.00
SSN	345-67-8909	Benefit	0.00	Benefit	0.00
Birth	11-02-55	Vacation Paid	0.00	Vacation Paid	0.00
Table	Oregon	Gross	0.00	Gross	20,700.00
Periods	24 /year				

Dependents		Deductions:		Deductions:	
Federal	2 allowances	FIT	0.00	FIT	3,615.93
Federal Status	Married	SIT	0.00	SIT	1,521.72
State	2 allowances	FICA	0.00	FICA	1,554.57
State Status	Married	SUTA	0.00	SUTA	0.00
Company:		SDI	0.00	SDI	0.00
Hire		Local	0.00	Local	0.00
Termination		Union	0.00	Union	1,035.00
FICAExempt	No	Medical	0.00	Medical	495.00
Regular	0.00 /hour	Dental	0.00	Dental	0.00
Overtime	0.00 /hour	Withheld	0.00	Withheld	8,222.22
Salary	2,300.00 /period	Net Pay	0.00	Net Pay	12,477.78

		Expenses:		Expenses:	
		FICA	0.00	FICA	1,554.57
		FUTA	0.00	FUTA	56.00
		SUTA	0.00	SUTA	112.00
		SDI	0.00	SDI	0.00
		Expense	0.00	Expense	1,722.57
		Advance Paid	0.00	Advance Paid	0.00

Americana Decorating Sales & Service Inc. FOR INSTRUCTIONAL USE ONLY   Page 5
EMPLOYEE Summary Sept. 30,1988

5 Washington, George   qtd   ytd

Personal:	Earnings:		Earnings:	
Street .... 3456 Apple Tree Lane	Regular	0.00	Regular	0.00
City .... Portland	Overtime	0.00	Overtime	0.00
State .... Oregon	Salary	0.00	Salary	26,322.03
Zip 89786-7544	Tips	0.00	Tips	0.00
Phone 503-254-6019	Commission	0.00	Commission	0.00
SSN 234-56-7890	Benefit	0.00	Benefit	0.00
Birth 10-02-63	Vacation Paid	0.00	Vacation Paid	0.00
Table .... Oregon	Gross	0.00	Gross	26,322.03
Periods .... 24 /year				
Dependents	Deductions:		Deductions:	
Federal .... 3 allowances	FIT	0.00	FIT	4,985.28
Federal Status .... Married	SIT	0.00	SIT	2,027.70
State .... 2 allowances	FICA	0.00	FICA	1,976.76
State Status .... Married	SUTA	0.00	SUTA	0.00
Company:	SDI	0.00	SDI	0.00
Hire	Local	0.00	Local	0.00
Termination	Union	0.00	Union	1,316.07
FICAExempt .... No	Medical	0.00	Medical	495.00
Regular .... 0.00 /hour	Dental	0.00	Dental	0.00
Overtime .... 0.00 /hour	Withheld	0.00	Withheld	10,800.81
Salary .... 2,924.67 /period	Net Pay	0.00	Net Pay	15,521.22
	Expenses:		Expenses:	
	FICA	0.00	FICA	1,976.76
	FUTA	0.00	FUTA	56.00
	SUTA	0.00	SUTA	112.00
	SDI	0.00	SDI	0.00
	Expense	0.00	Expense	2,144.76
	Advance Paid	0.00	Advance Paid	0.00

EMPLOYEES on File: 5

INSTRUCTION: 2.   Enter the integration accounts required for your General Ledger chart of accounts.

INSTRUCTION: 3.   Set the SYSTEM>Default>Module>Payroll>:

Automatic	Yes
FederalID	12-3456789
StateID	987654321
FUTARate	0.8%
SUTARate	0.8%
SDIRate	0%
Income A	Salary
Income B	
Deduction A	Comp. Pens
Deduction B	Medical
Deduction C	
Check	Yes
Address	Yes
Number	404
Port	Lpt1
Ready	Yes

INSTRUCTION: 4.   Enter the following transactions in the GENERAL, PAYABLE, RECEIVABLE and PAYROLL modules for month of October.

Oct.

1.   Received on account from Ollie North, $8,292.60, in full payment of invoice S411. R153.

1.   Received on account from S. Smith, $20,497.03, covering invoices S409 for $18,997.07 and S415 for $2,264.20 less Cm57 for $764.24. R154.

1.   Sold merchandise and services on account to Robert Redford: S416.

Item	Quantity	Unit	Detail	Price	Amount
2	60	Gallon	Eggshell Latex	22.00	$ 1,320.00
9	50	Roll	Select	14.00	700.00
15	70	Sq/Yd	Velvet	50.00	3,500.00
			Decorating Labour		4,378.89
			Freight		80.00
			SST @ 7%		386.40
					$10,365.29

8.   Paid on account to Zebra Color Stripes, $9,961.25, covering invoice P239 for $11,265.81 less Dm48 for $1,304.56. Ch404.

8.   Returned merchandise and realized purchases discounts from Munforte Paint & Paper, $1,013.34, covering purchase returns: paint, $123.34; wallpaper, $213.20; fabric, $345.67; and purchase discounts: paint, $87.89; wallpaper, $99.34; fabric, $143.90. Dm49.

8.   Paid on account to Munforte Paint & Paper, $6,191.65, covering invoice P240 for $7,204.99 less Dm49 for $1,013.34. Ch405.

8.   Purchased merchandise on account from Interior Supply: paint, $3,245.89; wallpaper, $1,345.78; fabric, $3,245.78; total, $7,837.45. P244.

16.   Recorded company pension owed to vendor Merrill Lynch Co., $616.23. M116.

16.   Paid Merrill Lynch Co. for company pension, $616.23. Ch406.

16.   Record medical plan owed to vendor Blue Cross, $270.00. M117.

16.   Paid Blue Cross for medical plan, $270.00. Ch407.

16.   Record sales tax owed vendor State Regulatory Body, $1,245.30. M118.

16.   Paid State Regulatory Body for sales tax, $1,245.30. Ch408.

16.   Record telephone expense as debt owing to vendor Bell Telephone, $165.89. P245.

16.   Paid Bell Telephone Co. for telephone expense, $165.89. Ch409.

16.   Record fuel expense as debt owing to vendor Texaco Oil Co., $86.34. P246.

16.   Paid Texaco Oil Co. for fuel expense, $86.34. Ch410.

16.   Record the withholding taxes payable as debt owing to vendor Internal Revenue Service: Federal Income Tax, $2,431.22; Federal Insurance; $1,851.16, total $4,282.38. M119.

Note: *You must enter all liabilities as a purchase to a vendor account so you can then run check payments.*

16. Paid withholding taxes to Internal Revenue Service, $4,282.38. Ch411.

16. Record State Income Tax payable, $944.03. M120.

   Note: You must record the debt owed to vendor State regulatory body so you can then process check using PAYABLE module.

16. Paid State of Oregon Regulatory Body for State Income Tax, $944.03. Ch412.

16. Record bank transfer from General to Payroll account. $3,697.40. M121.

16. Paid middle of month advance to Gary Carter, $660.00. Ch413.

   Note: With Payroll integrated into the System you no longer have to make two entries like you did if the employee was entered as a vendor payable.

16. Paid middle of month advance to Lou Gehrig, $720.00. Ch414.

16. Paid middle of month advance to Jackie Robinson, $750.00. Ch415.

16. Paid middle of month advance to Babe Ruth, $690.00. Ch416.

16. Paid middle of month advance to George Washington, $877.40. Ch417.

31. Record bank transfer from General to Payroll account, $3,440.21. M122.

31. Paid month end payroll to Gary Carter, $573.02, covering: Salary Expense, $2,200.00 plus employer's FICA Expense $165.22; less deductions of Federal Income Tax, $471.35; State Income Tax, $170.41; Employee and Employer FICA Payable, $330.44; Company Pension, $110.00; Medical, $50.00; Advances Receivable, $660.00. Ch418.

   Note: The Bedford Program will generate the employer's payroll taxes internally to save you making a separate entry.

31. Paid month end payroll to Lou Gehrig, $744.66, covering: Salary Expense, $2,400.00 plus employer's FICA Expense $180.24; less deductions of Federal Income Tax, $407.02; State Income Tax, $178.08; Employee and Employer FICA Payable, $360.48; Company Pension, $120.00; Medical, $50.00; Advances Receivable, $720.00. Ch419.

31. Paid month end payroll to Jackie Robinson, $578.93, covering: Salary Expense, $2,500.00 plus employer's FICA Expense $187.75; less deductions of Federal Income Tax, $597.16; State Income Tax, $201.16; Employee and Employer FICA Payable, $375.50; Company Pension, $125.00; Medical, $60.00; Advances Receivable, $750.00. Ch420.

31. Paid month end payroll to Babe Ruth, $696.42, covering: Salary Expense, $2,300.00 plus employer's FICA Expense $172.73; less deductions of Federal Income Tax, $401.77; State Income Tax, $169.08; Employee and Employer FICA Payable, $345.46; Company Pension, $115.00; Medical, $55.00; Advances Receivable, $690.00. Ch421.

31. Paid month end payroll to George Washington, $847.18, covering: Salary Expense, $2,924.67 plus employer's FICA Expense $219.64; less deductions of Federal Income Tax, $553.92; State Income Tax, $225.30; Employee and Employer FICA Payable, $439.28; Company Pension, $146.23; Medical, $55.00; Advances Receivable, $877.40. Ch422.

31. Recorded Bank Reconciliation adjustments: Short Term Loan Payment, $543.80; Mortgage Payment, $345.78; Interest Expense, $1,125.34; Bank Charges Expense, $14.23; Interest Income, $135.46; net total bank debit, $1,893.69. M123.

31. Recorded adjusting entry for insurance expense incurred, $400.00.

31. Recorded adjusting entry for office supplies expense incurred, $44.56.

31. Recorded adjusting entry for estimated depreciation expense incurred: Building, $1,750.00; Automotive, $185.00.

31. Recorded ending inventory change from end of last period, increasing: paint, $1,567.47; wallpaper, $456.44; fabric, $1,987.29; total, $4,011.20. Note: Modify the description of account Ending Inventory 09-30-88 to Inventory Change Oct. 1-31 before entering transaction.

INSTRUCTION: 6. Print individual employee's earnings records using Summary layout for current month and year to date.
Print payroll register of all employee's earnings records using Detail layout for current month and year to date.
Print Aging Schedule of Accounts Receivable in Summary and Detail form for all accounts.
Verify that the total of all customer's account balances agrees with the Accounts Receivable control account.
Print Aging Schedule of Accounts Payable in Summary and Detail form for all accounts.
Verify that the total of all vendor's account balances agrees with the Accounts Payable control account.
Print General Journal entries from 10-01-88 to 10-31-88.
Print Income Statement for 10-01-88 to 10-31-88.
Modify the description of Inventory Change Oct. 1-31 to Ending Inventory 10-31-88.
Print Income Statement for 01-01-88 to 10-31-88.
Print Balance Sheet for 10-31-88.

Chapter 10
INVENTORY

Chapter 10
INVENTORY

PREVIEW

In Chapter 10 you will become acquainted with the INVENTORY module of the Bedford Accounting System. You will first get an overview of the nature of inventory — types of inventory, how to handle purchase adjustments and federal taxes, how to record sales and adjustments for returns, the various inventory control methods, as well as the various methods of costing inventory.

The conversion process from a manual to a computerized inventory system is basically similar to that of the other modules: organizing inventory items, adding, deleting and modifying inventory items and entering historical inventory data. Then you will look at the various ways of displaying data entered and how to print various inventory reports. Before entering current inventory data, the system is put in the READY mode. You will learn about the major difference between the INVENTORY module and the other modules — additions to and reductions of inventory are made automatically as you enter purchases into the accounts PAYABLE module and as you enter sales into the accounts RECEIVABLE module.

The final section in this chapter lets you enter some current transactions — purchases, sales of goods, and transfers of inventory. Printing of invoices, generating an audit trail and exporting the files complete the chapter.

OBJECTIVES

After reading this chapter you should be able to explain:

1. The types of firm's that carry inventory;

2. How purchase adjustments are handled in accounting;

3. How sales and sales returns are recorded;

4. How state sales taxes are recorded;

5. How cost of goods sold is arrived at;

6. Methods of determining inventory costs;

7. How to convert a manual inventory system to a computerized system;

8. How to update the general ledger for the required accounts;

9. How to insert, modify, and delete inventory items into the INVENTORY module;

10. How to enter historical data;

11. How to display and print inventory reports;

12. How to change the system to READY mode for entering current data;

13. How inventory levels are increased and decreased by entering some purchases and sales into the appropriate modules;

14. What types of transactions are entered into the inventory module and how to enter them;

15. How to print invoices;

16. How to create an inventory audit trail, and why an audit trail is necessary.

    The data that we have so far entered into the Bedford accounting program is for Fast Delivery Inc., a service company. Service companies include gas stations, airlines, railroads, hotels, theatres, real estate brokerage firms, ski resorts, and so on. These companies get their revenue by providing services; their profit is the excess of their service fees over the cost of providing these services.

    However, there are also many manufacturing and merchandising firms. The former manufacture goods and then sell them to either wholesalers and retailers or merchandisers. A merchandising firm purchases goods, or inventory, and resells it to its customers. For a retailer, profit is dependent upon two factors:

a. The excess of sales over the cost of the goods that were sold (the *gross margin*), and

b. The excess of gross margin over the operating expenses necessary to earn the revenue.

    Figure 10.1 shows a typical income statement for a merchandising firm. It is different from a service business because it carries inventory. This inventory is purchased periodically throughout the year and reduced as sales are made. Thus sales revenue and cost of goods sold are two major factors on this income statement.

Fast Delivery Inc.
Income Statement
Jan 1, 1987 - Jan 31, 1987

Revenue		Expenses	
Product Sales		Cost of Goods Sold	
Product Line A	12,000	Product Line A	7,200
Product LIne B	40,000	Product Line B	24,000
Product Line C	7,000	Product LIne C	3,800
Total Product Sales	59,000	Total Cost of Goods Sold	35,000
Miscellaneous Sales		Administration Expenses	
Interest	500	Commissions	4,000
PST Commissions	1,500	Wages	2,000
		Interest - Bank Loan	700
Total Misc Sales	2,000	Telephone	300
		Accounting	500
Total Revenue	$ 61,000	Utilities	1,500
		Total Admin Expenses	9,000
		Total Expenses	44,000
		Income	$ 17,000

Figure 10.1 Typical income statement for a merchandising firm

From this statement, the company can calculate *gross margin,* which is total product sales minus cost of goods sold:

Total product sales	59,000
Total cost of goods sold	35,000
Gross margin	24,000

ACQUIRING INVENTORY

Inventory may be acquired in one of three ways:

1. Purchased from other manufacturers or suppliers

2. Manufactured

3. A combination of the above where the firm purchases raw materials and parts used in the manufacture of a finished product to particular specifications.

Inventory Purchased from Suppliers

The most common means of acquiring inventory is to buy it from manufacturers or wholesalers. To the basic cost of the inventory, the firm adds an amount to cover its expenses and provide a profit — the *markup.* Legally, the buyer is deemed to have acquired the goods when the responsibility for the goods was transferred from the seller to the purchaser. This actual transferring of responsibility for the goods from seller to purchaser is specified when the goods are ordered in the following way:

FOB (free on board) — FOB signifies that the shipper transfers the responsibility for the goods when it reaches a certain point. In other words, the shipper is free from responsibility when the goods are on board at the location designated. For example, FOB WAREHOUSE means that the goods are the responsibility of the purchaser as soon as they leave the warehouse. FOB DESTINATION means the goods are the responsibility of the purchaser when they reach their destination — the purchaser's receiving point.

FAS (free along side ship) — FAS is similar to FOB with the restriction that goods must be delivered to the ship for destination to some other point. Ship in this case need not literally mean via a ship but simply by some method of shipment.

CIF — CIF (cost, insurance and freight prepaid) indicates that the goods will transfer when the cost of the goods, the insurance for the transportation and the freight have been paid for.

Once the goods have been transferred to the purchaser, the following accounting entry is made:

```
Dr. Inventory                          xxx
     Cr. Accounts Payable (cash)              xxx
```

The inventory is always recorded in the books at cost. This includes the actual cost of the goods plus insurance, if required, and the cost of freight to bring the inventory to the site of sale.

Once the goods have been received, a receiving report should be filled out and passed on to the accounting department. The *receiving report* signifies to the accounting department that the goods have been actually received and should be paid for.

Manufactured Goods

Goods in inventory are often manufactured from raw materials. In this case, the purchase of the raw material would be entered into the accounting system at cost:

Dr. Inventory — raw materials xxx
    Cr. Accounts payable (cash) xxx

The raw materials will be transferred to new inventory items as they are consumed. A *manufacturing report* would be prepared showing the accounting department the amount or number of inventory items that were used in the manufacturing process. The new product cost will consist of the cost of raw materials used, plus the labor and overhead costs incurred in the production process. The accounting entry needed to record the new item would be:

Dr. Inventory — finished goods xxx
    Cr. Inventory — raw materials xxx
    Cr. Labor expenses xxx
    Cr. Overhead expenses xxx

Combination

It is quite possible that a firm incurs a combination of the two above costs, purchasing and manufacturing. A firm might purchase a variety of parts and various raw materials and turn out a new product worth more in the final form. This is also known as value added. The accounting entries would be virtually identical to the previous examples, making the finished goods material partly for resale and partly for transfer.

In entering the above items for inventory, the inventory module of a computerized accounting system keeps track of both the cost of the items as well as the number of items purchased. As you will see later in the chapter, it is important to be able to allocate a cost per item to the purchased or manufactured inventory items.

INVENTORY ADJUSTMENTS

Adjustments to inventory are necessary when the value of the inventory changes, when goods are returned, and when firms must add federal sales tax. Let's look at each more closely.

Value Adjustments

Sometimes the number of items purchased remains the same, but the value of these items either increases or decreases. We would want to reflect these changes in the cost of inventory. For example, a supplier may give a discount for purchasing a large quantity of product. The supplier might specify that if purchases of a particular item total $10,000 or more, the purchaser will get a 2% volume discount. Once we reach that level, our accounts payable to the supplier will be reduced by $200.00 ($10,000 x 2%). This adjustment would be reflected in the accounts as follows:

```
Dr. Accounts payable                          xxx
    Cr. Inventory                                        xxx
```

The recording of this entry will not affect the number of items purchased, but reduce the total cost of the items and therefore the unit cost.

On the other hand, inventory costs might have to be increased. For example, you might order some inventory items FOB manufacturer, but at the time the order is placed you do not know the freight cost. This cost will have to be added to the inventory at a later time. We would make the following entry when the inventory was received:

```
Dr. Inventory                                 xxx
    Cr. Accounts payable                                 xxx
```

When we have subsequently determined the cost of the freight, we would make an adjusting entry to the inventory item:

```
Dr. Inventory                                 xxx
    Cr. Freight payable                                  xxx
```

As in the previous example, the number of items is not adjusted, only the cost associated with the items received.

Purchase Returns

On occasion, you may purchase goods that are of the wrong type or defective. When returned, the goods must be taken out of inventory at the cost that they were recorded at. In addition, the number of items returned must also be recorded. The entry made in the books would be:

```
Dr. Accounts payable                          xxx
    Cr. Inventory                                        xxx
```

RECORDING SALES

For a retailer, total sales revenue equals the gross amount of the sale minus any returns or discounts. A sale of inventory for cash would be recorded in the books as follows:

```
Dr. Cash                                      xxx
    Cr. Sales                                            xxx
```

If the merchandise is bought on credit, the journal entry is

```
Dr. Accounts receivable                       xxx
    Cr. Sales                                            xxx
```

As mentioned earlier, the buyer legally becomes the owner of goods when responsibility for them is transferred from the seller to the buyer — FOB, FAS or CIF. Conversely, a good is deemed to have been sold when the responsibility for the item is transferred to the new owner. This means that often a sale is made without the cash being received immediately. Consequently, total sales in any given period is not likely to equal the amount of cash generated in that same period.

Sales Tax

When an item is sold the firm must often collect state and sometimes local sales taxes. Tax is usually added to the invoice in the following manner:

INVOICE

May 15, 1988

Customer: PFS Organics Inc.
556 Selma Cresd.
Bellingham, Wa. 97634

Item Number	Description	Number of Units	Cost per unit	Total
1234	Gaskets	12	3.50	$ 42.00
5678	Rings	14	6.10	85.40
Total Sales				$ 127.40
State sales Tax (7%)				8.92
				$ 136.32

The required journal entry for this sale would be:

Dr. Accounts receivable   151.25
   Cr. Sales   127.40
   Cr. State sales tax payable   8.92

The state sales tax will vary among states, however, it will not vary within the state.

If local sales taxes are also levied, it is usually combined with the state sales tax and then the combined rate is applied to the selling price. The journal entry would be identical to above.

Sales Returns

The opposite of purchase returns are sales returns from customers who found the goods unsuitable or defective. When customers return goods the entry that was originally made when the sale occurred must be reversed. The reversing entry is as follows:

Dr. Sales returns   xxx
   Cr. Accounts receivable   xxx

A special *Sales Returns* account is normally used instead of a debit to sales because management is interested in knowing the dollar value of returned items. A high level of sales returns and allowances in a given time period may indicate a high level of customer dissatisfaction with the product.

Cost of Goods Sold

One of the major differences between a service company and a merchandising company is the entries that are made on a sale. A service firm would proceed as follows:

Dr. Accounts receivable   xxx
     Cr. Revenue   xxx

This is the only entry required at the time of the sale. For a merchandising company, however, a second entry is required, which takes into account the reduction in the level of inventory. This entry takes the item out of inventory and puts it into an expense account — Cost of Goods Sold.

INVENTORY CONTROL METHODS

There are two methods of determining inventory and cost of goods sold for any given period — the periodic inventory system and the perpetual inventory system.

Periodic Inventory System

A business that sells a variety of merchandise at relatively low prices, most often uses a manual accounting method called the *periodic inventory system*. Sales are recorded on a daily basis as described above, and all purchases are recorded when received and debited to a *Purchased account*. No entry is made to record *Cost of Goods Sold* until the reporting date. At the report date, the ending inventory is physically counted to determine the level of inventory still on hand. Once the value of the remaining inventory is known, it is subtracted from the amount of inventory available for sale at the beginning of the period. The resulting amount, which could be plus or minus, is added to the total value of inventory purchased during the period. This amount is the value of the goods sold.

For example, let's assume that a company had the purchase records shown in Figure 10.2 for the month of January:

	Units	Per Unit	Total Cost
Opening inventory	20	5.00	100.00
Purchases			
January 10	30	5.10	153.00
January 15	50	5.20	260.00
January 25	100	5.15	515.00
Cost of Goods Available	200		$1,028.00

Figure 10.2 Purchase records for January

If at the end of January we determine that the level of inventory is $318.00 by actually counting and valuing the inventory, then the cost of goods sold would amount to $710.00 ($1,028.00 - $318.00). We would then adjust the purchases account and the opening inventory account to record cost of goods sold to be $710.00.

Dr. Cost of goods sold	710.00	
Cr. Purchases		928.00
Dr. Ending inventory	218.00	

Ending inventory will now be $318.00 ($100.00 from the opening entry and an increase of $218.00 in the above entry).

Perpetual Inventory System

The *perpetual inventory system* at one time was used almost exclusively by firms selling large items with a high unit value. These firms usually had only a few sales but each sale amounted to substantial sums. When a sale was made, these firms could make an immediate entry to credit Inventory and debit Cost of Goods Sold. Hence the inventory is perpetually updated.

With computerized accounting systems, however, even small firms with large numbers of transactions can use the perpetual inventory system. Computers can make the necessary entries automatically when a sale is made.

When using a perpetual inventory system it is necessary to make two entries each time there is a sale. First we record the sale:

Dr. Accounts receivable	xxx	
Cr. Sales		xxx

Then we record the cost of that sale:

Dr. Cost of goods sold	xxx	
Cr. Inventory		xxx

INVENTORY COSTING METHODS

The cost of the inventory sold depends on which items are sold. In some cases it is difficult to determine the actual cost of the item sold. As shown in the example in Figure 10.2, some inventory items were purchased at $5.10 per unit, some at $5.15 and some at $5.20. There were also some on hand that were purchased at $5.00. How do we know which of these was actually sold so that we can correctly reduce the amount from inventory and debit the Cost of Goods Sold account.

Four methods can be used for valuing inventory sold. They include:

a. FIFO (first-in, first-out)
b. LIFO (last-in, first-out)
c. specific item
d. average cost

FIFO

The *FIFO inventory valuation method* states that the first items purchased are the first items sold. For example, when a grocery store receives a new shipment of bread, the bread from the previous shipment not yet sold is placed on top of the newer bread so that it will sell first. In this case, the FIFO method of valuing inventory is appropriate as it stands to reason that the first one purchased is the first one sold, since it is on top of the new shipment.

Look back to Figure 10.2 for a moment. Let's assume that we sold 3 units at $10.00 apiece on January 11th. No matter which inventory system we use, the sale of the units would be recorded as follows:

Dr. Accounts receivable	30.00	
Cr. Sales		30.00

To record the cost of goods sold using the FIFO inventory system, the first three we purchased were the first three we sold. The three items that were sold would be valued at $5.00 each, totaling $15.00 (3 x $5.00). The journal entry would then be:

Dr. Cost of goods sold	15.00	
Cr. Inventory		15.00

To record a second sale of 18 units on January 18th, at $10.00 apiece, the entries made would be as follows:

Dr. Accounts receivable	180.00	
Cr. Sales		180.00
Dr. Cost of goods sold	90.10	
Cr. Inventory		90.10

The cost of goods sold on a FIFO basis is calculated to be $90.10.

17 units @ $5.00	85.00
1 unit @ $5.10	5.10
Total cost of goods sold	$90.10

LIFO

The *LIFO inventory valuation method* is the opposite to FIFO. In using this method we assume that the last items that we purchased are the first items sold. For example, a lumber yard will put new boards on top of the existing boards because the old boards will not spoil, within a reasonable time. In this case, LIFO is appropriate because the first ones sold are the last ones purchased.

Let's use the items shown in Figure 10.2, to see what the LIFO inventory valuation method will do to our cost of goods sold.

In our first sale, we sold 3 units at $10.00 apiece on January 11th. The sale of the units would be recorded as before:

Dr. Accounts receivable	30.00	
Cr. Sales		30.00

So, using the LIFO inventory valuation method to record the cost of goods sold, the three items that were sold would then be valued at $5.10 each, totaling $15.30 (3 x $5.10). We use $5.10 as the cost per item as the last purchase was on January 10th. The journal entry would then be:

Dr. Cost of goods sold	15.30	
Cr. Inventory		15.30

To record a second sale of 18 units on January 18th, at $10.00 apiece, the entries made would be as follows:

Dr. Accounts receivable	180.00	
Cr. Sales		180.00
Dr. Cost of goods sold	93.60	
Cr. Inventory		93.60

The cost of goods sold is calculated to be $93.60 on a LIFO basis:

18 Units @ $5.20	93.60

Here we use $5.20 because the last items purchased were 50 units on January 15th at $5.20 apiece. In LIFO, the timing of the sale is important as the cost of goods sold will depend on the last purchase.

Specific Item

The *specific item inventory valuation method* is generally used when the number of items sold is relatively low but each item represents a significant part of the inventory in terms of its cost. The automotive industry is a good example. Each vehicle is identified by a number, and by specific options. When that vehicle is sold it is easy to identify its cost and charge it out to cost of goods sold.

For the items shown in Figure 10.2, using the specific item inventory method would not be appropriate since we cannot identify one unit from the next.

Average Cost

The *average cost inventory valuation method* is based on the premise that for identical items we cannot tell which item was purchased prior to another one, and therefore cannot identify it specifically for cost of goods sold. Therefore we value each item at its average cost.

A good example is a bin of nails in a hardware store. When we replenish the stock of nails with a new purchase, we cannot tell which nails were purchased or sold first. Since they are all mixed together, it is appropriate to use the average cost inventory method — the cost of goods sold is based on the weighted average cost of the nails in the bin.

To the inventory items in Figure 10.2 we have added sales dates as shown in Figure 10.3. Notice that we have arranged sales and purchases in date order.

		Units	Per Unit	Total Cost
	Opening inventory	20	5.00	100.00
Sales	Purchases			
	Jan. 10	30	5.10	153.00
Jan. 11		3		
	Jan. 15	50	5.20	260.00
Jan. 18		18		
	Jan. 25	100	5.15	515.00
	Cost of goods available	200		$1,028.00

Figure 10.3 Purchases and sales of inventory items

For the first sale, the cost of goods sold would be calculated as 3 units times $5.06 equals $15.18.

	Units	Per Unit	Total Cost
Opening inventory	20	5.00	100.00
January 10 purchase	30	5.10	153.00
	50		$253.00
Average cost per unit	253	= $5.06	
	50		

The journal entry is then:

Dr. Cost of goods sold	15.18	
Cr. Inventory		15.18

The second sale entry for 18 units would be valued at the new average cost including the purchase on January 15. The cost of goods sold would then be 18 units times $5.13, which equals $92.34.

	Units	Per Unit	Total Cost
Units available	50		253.00
Units sold	3		15.18
Units remaining	47		237.82
January 15 purchase	50	$5.20	260.00
Total available	97		$497.82
Average cost per unit	497.82	= $5.13	
	97		

The entry to record cost of goods sold is then:

Dr. Cost of goods sold	92.34	
Cr. Inventory		92.34

All four of the above methods of valuing inventory are accepted as appropriate by the various accounting bodies; nevertheless, the retailer must pick one method and apply it consistently. **The inventory valuing method that applies to the greatest number of firms is the average cost method.** For this reason, the Bedford Accounting System uses this method in its calculation of inventory.

Although the average cost method would be virtually impossible to use with a manual accounting system, it presents no problems for a computerized system. The Bedford Accounting System only requires that you enter the sale. The program will automatically calculate the cost of goods sold and make the necessary entry to record the cost of goods sold and reduce the inventory based on the average cost. It will then produce the necessary reports so you can order, transfer or value the remaining inventory.

COMPUTERIZING INVENTORY

Converting your manual inventory accounting system to a computerized system can be done at any time during the year. It is not necessary to wait for year end or for some time in the year when inventory is at its lowest point.

Organizing Inventory Records

As was the case with each of the other modules, some manual preparation is required to convert the system prior to actually using the INVENTORY module of the Bedford Accounting System. You must do the following beforehand:

1. Prepare a listing of all inventory items that you stock on the conversion date.

2. Associate each inventory item with an inventory asset account, an inventory revenue account and an inventory expense account in the general ledger.

3. Ensure that the balance of all inventory items for each general ledger account agrees with those accounts.

▪ *Prepare a Listing of Inventory Items*

In the accounts **RECEIVABLE** and accounts **PAYABLE** modules, we made a list of all our customers and creditors. We have to make a similar list for the **INVENTORY** module. This listing must contain all the inventory items currently on hand. We may also want to include all items that we normally carry but which are temporarily out of stock. The more complete the listing is, the less work required when that stock is replenished.

For each of the inventory items in the list, we need the following data. This information is required by the Bedford Accounting System to calculate inventory levels for each item.

1. Item name

2. Unit description

3. Selling price per unit — this would be the unit price if the units are normally sold individually. If they are normally sold in pairs, it would mean the price per pair; if sold in dozens it would mean the price for 12 items, and so on.

4. Quantity — total quantity in units (as described in #3 above)on hand at the time of the conversion.

5. Amount — represents the total cost for all of the inventory items on hand. The Bedford Accounting System will take the total you enter and divide it by the quantity to determine the cost per unit.

6. Minimum Stock level — this number is used to indicate the point at which you would like to order more stock. For example, you may sell 5 units of a particular item per week. If it takes 3 weeks to get a new shipment, you would want to reorder the item when your inventory was down to 15 units. The reorder point should be carefully calculated because the Bedford Accounting System will tell you to reorder an item when the reorder point is reached.

This underscores one of the major objectives of good inventory management: **You should reduce inventory carrying costs by keeping your inventory at the lowest level possible but not so low that you run out of stock and loose substantial sales.** If you would like to know more about calculating the optimum level of inventory to reduce the various costs to their lowest point, you should consult an appropriate book on inventory management.

▪ *Associate Items to the General Ledger*

Unlike the other modules, the **INVENTORY** module does not have preset accounts in the general ledger to record purchases and sales. It is up to you to determine the asset account, revenue account and expense account to be associated with each inventory item. This means assigning one account between 100-199 (asset), one between 400-499 (revenue) and one between 500-599 (expense) for each item.

If your company only has one type of inventory, such as grocery items, you would only need one set of the three above mentioned accounts. However, if you wish to break the inventory items into categories — produce, canned goods and pop — you would have three groups of items and therefore, require three groups of asset, revenue and expense accounts.

Once the accounts have been assigned, it is necessary to set them up in the general ledger module before proceeding. This will be the first step in the conversion process. See Beginning Inventory Conversion below.

▪ *Agree to Control*

The final step before conversion is to ensure that the total amount of inventory associated with each asset account agrees with the balance of that inventory asset account in the general ledger. The Bedford Accounting System will not allow you to set the **INVENTORY** module to READY until that is accomplished.

Beginning the Inventory Conversion

After performing the above three steps you are ready to begin the inventory conversion. Start the Bedford Accounting System program as before by typing:

```
BEDFORD [Ret]          or if you have a monochrome monitor

BEDFORD mono [Ret]
```

After a few seconds, the Bedford opening screen will be displayed as shown in Figure 10.4.

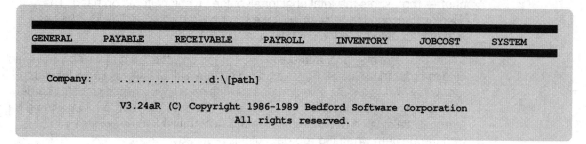

Figure 10.4 Bedford start-up menu

Enter the location of the data files.

```
B:\FASTDEL          C:\FASTDEL
013188         To enter the Using date
```

The main menubar of the Bedford Accounting System will now appear, as shown in Figure 10.5.

Figure 10.5 Bedford main menubar

Our conversion process will use two categories of inventory items, Widget A and Widget B, and use the information presented in Figure 10.3 as our inventory data for Widget A.

▪ Adding Asset Accounts to the General Ledger

In Figure 10.3 we indicated that 20 units of Widget A were on hand at the beginning of the year for a total cost of $100.00. We will assign the Widget A inventory item to the following accounts:

Asset Account	126 (already set up)
Revenue Account	401
Expense Account	501

The first task is to enter the accounts into the general ledger. With the word **GENERAL** highlighted on the main menubar, press the following keys:

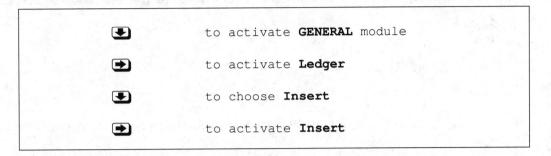

You can use the up and down arrow keys to view the existing chart of accounts. You will notice that the account #126 for inventory already exists in the general ledger. The accounts for revenue, #401, and for expenses, #501, do not.

Let's insert these accounts. Type

```
Sales — Widgets Ret    to enter Account name

        401            to enter the account Number

         R             to enter account type, R for right

         Y             to Suppress the account if the
                       balance is zero.

        ⬅             to accept account definition data entered
```

- *Practice Exercise*

Repeat the above steps to enter the account #501 that we will call "Cost of sales — Widgets".

- *Entering Inventory Items*

Now that you have updated the general ledger, you are ready to enter the first inventory item, Widget A. Press

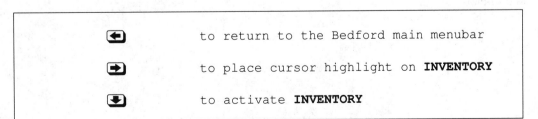

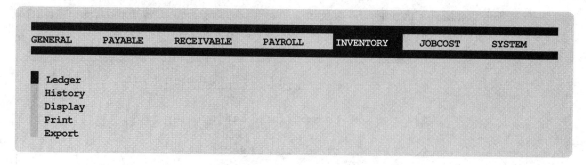

Figure 10.6 Inventory submenu

Your screen will now display Figure 10.6. With your cursor next to the word **Ledger,** press

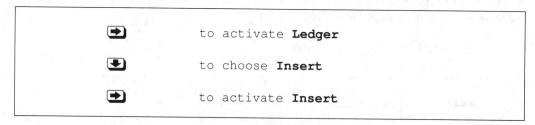

Your screen will now resemble Figure 10.7.

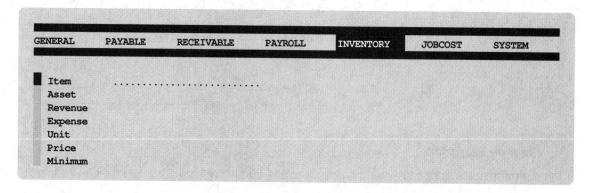

Figure 10.7 Inventory item entry screen

You can now enter details about inventory items. As you input the name of the item, remember that the first letter you type will be automatically capitalized. Now enter the requested information:

Widget A `Esc`   to enter the **Item** name. You normally
enter the name in such a way that when
the items are listed on the screen, they
will be in alphabetical order so that
you can easily look up the inventory
number.

126   to enter the **Asset** account number for
this inventory item. The available
accounts in the chart of accounts will
be displayed on the right side of the
screen. (See Figure 10.8 which shows a
portion of the chart of accounts.) Use
the up and down arrow keys to see the
available accounts. Notice that after
you enter the account number, the name
of the account will replace the number
you have typed in.

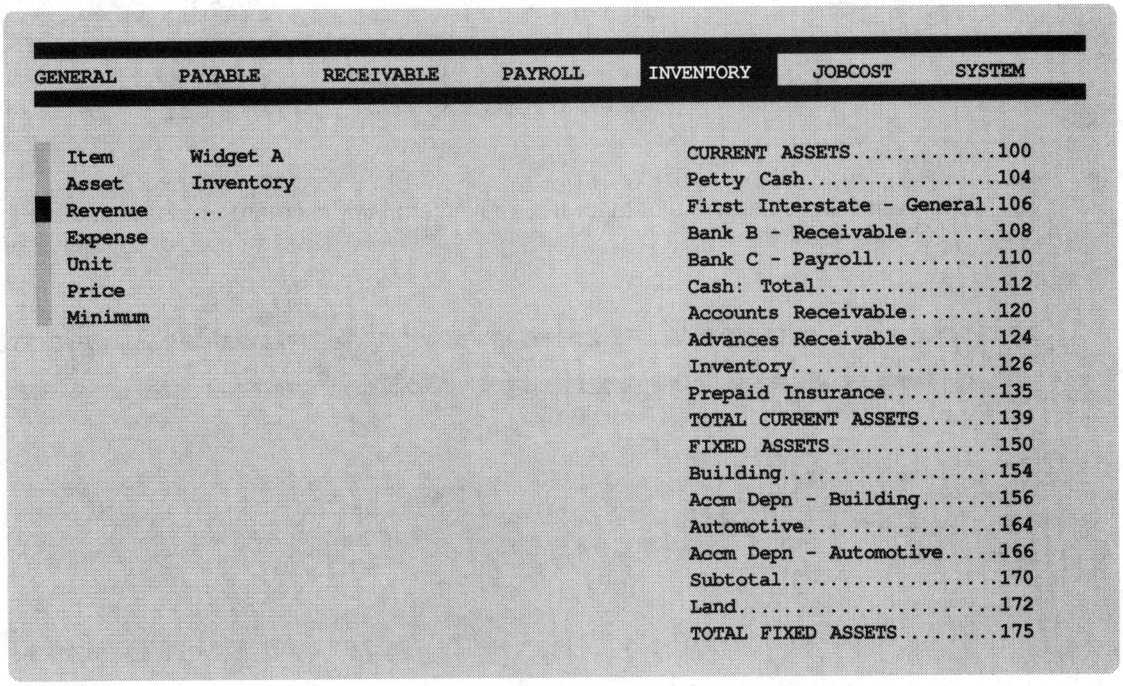

GENERAL	PAYABLE	RECEIVABLE	PAYROLL	INVENTORY	JOBCOST	SYSTEM

```
Item      Widget A                CURRENT ASSETS............100
Asset     Inventory               Petty Cash................104
Revenue   ...                     First Interstate - General.106
Expense                           Bank B - Receivable.......108
Unit                              Bank C - Payroll..........110
Price                             Cash: Total...............112
Minimum                           Accounts Receivable.......120
                                  Advances Receivable.......124
                                  Inventory.................126
                                  Prepaid Insurance.........135
                                  TOTAL CURRENT ASSETS......139
                                  FIXED ASSETS..............150
                                  Building..................154
                                  Accm Depn - Building......156
                                  Automotive................164
                                  Accm Depn - Automotive....166
                                  Subtotal..................170
                                  Land......................172
                                  TOTAL FIXED ASSETS........175
```

Figure 10.8 A portion of the chart of accounts from which you
choose the asset account for this item

401	to enter the **Revenue** account number for the item.
501	to enter the **Expense** account number of the item.
1 [Ret]	to enter the number of items in a **Unit**. As this particular item is sold as single units, you enter the number 1.
10 [Ret]	to enter the selling **Price** per unit of the item – $10.00 in our case. This value is provided as a default for an item's price. A default value for the price is useful when repeatedly entering items with the same price. The default price value can be changed at any time if the selling price changes or you can override it by entering a different price from the default value.
10 [Ret]	to enter the **Minimum** number of units at which point you want to reorder.

When you have entered the data for the above item, your screen should resemble Figure 10.9.

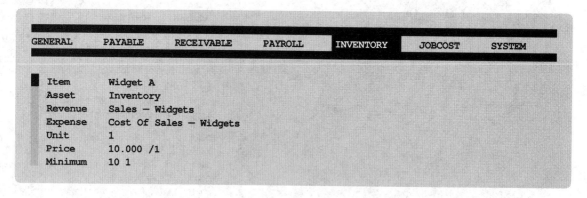

Figure 10.9 Inventory data entered for one item

You can use the up and down arrow keys to move to any item and change an incorrect entry. Let's try it. Move the cursor to the word **Expense** and press the right arrow key. Notice that the chart of accounts reappears. We could now change the account if we wished. Since we do not want to make that change at this time, enter 501 again.

When you are certain that the information is correct, press the left arrow key to accept the data entered. The program will now create an inventory record which includes the details of all items entered. Press

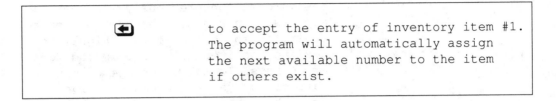

to accept the entry of inventory item #1.
The program will automatically assign
the next available number to the item
if others exist.

▪ Practice Exercise

Enter a second inventory item, Widget B, using the following data:

Item	Widget B
Asset	126
Revenue	401
Expense	501
Unit	1
Price	15
Minimum	12

▪ Modifying Inventory Items

Inventory item data may have to be modified at times. For example, a price could change, or you might want to change the reorder point. To make a change use the **Modify** command on the menu.

To modify an account, press

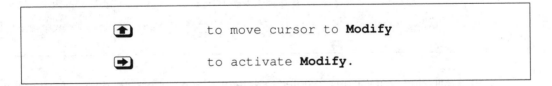

to move cursor to **Modify**

to activate **Modify**.

Your screen should look like Figure 10.10.

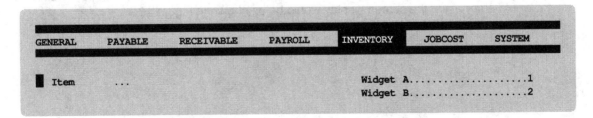

Figure 10.10 Inventory item modify screen

```
     1 [Ret]          to enter the inventory Item to modify.
                       Inventory item Number 1 is Widget - A.
                       Notice that once you press the [Ret] key,
                       the information previously entered
                       appears. You can now choose the item to
                       modify by moving the cursor highlight
                       next to the item using the up and down
                       arrow keys. To make a change to any
                       part of the record, press the right
                       arrow key when the cursor is next to
                       that item. Then type in the correct in-
                       formation.
```

After making changes press the left arrow key to accept the data. If you do not wish to change the previous information, then press the ESCape key. In this case you do not want to change anything, so press

```
     [Esc]            to leave inventory item Modify screen
```

■ *Deleting Inventory Records*

There may be times when you have to delete an inventory record if, for example, the item is no longer sold by the company. To do so, press

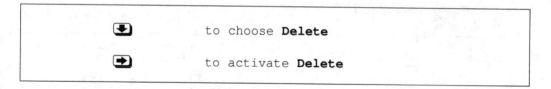

```
     [↓]              to choose Delete

     [→]              to activate Delete
```

Once activated, you will be prompted to enter the item you wish to delete. A list of the inventory items currently on the system will be displayed at the right side of the screen. If you had many items you might have to press the up or down arrow key to view other screens. To delete an item, enter the appropriate number. For example, if you wanted to delete item #2, Widget B, you would enter 2 and the screen display would be as shown in Figure 10.11.

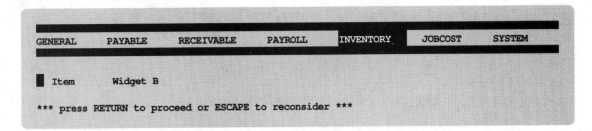

Figure 10.11 Message confirming the deletion of an item

To delete the item, you must press ENTER (RETURN). If you wish to reconsider your action, you can press ESCape and leave the inventory item on file. In this case do <u>not</u> delete an item. Press

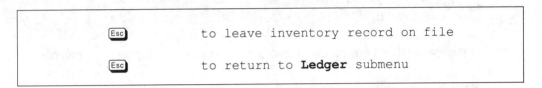

Note: You can delete any inventory records while the INVENTORY module is in the NOT READY mode. However, once the INVENTORY module is in the READY mode, you can only delete those inventory records for which there is no existing stock.

▪ Entering Opening Balances

The second step in our conversion, is to enter the amount of inventory on hand at the conversion date. In our case, Widget A had 20 units on hand worth a total of $100.00.

When the **INVENTORY** module is NOT READY, the main menu will resemble Figure 10.13. The second item on the menu is **History.** You use this menu item to change or set up the inventory record's balances at the conversion date. All of these items are set to zero when the record is created.

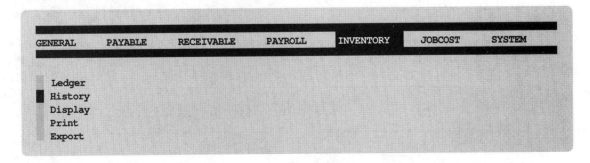

Figure 10.12 INVENTORY submenu

To enter these amounts, choose **History** from the main menu.

⬇	to choose **History**
➡	to activate **History**

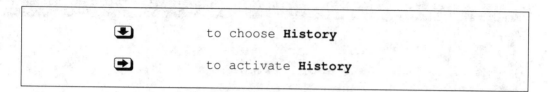

GENERAL	PAYABLE	RECEIVABLE	PAYROLL	INVENTORY	JOBCOST	SYSTEM

```
■ Item        ...                        Widget A...................1
  Quantity                               Widget B...................2
  Amount
```

Figure 10.13 Choosing an inventory item to enter quantity on hand balances

Your screen should now resemble Figure 10.13, listing the inventory records entered with their corresponding numbers on the right and the balances to be filled in on the left. Choose inventory record #1 to enter historical balances.

1 [Ret]	to choose **Item** "Widget A". The "1" will disappear and the name will take its place.
20 [Ret]	to enter the **Quantity** of inventory items on hand at the conversion date. The quantity based on units of product.
100 [Ret]	to enter the total **Amount** of the inventory items entered above.

Once all the items are entered, and you are satisfied that all entries are correct, you can accept the entry by pressing the

⬅	to accept entry of the historical data

Displaying Inventory Reports

Displaying inventory reports is similar to displaying the reports in other modules. From the **INVENTORY** submenu, press

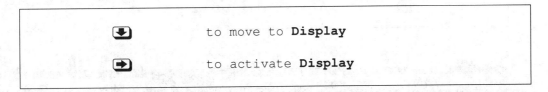

Your screen will show the information similar to Figure 10.14, listing the displays available in the **INVENTORY** module.

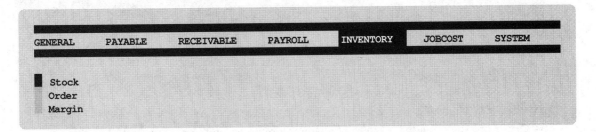

Figure 10.14 Display submenu for inventory items

▪ *Stock Display*

The first of the displays is the stock report. The **Stock** display gives you an alphabetical listing of each inventory item in a group, the average cost of those items, and their total value. The stock display is particularly useful to check if enough items of a particular type are on hand to fill an order. You may also use it as a control listing to show what the general ledger inventory account consists of.

To display a listing press

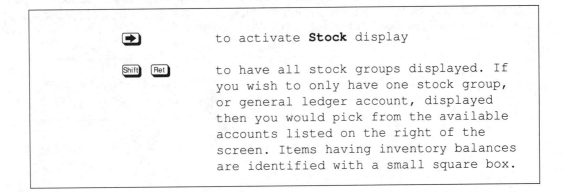

The listing will resemble Figure 10.15. Once you have seen the listing and wish to go to another, press

       ⌨ Esc   to exit the **Display**

GENERAL	PAYABLE	RECEIVABLE	PAYROLL	INVENTORY	JOBCOST	SYSTEM
				stock	cost	value
1 Widget A				1 20	5.000	100.00
2 Widget B				1 0	0.000	0.00
						100.00

Figure 10.15 Inventory stock display listing the two inventory items entered

▪ Order Display

The **Order** display provides a listing of all inventory items on the system including the amount of stock on hand and the minimum stock level. Those items with a stock on hand below the minimum order level will be highlighted. This display quickly identifies which items need to be reordered.

From the **Display** submenu, press

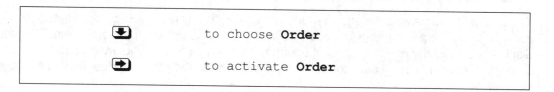

       ⬇   to choose **Order**

       ➡   to activate **Order**

You must now identify which group of inventory items you wish to display based on the asset account that you set up earlier for each group of inventory items. You can choose a particular group from the accounts in the general ledger listing displayed on the right of the screen, or you can choose all inventory items as we will do

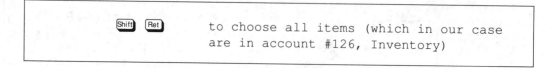

     Shift   Ret   to choose all items (which in our case are in account #126, Inventory)

Your screen will now resemble Figure 10.16.

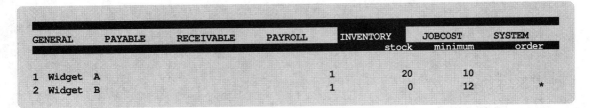

GENERAL	PAYABLE	RECEIVABLE	PAYROLL	INVENTORY	JOBCOST	SYSTEM	
				stock	minimum	order	
1 Widget A				1	20	10	
2 Widget B				1	0	12	*

Figure 10.16 Order display of all stock items

If you had more than a screenful of items you could use the up and down arrows to see more items. Because we have only two items we do not have to do that. You will notice that item #2 has an asterisk (*) in the order column. This means that the amount on hand is lower than the minimum we have established for that item. This warning signal indicates that we should reorder the item.

When you are through with the display press

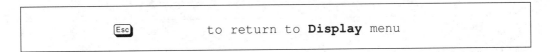

Esc   to return to **Display** menu

▪ Margin Display

The **Margin** display provides a listing of all inventory items on the system, the cost of each item, the selling price, and the margin for that item. **Margin** is the percentage that the cost price is of the selling price. With this display, you can easily identify whether or not your selling price is sufficient to meet the markup requirements of your business. Since your costs may change from shipment to shipment, the margin report can give you a good idea of whether or not your markup on the various items is still adequate to cover your expenses and make a profit.

From the **Display** submenu, press

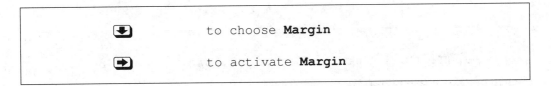

⬇   to choose **Margin**

➡   to activate **Margin**

As in the two previous displays, **Stock** and **Order**, you will be asked to identify which group of inventory items you wish to display. You can choose the group from the general ledger listing displayed on the right of the screen, or you can choose all inventory items as we will do:

Shift   Ret   to choose all items

Your screen will now resemble Figure 10.17.

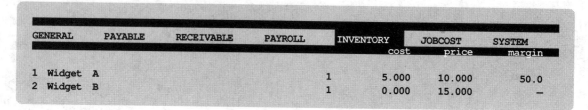

Figure 10.17 Margin display

As mentioned previously, if you have many inventory items you can use the up and down arrows keys to view additional screens. When you have viewed the display, press

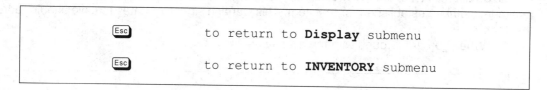

Printing the Inventory Reports

The printing of inventory reports is similar to the printing of the reports in other modules and to the display command. The inventory report gives you a combination of the three display reports all in one. Make sure you are in the **INVENTORY** submenu. Press

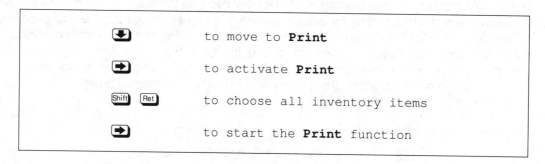

The printed report should resemble the report shown in Figure 10.18.

Fast Delivery Inc. FOR INSTRUCTIONAL USE ONLY

INVENTORY Jan 31, 1988

Page 1

			price	stock	minimum	cost	value	margin
1	Widget A	1	10.000	20	10	5.000	100.00	50.0
2	Widget B	1	15.00	0	12	0.000	0.00	
							100.00	

Figure 10.18 Printed inventory report

When the report has been printed return to the Bedford main menubar.

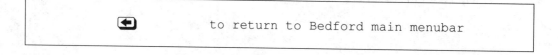

Changing to Ready Mode

Having entered our historical (opening balances), the conversion process from a manual to a computerized inventory system is complete.

Before we can enter current data into the inventory system we must change the inventory module from the NOT READY mode to the READY mode. Remember, once you change to the READY mode you cannot return to the NOT READY mode for changing historical data. Therefore you must be absolutely sure that the data you entered prior to changing to READY mode is accurate.

The Bedford Accounting System will not allow you to change a module to the READY mode until

a. the general ledger is in READY mode, and

b. the subledger is in balance with the control account — inventory, in the general ledger.

If the **GENERAL** ledger module is in the NOT READY mode you cannot change the **INVENTORY** module to the READY mode. A screen message will tell you so. You must then go to the **GENERAL** ledger module and make it READY first.

If the totals in the **INVENTORY** module are not in balance with the respective inventory account(s) in the general ledger, Bedford displays a message informing you of the problem. You must rectify the situation before you can make the **INVENTORY** module READY.

To make the **INVENTORY** module READY, start from the Bedford main menubar. Press

➡	to move cursor to **SYSTEM**
⬇	to activate **SYSTEM**
⬇	to choose **Default**
➡	to activate **Default**
➡	to activate **Module**
⬇	to choose **Inventory**
➡	to activate **Inventory**

You will now be presented with a two item menu as in Figure 10.19.

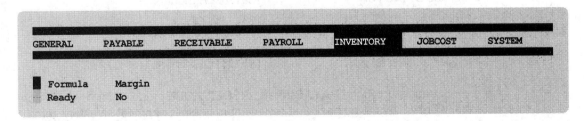

Figure 10.19 SYSTEM inventory READY display

To change to the READY mode, press

⬇	to choose **Ready**
➡	to change **No** to **Yes**

While you are at the READY display, there is one other item that you can change. This is the item, **Formula**. This item allows you to change the method used by the Bedford Accounting System to report the difference between the average cost of your inventory and the selling costs in the display and the printing of reports.

The default setting is to show the **Margin.** If you prefer you can change it to **Markup**. With this change the reports will display the percentage markup instead of the percentage margin. The difference is as follows:

MARGIN	MARKUP
$\dfrac{\text{PRICE - COST}}{\text{PRICE}}$	$\dfrac{\text{PRICE - COST}}{\text{COST}}$

To select the markup method, press the right arrow key. You can now insert the number that corresponds to either method. When you press the left arrow key the program will accept the change. If you wish to see the effect of this change, go back to **Display** in the **INVENTORY** module and display the reports again. Let's keep it at the default, **Margin**.

Return to the Bedford main menubar

⬅	to save change to READY mode
⬅	to exit **SYSTEM** module

ENTERING CURRENT PURCHASES AND SALES DATA

We are now ready to enter current data into our system. Unlike the other modules that we have looked at so far, the entry of inventory items is not only done in the **INVENTORY** module but in three modules.

Purchase of inventory	**PAYABLE** module
Sale of inventory	**RECEIVABLE** module
Transfer of inventory	**INVENTORY** module

We have already studied the **PAYABLE** and **RECEIVABLE** modules for non-inventory transactions. We will now have to go back and review them again for entry of inventory items. If you are not familiar with those chapters, you may want to return and review them before proceeding.

Purchase of Inventory

Purchases of inventory are made through the **PAYABLE** module. Be sure you are at the Bedford main menubar.

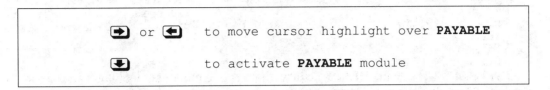

Now let's record the purchases that were made during the month of January. The information we had on Widget A was as follows:

	Units	Per unit	Total Cost
Purchases			
Opening inventory	20	5.00	100.00
Purchases			
January 10	30	5.10	153.00
January 15	50	5.20	260.00
January 25	100	5.15	515.00
Cost of Goods Available	200		$1,028.00
Sales January 11	3	10.00	
January 18	18	10.00	

Let's record the purchase on January 10. With the **PAYABLE** module activated, press

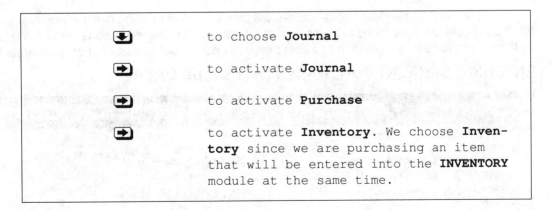

Your screen will now look like Figure 10.20.

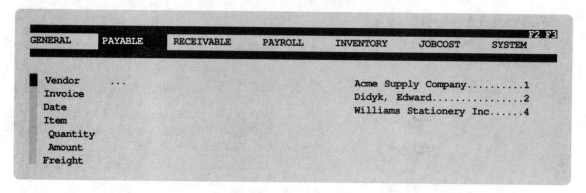

Figure 10.20 Inventory purchase screen

We will assume that the inventory items are purchased from Acme Supply Company, vendor #1. To enter the invoice for payment, we enter the following:

1 Ret to choose **Vendor** #1. Notice that the number will be replaced by the name of the vendor. If the number of vendors requires more than one screen you can use the down arrow key to read the vendors, listed in alphabetical order, on subsequent screens.

2466 Ret to enter the **Invoice** number.

011088 to enter the purchase **Date** of January 10, 1988.

Now the right hand side of the screen will give you a listing of the items in the inventory file. You should have two items listed as shown in Figure 10.21. We will choose item #1, Widget A. If you are purchasing more than one item then each item should be entered on a separate line.

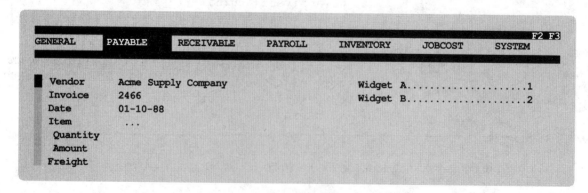

Figure 10.21 Entering the purchase of an inventory item

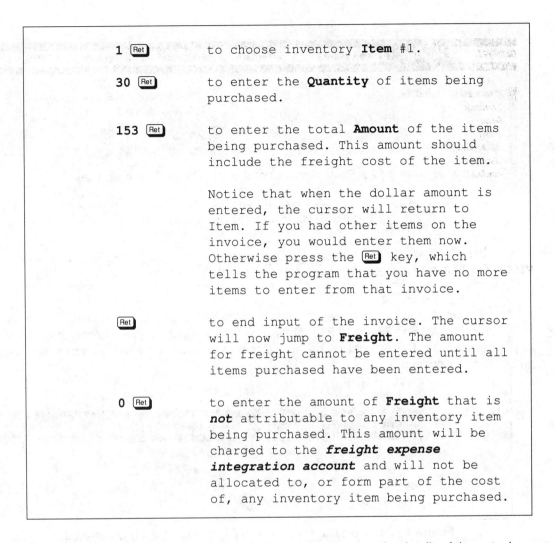

1 [Ret]   to choose inventory **Item** #1.

30 [Ret]   to enter the **Quantity** of items being
                           purchased.

153 [Ret]   to enter the total **Amount** of the items
                           being purchased. This amount should
                           include the freight cost of the item.

                           Notice that when the dollar amount is
                           entered, the cursor will return to
                           Item. If you had other items on the
                           invoice, you would enter them now.
                           Otherwise press the [Ret] key, which
                           tells the program that you have no more
                           items to enter from that invoice.

[Ret]   to end input of the invoice. The cursor
                           will now jump to **Freight**. The amount
                           for freight cannot be entered until all
                           items purchased have been entered.

0 [Ret]   to enter the amount of **Freight** that is
                           not attributable to any inventory item
                           being purchased. This amount will be
                           charged to the *freight expense
                           integration account* and will not be
                           allocated to, or form part of the cost
                           of, any inventory item being purchased.

At any time during the entering of an invoice you can view the details of the entry by pressing [F2] or [F3].

[F2]   to review entry

[F2] will give you the details of the journal entry being prepared as shown in Figure 10.22. Notice that the integration accounts have been entered automatically by the Bedford Accounting System. After your review of the entry, press [F2] again to return to the entry.

GENERAL	PAYABLE	RECEIVABLE	PAYROLL	INVENTORY	JOBCOST	SYSTEM	F2
J15				debits	credits		
220 Accounts Payable					153.00		
126 Inventory				153.00			
				153.00	153.00		

Figure 10.22 Reviewing a journal entry with the F2 function key

[F2]	to return to entry mode
[F3]	to review inventory detail

[F3] will display on the screen the details of the invoice as it will be entered into the **IN-VENTORY** module (See Figure 10.23). At this point you will see the average cost of the inventory just purchased. This amount will be integrated with the inventory already on hand and the average cost recalculated.

GENERAL	PAYABLE	RECEIVABLE	PAYROLL	INVENTORY	JOBCOST	SYSTEM	F3
# quantity	units	description			cost	amount	
1 30	1	Widget A			5.100	153.00	
						153.00	

Figure 10.23 Displaying the details of the invoice as it will be entered into the inventory module

After your review of the entry, return to the input screen. Press

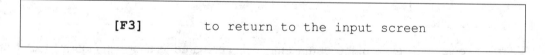

[F3]	to return to the input screen

Once you are satisfied with the entry, accept it into the system by pressing the left arrow key.

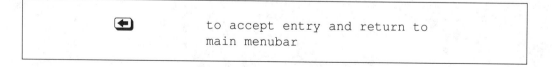

⬅	to accept entry and return to main menubar

Sale of Inventory Items

The sale of an inventory item is not entered through the **INVENTORY** module either but through the **RECEIVABLE** module as a regular sale. Recall that the first sale consists of 3 units at a price of $10.00 per unit. To enter the sale, return to the Bedford main menubar and place your cursor on **RECEIVABLE**. Press

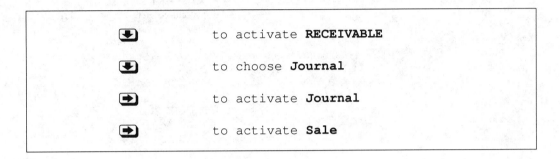

Your screen will now resemble Figure 10.24.

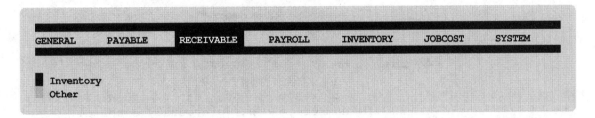

Figure 10.24 Sale submenu in accounts receivable module

When you entered sales in the accounts receivable chapter, you did not see this menu because the **INVENTORY** module had not been made READY. Now that the **INVENTORY** module is in READY mode, when entering a sale you must identify whether the sale involves inventory items or is a service revenue. Press

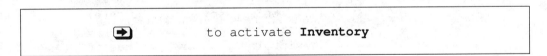

This will bring up an entry screen as displayed in Figure 10.25. Now continue to enter the sale from the source document. In entering this sale, assume that the source document (i.e., the invoice), has been prepared by hand and you are only entering the information from the document. Later in the chapter, we will discuss invoices prepared and printed by the computer.

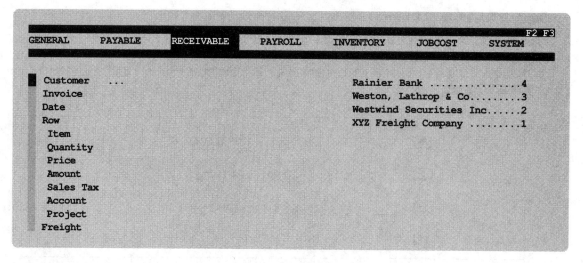

Figure 10.25 Entry screen for entering sales information in accounts receivable module

1 Ret	to enter **Customer** #1. This is the customer we are selling the goods to.
222 Ret	to enter the **Invoice** number of the source document. The program will not allow you to enter an invoice with a number that was previously entered.
011188	to enter the **Date** of the invoice. This date must be between the start date and the using date.
1 Ret	to enter the **Row** number of the invoice that will show the description of the item sold. If only one item is sold, as in this case, you will enter a 1. If more than one item will appear on the invoice you can continue to specify other row numbers after you complete each item entry.
1 Ret	to enter on the invoice the **Item** number being sold. The item numbers will appear on the right hand side of the screen. If there are more items than will fit on one screen you can use the up and down arrow keys to view the remainder of the inventory items.

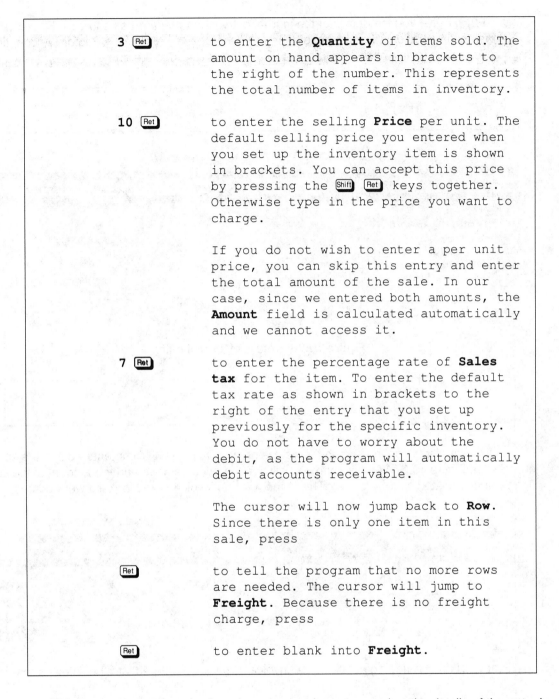

3 [Ret]   to enter the **Quantity** of items sold. The
               amount on hand appears in brackets to
               the right of the number. This represents
               the total number of items in inventory.

10 [Ret]   to enter the selling **Price** per unit. The
               default selling price you entered when
               you set up the inventory item is shown
               in brackets. You can accept this price
               by pressing the [Shift] [Ret] keys together.
               Otherwise type in the price you want to
               charge.

               If you do not wish to enter a per unit
               price, you can skip this entry and enter
               the total amount of the sale. In our
               case, since we entered both amounts, the
               Amount field is calculated automatically
               and we cannot access it.

7 [Ret]   to enter the percentage rate of **Sales
               tax** for the item. To enter the default
               tax rate as shown in brackets to the
               right of the entry that you set up
               previously for the specific inventory.
               You do not have to worry about the
               debit, as the program will automatically
               debit accounts receivable.

               The cursor will now jump back to **Row**.
               Since there is only one item in this
               sale, press

[Ret]   to tell the program that no more rows
               are needed. The cursor will jump to
               Freight. Because there is no freight
               charge, press

[Ret]   to enter blank into **Freight**.

At any time during the entering of a sales invoice you can view the details of the entry by pressing [F2] or [F3].

[F2]   to review entry

[F2] will give you the details of the journal entry being prepared as shown in Figure 10.26. Notice that the integration accounts have been entered automatically by the Bedford Accounting System. After your review of the entry, press [F2] again to return to the entry.

```
[F2]          to return to entry mode
```

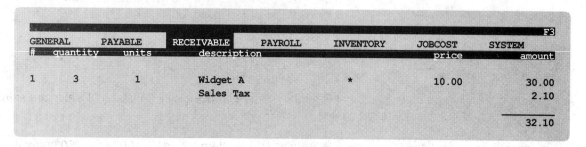

```
                                                                    F2
GENERAL     PAYABLE    RECEIVABLE    PAYROLL    INVENTORY   JOBCOST    SYSTEM
J16                                             debits      credits

120 Accounts Receivable                          32.10
126 Inventory                                                15.18
501 Cost Of Sales — Widgets                      15.18
401 Sales — Widgets                                          30.00
260 Sales Tax Payable                                         2.10
                                                _____     _____
                                                 47.28       47.28
```

Figure 10.26 Details of journal entry

```
[F3]          to review invoice detail
```

[F3] will display on the screen the details of the invoice as it will be entered into the sales journal (See Figure 10.27). At this point you will see the price per item and the amount of the sale along with the related state sales tax. This is the way the invoice would look if it were printed out.

```
                                                                    F3
GENERAL     PAYABLE    RECEIVABLE    PAYROLL    INVENTORY   JOBCOST    SYSTEM
#   quantity   units        description                      price      amount

1      3         1        Widget A              *            10.00       30.00
                         Sales Tax                                        2.10
                                                                        _____
                                                                         32.10
```

Figure 10.27 Reviewing details of the invoice as it will be entered into the sales journal

After you have reviewed the entry, return to the input screen.

```
[F3]          to return to the input screen
```

Once you are satisfied with the entry, accept it into the system by pressing the left arrow key.

⬅	to accept entry and return to **RECEIVABLE** submenu

Displaying or Printing Reports

To display various reports, make sure you are in the **RECEIVABLE** submenu. Press

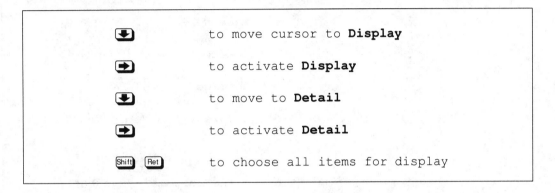

⬇	to move cursor to **Display**
➡	to activate **Display**
⬇	to move to **Detail**
➡	to activate **Detail**
Shift Ret	to choose all items for display

Your screen will now show you the details of the entered invoices. After reviewing them, return to the previous menu and print out the detail to establish an audit trail. Press

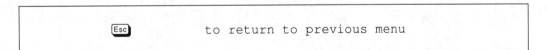

Esc	to return to previous menu

- *Practice Exercise*

Enter the following purchases and sales as they occur chronologically. Assume all sales are sales tax exempt and there is no freight charge.

Purchase	Vendor #1	Inv # 282 Jan 15	Item 1	50 units 260.00 total
Sale	Customer #2	Inv # 461 Jan 18	Item 1	18 " 10.00 each
Purchase	Vendor #1	Inv # 293 Jan 25	Item 1	100 " 515.00 total

Remember that purchases are entered through **PAYABLE** module and sales through the **RECEIVABLE** module.

Printing Sales Invoices

We did not print invoices for the sales we just entered. With the Bedford Accounting System we can print the invoices at the same time as sales information is entered and thereby eliminate writing out an invoice by hand.

So that the Bedford Accounting System can print the invoices, we must change the default setting in the **SYSTEM** module. To do so, return to the Bedford main menubar, and press

➡	to move cursor to **SYSTEM**
⬇	to activate **SYSTEM**
⬇	to choose **Default**
➡	to activate **Default**
➡	to activate **Module**
⬇	to choose **Receivable**
➡	to activate **Receivable**
⬇	to choose **Invoice**
➡	to change **Invoice** from **No** to **Yes**
⬅	to save change
⬅	to return to Bedford main menubar

Now enter another sales invoice based on the following information:

Date:	January 25
Sold to:	Customer #2
Invoice #	305
Item:	Widget — A
No. of items:	15
Price per item:	$10.00
Sales Tax:	7%
Freight:	$0.00

From the Bedford main menubar, move cursor to the **RECEIVABLE** module and proceed to enter the invoice. Press

⬇	to activate **RECEIVABLE**
⬇	to choose **Journal**
➡	to activate **Journal**
➡	to activate **Sale**
➡	to activate **Inventory**

The input screen as displayed in Figure 10.28 has undergone some minor changes from the one we saw earlier. At the top of the entry screen is a space to identify who the shipment will be sent to. Part way down, under **Row**, is a line for entering the **Detail** (description) of the item being sold. Near the bottom of the screen is a line for inserting a comment on the invoice such as "NET 30 DAYS".

```
                                                                F2 F3
GENERAL      PAYABLE      RECEIVABLE      PAYROLL      INVENTORY     JOBCOST      SYSTEM

  Customer    ...                          Rainier Bank ...............4
  Date                                     Weston, Lathrop & Co........3
  Ship To                                  Westwind Securities Inc.....2
   Street                                  XYZ Freight Company ........1
   City
   State
   Zip
  Row
   Item
   Quantity
   Unit
   Detail
   Price
   Amount
   Sales Tax
   Account
   Project
  Freight
  Comment
  Print
```

Figure 10.28 The accounts receivable invoice entry screen enabled for printing invoices

Now let's enter the invoice:

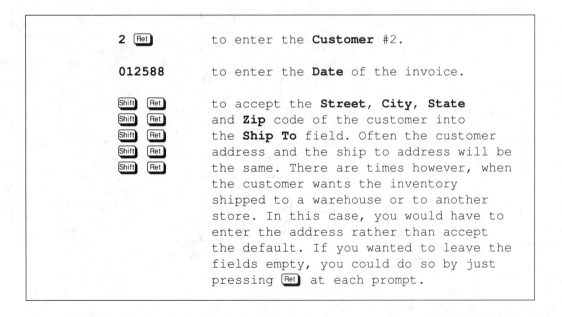

2 Ret	to enter the **Customer** #2.
012588	to enter the **Date** of the invoice.
Shift Ret Shift Ret Shift Ret Shift Ret Shift Ret	to accept the **Street, City, State** and **Zip** code of the customer into the **Ship To** field. Often the customer address and the ship to address will be the same. There are times however, when the customer wants the inventory shipped to a warehouse or to another store. In this case, you would have to enter the address rather than accept the default. If you wanted to leave the fields empty, you could do so by just pressing Ret at each prompt.

[Shift] [Ret]	to enter the **Row** of the invoice being entered. The default row is the next consecutive row of the invoice that you are creating, leaving one row for each different item on the invoice. If your invoice is longer than 16 items or rows, the program will automatically skip to the first printing line of the next page of the invoice. The invoice however, must not exceed 99 lines.
1 [Ret]	to enter the **Item** number being sold. The item numbers will appear on the right hand side of the screen.
15 [Ret]	to enter the **Quantity** of items being sold.
[Shift] [Ret]	to enter the **Unit** size.
[Shift] [Ret]	to accept the **Detail** description of the item being sold.
10 [Ret]	to enter the selling **Price** per unit. The default selling price you entered in setting up the inventory item can be entered by pressing the [Shift] [Ret] keys together. If you wish to enter a different price, or just want to type in the default amount, you could do so here.
7	to enter the **Sales Tax** percent
	Now you are prompted to enter the **Account** number to which the sale will be credited to. We do not have to worry about the debit, as the program will automatically debit accounts receivable. In brackets to the right of the entry will be the default revenue account that was set up for the specific inventory item — Sales — Widgets. We can accept this as our credit account by pressing [Shift] [Ret]. If we wish to enter some other account number, we can do so here.
[Shift] [Ret]	to accept default **Account**.

The cursor will now jump back to **Row**. As we do not want to enter any more data for this invoice, pressing the [ENTER] key now will cause the cursor to jump to the item **Freight**. Since we are not shipping this item out, we would leave this item blank.

[Ret]	to end entry.
[Ret]	to enter 0 into **Freight**.
TERMS NET 30 DAYS [Ret]	to enter a **Comment**. This comment field can be used to record customer information such as special deals coming up or new items on hand. If you have entered a default comment in the **SYSTEM** module, pressing the [Shift] [Ret] keys will cause that default comment to appear.

If you are not satisfied with the entry, or if it is wrong, you can clear the data by pressing the ESCape key. You can then reenter the information again.

At any time during the entering of a sales invoice you can view the details of the entry by pressing [F2] or [F3].

[F2]	to review entry

[F2] will give you the details of the journal entry being prepared as shown in Figure 10.29. Notice that the integration accounts have been entered automatically by the Bedford Accounting System. After your review of the entry, press [F2] again to return to the entry.

[F2]	to return to entry mode

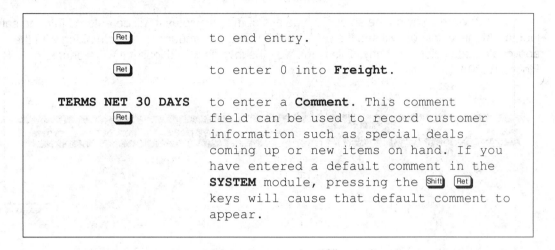

GENERAL	PAYABLE	RECEIVABLE	PAYROLL	INVENTORY	JOBCOST	SYSTEM
J20				debits	credits	
120 Accounts Receivable				160.50		
126 Inventory					77.13	
501 Cost Of Sales — Widgets				77.13		
401 Sales — Widgets					150.00	
260 Sales Tax Payable					10.50	
				237.63	237.63	

Figure 10.29 Details of journal entry can be viewed by pressing F2 function key

```
[F3]              to review invoice detail
```

[F3] will display on the screen the details of the invoice as it will be entered into the sales journal. At this point you will see the price per item and the amount of the sale along with the applicable state sales tax if any. This is the way the invoice would look if it were printed out. (See Figure 10.30.)

							F3
GENERAL	PAYABLE	RECEIVABLE	PAYROLL	INVENTORY	JOBCOST	SYSTEM	
# quantity	units	description			price	amount	
1 15	1	Widget — A	*		10.000	150.00	
		Sales Tax				10.50	
						150.00	

Figure 10.30 Invoice detail can be viewed by pressing F3 function key

After your review of the entry, return to the input screen.

```
[F3]              to return to the input screen
```

Now we are ready to print the invoice.

```
⬇          to move cursor beside the word Print.
            Make sure your printer is turned on and
            is loaded with paper.

➡          to print the invoice. A program
            generated invoice number will be
            printed at the top right hand corner of
            the invoice. If you wish to print the
            invoice again, you may do so by
            pressing the right arrow key again. The
            program does not create a journal entry
            for the invoice until it is accepted
            with the left arrow key. This will
            prevent multiple journal entries or
            invoice numbers from being generated
            when printing extra invoices.
```

Once you are satisfied with the entry and its printed invoice, accept it into the system by pressing the left arrow key. If not, you can make changes by moving the cursor to any item and pressing the right arrow key to enter that field. If you want to cancel the information entered press the ESCape key and reenter the information. If you do, make sure that you also destroy any hard copies of the invoice so that there is no confusion as to what the computer has accepted.

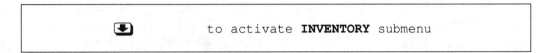

```
   ⬅    to accept entry
```

Transfer of Inventory

We can now return to the **INVENTORY** module for the first time since setting up our individual items. With the Bedford main menubar displayed and the cursor highlight over **INVENTORY**, press

```
   ⬇    to activate INVENTORY submenu
```

As with previous modules, when the module is made READY, the **History** item in the **INVENTORY** submenu is changed to **Journal**. The **Journal** item is the menu item that we will activate to record all journal entries to the system.

The **INVENTORY** module is only used to record transfers and adjustments to inventory and may therefore be seldom used for creating journal entries. **Transfer** is used when you wish to reclassify some or all of an inventory item or to transfer it as a component to a larger item you were manufacturing. **Adjustment** is used when you wish to write off the value of some inventory which was perhaps used for promotion, given away, or stolen.

For our example, lets assume that one of the Widgets in item #1 was a very popular item and therefore we want to sell this item at $12.00 instead of the regular $10.00. We have 20 of these items on hand. We will transfer these items to Widget B to reclassify them. With your **INVENTORY** submenu displayed press the following keys:

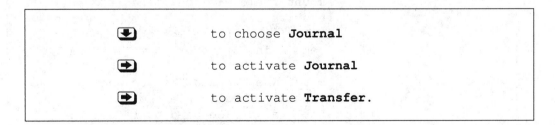

```
   ⬇    to choose Journal
   ➡    to activate Journal
   ➡    to activate Transfer.
```

Your screen will now resemble Figure 10.31.

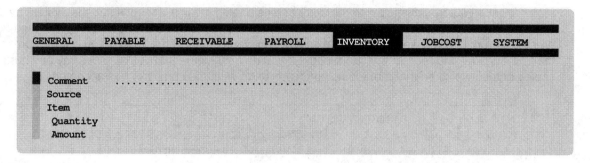

Figure 10.31 Inventory transfer entry screen

Transfer A to B Ret
to enter a **Comment** as to why the transfer is being made.

299 Ret
to enter the **Source** document you would like stored with the journal entry.

1 Ret
to enter the **Item** number to be transferred. Items for which the quantity is being reduced are always entered first. This is done so the cost of the transferred item will be properly deducted from the account.

-20 Ret
to enter the **Quantity** of items being transferred. In our case we are reducing the amount of #1 items, so we enter a negative number. If we wish to add to the inventory amount, we would add a positive number.

Shift Ret
when we enter a negative item, the **Amount** field will be opened and a negative amount equal to the average cost of the item times the number of items being transferred will appear. This amount will then be the default amount when we add them to another category. This is the amount that should always be used to reduce the value of the inventory.

2 Ret
to enter the **Item** number to transfer to

20 Ret
to enter the **Quantity** assigned

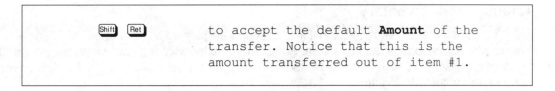

The cursor will now return to the **Item** field. You must transfer all of the items in the entry before you can accept the entry. If the entry does not balance, the computer will beep when you attempt to accept it. We can review the effect of the entry by pressing [F2] and [F3] prior to acceptance of the entry.

| **[F3]** | to reveal detail of inventory adjustments (See Figure 10.32.) |

						F3
GENERAL	PAYABLE	RECEIVABLE	PAYROLL	INVENTORY	JOBCOST	SYSTEM
#	quantity	units	description		cost	amount
1	20-	1	Widget A		5.142	102.84-
2	20	1	Widget B		5.142	102.84
						0.00

Figure 10.32 Detail of inventory adjustment journal entry

| **[F3]** | to return to the entry. |

When you are ready to accept the entry press

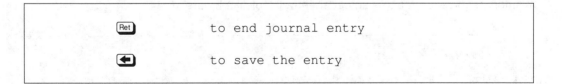

Adjustment of Inventory

Making adjustments to inventory is similar to making transfers. An adjustment is made when inventory items are lost, broken or stolen. For example, after counting your inventory you find that one item is missing. To adjust your inventory you would make an entry through the Adjustment menu to record the missing item.

The entry that would be made for a lost item would be:

> Dr. Loss on Inventory (expense)   xxx
> > Cr. Inventory   xxx

The entry screen for adjustments reached through the **INVENTORY - Journal** submenu is displayed in Figure 10.33.

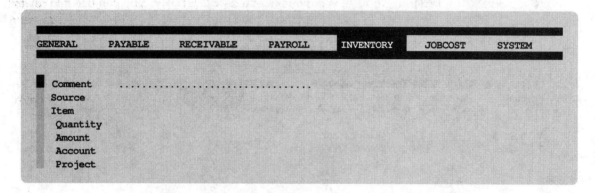

Figure 10.33 Inventory adjustment entry screen

As you can see this screen closely resembles the **Transfer** screen except that it allows you to enter the account to which the loss will be debited and the project cost that might be associated with the loss. All other entry rules are the same as described under **Transfer**.

EXPORTING INVENTORY FILES

The inventory report is the only report in the module that can be exported to a spreadsheet. The inventory report exported to a spreadsheet will look like Figure 10.34.

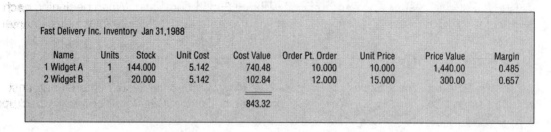

Name	Units	Stock	Unit Cost	Cost Value	Order Pt. Order	Unit Price	Price Value	Margin
1 Widget A	1	144.000	5.142	740.48	10.000	10.000	1,440.00	0.485
2 Widget B	1	20.000	5.142	102.84	12.000	15.000	300.00	0.657
				843.32				

Fast Delivery Inc. Inventory Jan 31,1988

Figure 10.34 Inventory report exported to Lotus 1-2-3 spreadsheet

The exported file will be called INVENT.EXT, with .EXT taking on one of the following — WKS, WK1, WR1 or TXT depending on the file format you chose for exporting. If you repeatedly export a file with the same name, it will be copied over the previous one. Therefore, if you wish to save the old one you must change its name before you export the same file again.

MAINTAINING AN AUDIT TRAIL

As in other modules, it is important for you to establish an audit trail to have a record of all accounting entries made. An audit trail means that you have a printed list (hard copy) for the items you entered. For the **INVENTORY** module, this encompasses printing out a copy of the journal entries made in each module — accounts **PAYABLE**, accounts **RECEIVABLE** and **INVENTORY**. Return to the **GENERAL** module and activate it, then choose **Print** and activate it, then choose **Journal** and activate it. You can now print journal entries for each of the modules. Store the printout of the journal entries in a binder marked <u>**INVENTORY**</u>. You can use it to review any of the entries made or re-enter journal entries in the event that the data files on the disk were destroyed.

FINISHING THE SESSION

You have now completed the inventory tutorial. You should finish this session to save your data to disk. After activating the **Finish** command you will be returned to the disk operating system.

To finish this session, press

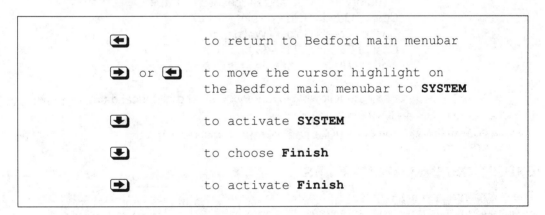

```
←              to return to Bedford main menubar

→ or ←         to move the cursor highlight on
               the Bedford main menubar to SYSTEM

↓              to activate SYSTEM

↓              to choose Finish

→              to activate Finish
```

You should always end each session with the **Finish** command. When beginning each chapter in this tutorial start the Bedford Accounting Program as described earlier in this chapter

BACKING UP YOUR DATA FILES

You should always make a backup of the data files on your computer system to guard against loss of files or hardware failure. Follow the procedures outlined in Chapter 4 for making backups.

BEDFORD PRACTICE SET

AMERICANA HOME DECORATING AND SERVICE COMPANY

Part V — Inventory Module

OBJECTIVE

After completing this practice set on inventory, you should be able to:

1. Create inventory item files.

2. Enter historical data to inventory items.

3. Enter necessary defaults and integration accounts.

4. Set the System to Ready.

5. Enter transactions for: Inventory sales and sales returns with the system on-line for generating invoices; sales discounts with the system off-line for generating invoices; end of month adjustments to inventory accounts.

6. Print detailed stock report of all inventory items.

INSTRUCTION: 1 Insert the three following cost accounts between your accounts Opening Inventory 01-01-88 and Purchases — Paint:
Cost of Goods Sold — Paint
Cost of Goods Sold — Wallpaper
Cost of Goods Sold — Fabric
Note: The account type should be L and suppress Yes.

INSTRUCTION: 2. Enter the following inventory items and historical data.

Americana Decorating Sales & Service Inc. FOR INSTRUCTIONAL USE ONLY   Page 1
INVENTORY Oct 31,1988

			price	stock	minimum	cost	value	margin
1	Ceiling Flat Latex	Gallon	16.000	600	300	8.000	4,800.00	50.0
6	Colorol	Roll	8.000	524	400	4.000	2,096.00	50.0
11	Cotton	Sq/Yd	20.000	967	200	10.000	9,670.00	50.0
12	Cotton/Polyester	Sq/Yd	30.000	756	300	15.000	11,340.00	50.0
7	Dimensional Living	Roll	10.000	1,000	200	5.000	5,000.00	50.0
2	Eggshell Latex	Gallon	22.000	400	200	11.000	4,400.00	50.0
8	Jack & Jill	Roll	12.000	876	150	6.000	5,256.00	50.0
13	Lace	Sq/Yd	40.000	486	300	20.000	9,720.00	50.0
3	Oil Base	Gallon	32.000	500	200	16.000	8,000.00	50.0
4	Satin Latex	Gallon	18.000	600	150	9.000	5,400.00	50.0
9	Select	Roll	14.000	834	150	7.000	5,838.00	50.0
5	Semi-Gloss Latex	Gallon	24.000	721	200	12.006	8,675.00	49.9
14	Sheer	Sq/Yd	10.000	1,881	200	5.000	9,405.00	50.0
15	Velvet	Sq/Yd	50.000	419	150	25.033	10,489.00	49.9
10	Waldec	Roll	16.000	858	150	8.002	6,866.00	49.9
							106,937.00	

INSTRUCTION: 3. Enter the integration accounts required for your General Ledger chart of accounts.

INSTRUCTION: 4. Set the SYSTEM>Default>Module>Inventory>:
Formula   Margin
Ready   Yes

Note: $\dfrac{Selling\ Price\ -\ Cost\ Price}{Selling\ Price} = Margin$

INSTRUCTION: 5. Enter the following transaction on 11-01-88 to convert your current books from a periodic inventory system to a perpetual inventory system.

Nov.   1. Close out the year to date balances for all Purchases, Purchase Returns & Allowances, Opening Inventory, and Ending Inventory accounts to: Cost of Goods Sold — Paint, $35,264.60; Cost of Goods Sold — Wallpaper, $24,690.43; Cost of Goods Sold — Fabric, $69,156.65. No source document required. Set Suppress to Yes for accounts being closed out so they will not appear on the financial statements.

Display an Income Statement for 01-01-88 to 11-02-88 and you will see a perpetual inventory system's financial statement. There is no need for Opening Inventory, Ending Inventory, Purchases, and Purchases Returns accounts, since inventory will be up-dated with each entry.

If you display an Income Statement ending before 11-02-88 you will convert back automatically to a periodic inventory system.

INSTRUCTION: 6. Enter the following transactions in the GENERAL, PAYABLE, RECEIVABLE, PAYROLL, and INVENTORY modules for month of November.

Note: Entries will begin on the second of the month and not the first, since we used that date exclusively for the change over of periodic inventory to perpetual inventory.

Nov   2. Sold merchandise and services on account to Marlo Thomas. S417.

Item	Quantity	Unit	Detai	Price	Amount
2	120	Gallon	Eggshell	$22.00	$ 2,640.00
6	150	Roll	Colorol	8.00	1,200.00
15	180	Sq/Yd	Velvet	50.00	9,000.00
			Decorating Labor		5,467.67
			Freight		120.00
			SST @ 7%		898.80
					$19,326.47

Note: Press the F2 key to observe how the program automatically calculates the changes to Cost of Goods Sold and Inventory Accounts.

After saving entry escape back to the Main Menu bar and select INVENTORY module. Display stock order to screen and inventory item Colorol, #6, is below the minimum quantity on hand. An efficient business must monitor its stock at all times so a stock out will not occur.

2. Sold merchandise and services on account to Wayne Gretzky. S418.

Item	Quantity	Unit	Detail	Price	Amount
3	120	Gallon	Oil Base	$32.00	$ 3,840.00
7	245	Roll	Dimensional Living	10.00	2,450.00
14	357	Sq/Yd	Sheer	10.00	3,570.00
			Decorating Labor		6,783.45
			Freight		135.00
			SST @ 7%		690.20
					$17,468.65

2. Sold merchandise and services on account to Ronald MacDonald. S419.

Item	Quantity	Unit	Detail	Price	Amount
5	100	Gallon	Semi-Gloss	$24.00	$ 2,400
8	90	Roll	Jack & Jill	12.00	1,080.00
13	95	Sq/Yd	Lace	40.00	3,800.00
			Decorating Labor		5,690.34
			Freight		135.00
			SST @ 7%		509.60
					$13,614.94

2. Received on account from Fuzzy Zeller, $5,900.80, in full payment of invoice S412. R155.

2. Granted credit to Marlo Thomas for sales discounts: paint, $65.34; wallpaper, $44.23; fabric, 270.00; total, $379.57. Cm59.

   Note: To process this transaction you must take RECEIVABLE module invoice option off-line by going to SYSTEM>Default>Module>Receivable> Invoice>No. Make sure to put RECEIVABLE module back on-line after entering transaction.

2. Received on account from Marlo Thomas, $18,946.90, covering invoice S417 for $19,326.47 less Cm59 for $379.57. R156.

16. Granted credit to Ronald MacDonald for merchandise returns. S420.

   Note: If you were processing this transaction off-line the source document would be a credit memo but on-line it will a negative sales invoice.
   Enter Customer Return in the Ship to field to identify this transaction as a negative sale.

Item	Quantity	Unit	Detail	Price	Amount
5	10-	Gallon	Semi-Gloss Latex	$24.00	$ 240.00-
8	15-	Roll	Jack & Jill	12.00	180.00-
13	20-	Sq/Yd	Lace	40.00	800.00-
			SST @ 7%		85.40-
					$1,305.40-

16. Received on account from Ronald MacDonald, $12,309.54, covering invoice S419 for $13,614.94 less invoice S420 for $1,305.40. R157.

16. Received on account from Fred Flinstone, $3,856.40, in full payment of invoice S413. R158.

16. Paid on account to Interior Supply, $7,837.45, in full payment of invoice P244. Ch423.

16. Purchased merchandise on account from Seattle Paint & Paper. P247.

Item	Quantity	Unit	Detail	Price	Amount
6	200	Roll	Colorol	$ 4.00	$ 800.00
			Freight expense		30.00
					$ 830.00

16. Record bank transfer from General to Payroll account. $3,697.40. M124.

16. Paid middle of month advance to Gary Carter, $660.00. Ch424.

   Note: With Payroll integrated into the System you no longer have to make two entries like you did if the employee was entered as a vendor payable.

16. Paid middle of month advance to Lou Gehrig, $720.00. Ch425.

16. Paid middle of month advance to Jackie Robinson, $750.00. Ch426.

16. Paid middle of month advance to Babe Ruth, $690.00. Ch427.

16. Paid middle of month advance to George Washington, $877.40. Ch428.

16. Recorded company pension owed to vendor Merrill Lynch Co., $616.23. M125.

16. Paid Merrill Lynch Co. for company pension, $616.23. Ch429.

16. Record utilities expense to vendor Northwestern Hydro, $235.40. P248.

16. Paid Northwestern Hydro for utilities expense, $235.40. Ch430.

16. Record sales tax owed vendor Oregon State Regulatory Body, $386.40. M126.

16. Paid State of Oregon for sales tax, $386.40. Ch431.

16. Bank debited Americana account for partial principal payment of short term loan, $15,000.00. M127.

16. Record the withholding taxes payable as debt owing to vendor Internal Revenue Service: Federal Income Tax, $2,431.22; Federal Insurance; $1,851.16, total $4,282.38. M128.

   Note: You must enter all liabilities as a purchase to a vendor account so you can then run check payments.

16. Paid withholding taxes to Internal Revenue Service, $4,282.38. Ch432.

16. Record State Income Tax payable, $944.03. M129.

   Note: You must record the debt owed to vendor State regulatory body so you can then process check using PAYABLE module.

16. Paid State of Oregon Regulatory Body for State Income Tax, $944.03. Ch433.

16. Record medical plan owed to vendor Blue Cross, $270.00. M130.

16. Paid Blue Cross for medical plan, $270.00. Ch434.

16. Record telephone expense as debt owing to vendor Bell Telephone, $145.89. P249.

16. Paid Bell Telephone for telephone expense, $145.89. Ch435.

16. Record fuel expense as debt owing to vendor Texaco Oil Co., $98.78. P250.

16. Paid Texaco Oil Co. for fuel expense, $98.78. Ch436.

16. Purchased office supplies on account from Wilson Stationery, $789.76. P251.

30. Paid on account to Wilson Stationery, $789.76, in full payment of invoice P251. Ch437.

30. Record bank transfer from General to Payroll account, $3,440.21. M131.

30. Paid month end payroll to Gary Carter, $573.02, covering: Salary Expense, $2,200.00 plus employer's FICA Expense $165.22; less deductions of Federal Income Tax, $471.35; State Income Tax, $170.41; Employee and Employer FICA Payable, $330.44; Company Pension, $110.00; Medical, $50.00; Advances Receivable, $660.00. Ch438.

Note: The Bedford Program will generate the employer's payroll taxes internally to save you making a separate entry.

31. Paid month end payroll to Lou Gehrig, $744.66, covering: Salary Expense, $2,400.00 plus employer's FICA Expense $180.24; less deductions of Federal Income Tax, $407.02; State Income Tax, $178.08; Employee and Employer FICA Payable, $360.48; Company Pension, $120.00; Medical, $50.00; Advances Receivable, $720.00. Ch439.

30. Paid month end payroll to Jackie Robinson, $578.93, covering: Salary Expense, $2,500.00 plus employer's FICA Expense $187.75; less deductions of Federal Income Tax, $597.16; State Income Tax, $201.16; Employee and Employer FICA Payable, $375.50; Company Pension, $125.00; Medical, $60.00; Advances Receivable, $750.00. Ch440.

30. Paid month end payroll to Babe Ruth, $696.42, covering: Salary Expense, $2,300.00 plus employer's FICA Expense $172.73; less deductions of Federal Income Tax, $401.77; State Income Tax, $169.08; Employee and Employer FICA Payable, $345.46; Company Pension, $115.00; Medical, $55.00; Advances Receivable, $690.00. Ch441.

30. Paid month end payroll to George Washington, $847.18, covering: Salary Expense, $2,924.67 plus employer's FICA Expense $219.64; less deductions of Federal Income Tax, $553.92; State Income Tax, $225.30; Employee and Employer FICA Payable, $439.28; Company Pension, $146.23; Medical, $55.00; Advances Receivable, $877.40. Ch442.

30. Recorded Bank Reconciliation adjustments: Short Term Loan Payment, $543.80; Mortgage Payment, $345.78; Interest Expense, $925.89; Bank Charges Expense, $35.98; Interest Income, $125.45; net total bank debit, $1,726.00. M132.

30. Recorded adjusting entry for insurance expense incurred, $400.

30. Recorded adjusting entry for office supplies expense incurred, $165.89.

30. Recorded adjusting entry for estimated depreciation expense incurred: Building, $1,750.00; Automotive, $185.00.

30. Recorded ending inventory change from end of last period.

Item	Quantity	Unit	Detail	Cost Price	Amount
4	5-	Gallon	Satin Latex	$ 9.00	$ 45.00-
7	7-	Roll	Dimensional Living	5.00	35.00-
12	15-	Sq/Yd	Cotton/Polyester	15.00	225.00-
					$ 305.00-

Note: Since you have set the INVENTORY module to ready you must make your adjustments to inventory in that module. The program is integrated to the Inventory and Cost of Goods Sold accounts so just enter the figures and accept the defaults.

INSTRUCTION: 7.   Print list of all stock showing: price; stock; minimum; cost; value; margin. Print list of stock by department showing: price; stock; minimum; cost; value; margin.
Verify that the total stock by department agrees with the Inventory control accounts in the General Ledger.
Print individual employee's earnings records using Summary layout for current month and year to date.
Print payroll register of all employee's earnings records using Detail layout for current month and year to date.
Print Aging Schedule of Accounts Receivable in Summary and Detail form for all accounts.
Verify that the total of all customer's account balances agrees with the Accounts Receivable control account.
Print Aging Schedule of Accounts Payable in Summary and Detail form for all accounts.
Verify that the total of all vendor's account balances agrees with the Accounts Payable control account.
Print General Journal entries from 11-01-88 to 11-30-88.
Print Income Statement for 11-02-88 to 11-30-88

Note: The period of time for November's Income Statement must begin on Nov. 2 since Nov.1 was used as the conversion date from periodic inventory to perpetual inventory.

Print Income Statement for 01-01-88 to 11-30-88.
Print Balance Sheet for 11-30-88.

Chapter 11
JOB COSTING

Chapter 11
JOB COSTING

PREVIEW

In Chapter 11 you will acquire a basic understanding of the purpose of the JOBCOST module of the Bedford Accounting System. You will learn how to organize this module, how to add and delete cost centers, and how to modify information about a cost center. Then you will make some entries into jobcost accounts through the various subledgers. Finally you will display and print the various reports available, as well as export a file for manipulation in a spreadsheet.

OBJECTIVES

After completing this Chapter, you should be able to explain:

1. The function of the JOBCOST module of the Bedford Accounting System;

2. How to prepare for using the JOBCOST module — adding and deleting cost centers, as well as modifying information about them.

3. How to make entries into the various JOBCOST centers that have been set up;

4. How to display information in report form and how to print the various reports;

5. How to export jobcost data for use in a spreadsheet or text file.

In working through the preceding chapters you learned how the general ledger provides overall control of business transactions and accounting data and ties the various subledgers of accounts payable, accounts receivable, payroll and inventory together. With an accounting system we can measure the state of the company's financial health through the balance sheet. The success of the firm's operation is shown by the income statement. But these statements may not be enough for purposes of decision making.

Fast Delivery Inc., the company that we have been using as an example, has three sources of revenue.

   a) freight delivery
   b) goods storage
   c) truck rental

The accounting system will tell us whether a firm, overall, is profitable, but management might also want to know which divisions are making money and which ones are loosing money. Are all divisions contributing to the profitability of the firm? Is one division supporting another?

WHAT IS COST ACCOUNTING?

Cost accounting is the developing of cost information pertaining to a division, department, project or manufactured product within the framework of the general ledger. The cost information is provided by the transactions that the company completes during a particular cycle. We can compare these costs to the revenue produced by a particular activity to determine if costs and revenues are within budget.

Thus in cost accounting, also known as *job costing,* we allocate the various revenues and costs to departments, divisions, or profit centers, rather than just record the costs as part of the total entity of Fast Delivery, Inc.

For example, an employee of Fast Delivery, Inc., works in all three areas mentioned above. For her duties she is paid $2,500 per month. Our accounting entry to record this wage at the end of each month, (not considering withholding taxes) would be as follows:

Dr. Wage Expense	$2,500.00	
Cr. Cash		$2,500.00

This entry will adequately record as an expense to the company the payment for the monthly salary. However, if we wanted to treat each department as a separate profit center, or *job cost center,* we would have to distribute that employee's salary according to some percentage of time spent in each department. If she worked 50% of her time in the delivery division, 30% of the time in the storage division, and 20% of the time in the truck rental division, we would show this distribution by splitting the wage cost and allocating it to each center:

	Dept 1 Delivery	Dept 2 Storage	Dept 3 Rental
Wage expense	1,250.00	750.00	500.00

Similarly, other costs and revenues would be assigned to these departments, either in total or in part. At the end of each period, we can prepare a report by jobcost center as shown in Figure 11.1 that will tell us whether or not that particular function of the business was profitable. We could also compare the department's results against the budget to determine the success of that part of the firm in meeting its plans and objectives.

	Dept 1 Delivery	Dept 2 Storage	Dept 3 Rental
Revenue	13,480.00	6,500.00	4,300.00
Expenses			
Fuel	4,350.00	1,250.00	250.00
Rent	2,100.00	2,100.00	2,100.00
Wages	1,250.00	750.00	500.00
Total	7,700.00	4,100.00	2,850.00
Profit	5,780.00	2,400.00	1,450.00

Figure 11.1 Report by jobcost center, Fast Delivery Inc.

Allocating Overhead

Not all costs can be easily broken down between departments. Overhead costs, for example, (telephone, utilities, janitorial, accounting services, etc.,) are allocated according to a formula devised by management. The formula may be based on the amount of revenue produced by the department, or on the amount of direct labor used in relation to the total labor for the firm. Whatever the method used, it must be applied consistently so the results can be compared to other periods.

PREPARING TO USE THE JOBCOST MODULE

The **JOBCOST** module is unlike any of the other modules. Its function is to allocate expenses and revenues to various projects or departments. To do so, the Bedford program uses information entered with journal entries made through other modules. Therefore this module cannot be used unless all of the other modules are in the READY stage. This also means that the **JOBCOST** module is always in the READY mode.

Identifying Cost and Revenue Centers

Before you can begin to convert your **JOBCOST** module to the Bedford Accounting System, you must organize existing data and have it ready for entry to the system. While in other modules this included making a listing of existing amounts, for the **JOBCOST** module you only have to identify the projects or departments among which you want the costs allocated.

Identifying cost or profit centers is not a difficult task but requires some thought. The centers that you identify should be meaningful and should be measurable. If the centers are composed of too many different activities, for example, there is little benefit in identifying them separately.

As an example, let's use the three centers that we identified earlier for Fast Delivery Inc.

1. freight delivery
2. goods storage
3. truck rental

Setting Up Bedford for Using the JOBCOST Module

Having decided on meaningful cost or profit centers, you are ready to enter them into the Bedford Accounting System. Start the Bedford program by typing

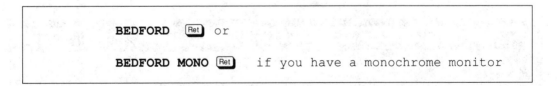

```
BEDFORD  [Ret]  or

BEDFORD MONO [Ret]   if you have a monochrome monitor
```

After a few seconds, the main menu will appear, as displayed in Figure 11.2.

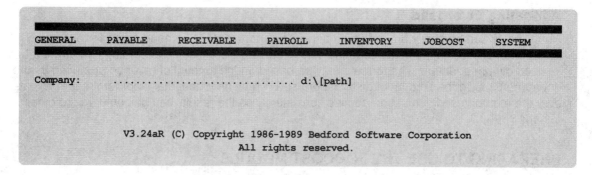

Figure 11.2 Bedford opening menu

Enter the location of the data files as in previous modules

```
        B:\FASTDEL              C:\FASTDEL
```

Now enter the **Using** date

```
        013188
```

The main menubar of the Bedford Accounting System will now appear. The word **GENERAL** should be highlighted. Press

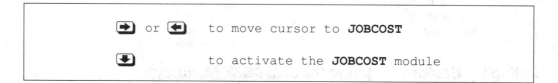

Your screen will now show the **JOBCOST** submenu as seen in Figure 11.3.

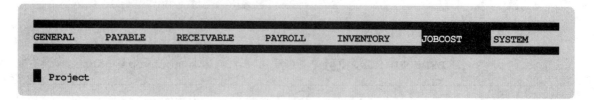

Figure 11.3 JOBCOST module submenu

You can now enter jobcost centers

Adding Jobcost Centers

Using the listing made earlier, you can now add the cost centers to the **JOBCOST** module in the Bedford Accounting System. Let's start by entering the following center:

> Jobcost center   Freight

With the **JOBCOST** submenu showing, press

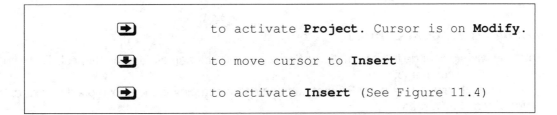

➡	to activate **Project**. Cursor is on **Modify**.
⬇	to move cursor to **Insert**
➡	to activate **Insert** (See Figure 11.4)

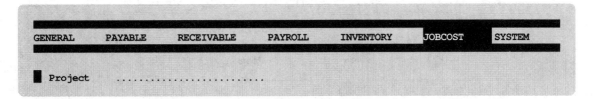

Figure 11.4 Project entry screen

Now enter the name of the cost center, **Freight**. Remember the program automatically capitalizes the first character for you.

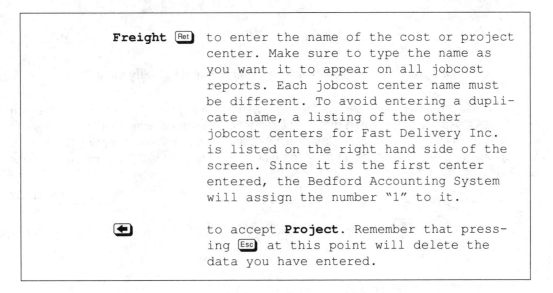

Freight [Ret]	to enter the name of the cost or project center. Make sure to type the name as you want it to appear on all jobcost reports. Each jobcost center name must be different. To avoid entering a dupli-cate name, a listing of the other jobcost centers for Fast Delivery Inc. is listed on the right hand side of the screen. Since it is the first center entered, the Bedford Accounting System will assign the number "1" to it.
⬅	to accept **Project**. Remember that pressing [Esc] at this point will delete the data you have entered.

▪ *Practice Exercise*

Repeat the above steps to enter the following three cost centers:

Center #2	Warehouse
Center #3	Rentals
Center #4	Other

When complete, return to the **JOBCOST** submenu.

Modifying Jobcost Centers

You may wish to change the information entered to make the name more meaningful. To do so, use the **Modify** command.

You should still be in the **Project** submenu after completing the above practice exercise. To **Modify** a center, press

| ⬆ | to choose **Modify** |
| ➡ | to activate **Modify** |

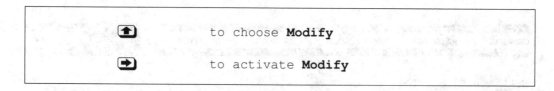

| GENERAL | PAYABLE | RECEIVABLE | PAYROLL | INVENTORY | JOBCOST | SYSTEM |

■ Project   ...

```
Freight.....................1
Other.......................4
Rentals.....................3
Warehouse...................2
```

Figure 11.5 Screen display after activating **Project-Modify** menu item

Your screen will now resemble the display shown in Figure 11.5. Notice that the menu on the left looks identical to the **Insert** menu. At the right of the screen, you will see a listing of the four projects that we have entered. After thinking about the name Warehouse we come to the conclusion that Storage might be a better name because it is more inclusive. To modify project #2, type:

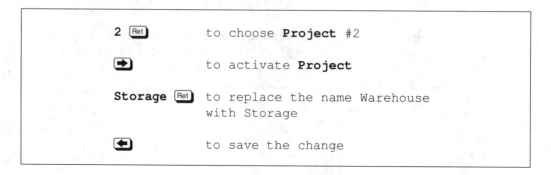

2 Ret	to choose **Project** #2
➡	to activate **Project**
Storage Ret	to replace the name Warehouse with Storage
⬅	to save the change

Once you have made the change, press the LEFT ARROW key to have the program accept the change. If you did not want to make a change you could simply press the ESCape key to get out of the **Modify** menu.

Deleting Jobcost Centers

If you no longer want a particular department, or when a project is completed, you can delete it. Make sure you are still in the **Project** submenu. To delete a project press

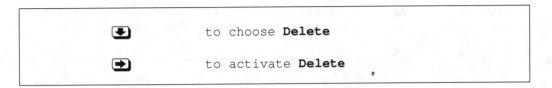

You will now be prompted for the number of the project you wish to delete. A list of the projects on the system will appear on the right hand side of the screen. Choose #4. You will be asked if you wish to delete it. Let's delete this cost center.

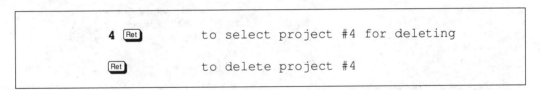

A project should be kept on the system until it is completed, no longer required or when you have finished analyzing it. Deleting a project will not free up much space since it only records an allocation of an existing journal entry and does not store new data. When a project is inserted into the **JOBCOST** module, an internal starting date specifically for that project is assigned. This date is the **Conversion** date if the system is in the NOT READY mode and the **Using** date if in READY mode. When the project is deleted, these dates are removed and can not be retrieved. Therefore, no further analysis can ever be done on the costs or revenue allocated to that project.

Change to Ready Mode

Since the data for the **JOBCOST** module is taken from the journal entries made in other modules, the **JOBCOST** module is in the READY stage by default. When you have entered the project names, you have completed the conversion process. You can immediately enter real data into the accounts system.

ALLOCATING REVENUES OR EXPENSES TO PROJECTS

Only revenue and expense items can be allocated to the jobcost centers. To understand how to allocate costs to a **JOBCOST** center, let's use the accounts **PAYABLE** module to make the following entry:

Freight $150.00   Vendor #1

Return to the Bedford main menubar, place your cursor on **PAYABLE** and press

⬇	to activate **PAYABLE** module
⬇	to choose **Journal**
➡	to activate **Journal**
➡	to activate **Purchase**
⬇	to choose **Other** since freight is not a purchase of an inventory item.
➡	to activate **Other**

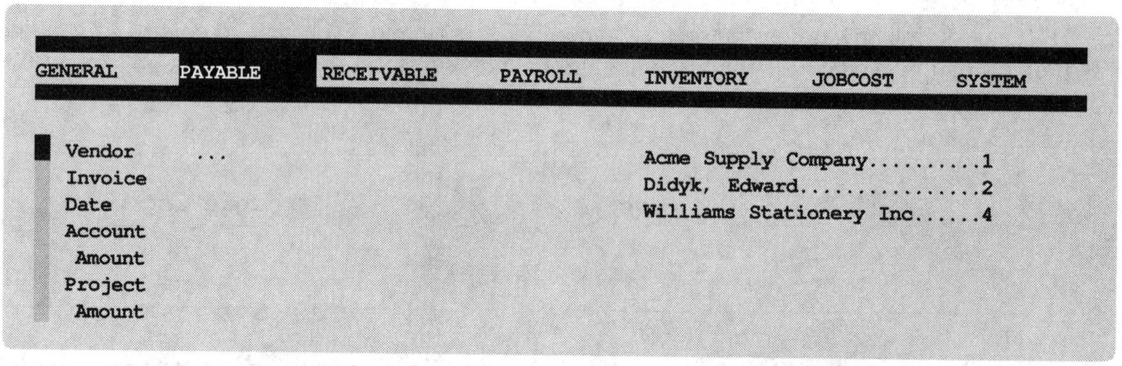

GENERAL   PAYABLE   RECEIVABLE   PAYROLL   INVENTORY   JOBCOST   SYSTEM

```
Vendor    ...                          Acme Supply Company.........1
Invoice                                Didyk, Edward...............2
Date                                   Williams Stationery Inc.....4
Account
 Amount
Project
 Amount
```

Figure 11.6 Accounts Payable purchase entry screen. Freight will be entered through the purchase entry screen and allocated to an expense account.

Your screen will now resemble Figure 11.6. You have seen this input screen before when you entered a purchase in Chapter 6. This entry will be similar except that you will allocate the cost of the purchase to a **JOBCOST** center.

1 Ret	to input **Vendor** #1
999 Ret	to enter **Invoice** number
013188	to enter **Date** of the invoice
520	to enter **Account** number that the invoice will be allocated to in the general ledger
150 Ret	to enter the **Amount** of the invoice

GENERAL	PAYABLE	RECEIVABLE	PAYROLL	INVENTORY	JOBCOST	SYSTEM	F2

```
     Vendor      Acme Supply Company      Freight.....................1
     Invoice     999                      Rentals.....................3
     Date        01-31-88                 Storage.....................2
     Account     Freight Expense
     Amount      150.00
 ▪   Project     ...
     Amount
```

Figure 11.7 Accounts payable purchase entry screen. Choose from the cost centers on the right and enter that number to allocate freight expense.

Your cursor is now beside the word **Project** and a listing of the project numbers will appear on the right hand side of the screen (See Figure 11.7). You entered three projects earlier which are now listed on your screen. You will allocate the entire amount to project #3, Rental. If you wanted to allocate it to more than one center you would distribute portions of the total to the other cost centers.

3 [Ret]	to choose **Project** #3
[Shift] [Ret]	to allocate the entire $150.00 to the project. Notice that the amount unallocated will appear to the right of the word **Amount**. Pressing [Shift] [Ret] will cause the default amount to be allocated to the Project.
[F2]	If you press F2, you can see how the journal entry has been allocated (See Figure 11.8). Notice that the allocation to **Project** #3 is listed below the entry. This will be stored with the entry and each time a report is generated in the **JOBCOST** module, it will be picked up and reported.

GENERAL	PAYABLE	RECEIVABLE	PAYROLL	INVENTORY	JOBCOST	SYSTEM	F2
J21				debits	credits	project	

```
220 Accounts Payable                                    150.00
520 Freight Expense                          150.00
   ▪  3 Rentals                                                    150.00
                                          _____      _____
                                            150.00        150.00
```

Figure 11.8 Journal entry (J21) has been allocated to a project

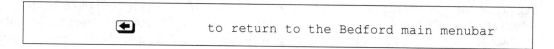

[F2]	to return to the entry mode
Ret	to complete allocation of costs
Ret	to complete journal entry
←	to record entry permanently

Each entry can be allocated among a revenue and expense account in each of the modules. However, it is not necessary to allocate all or any of the expense or revenue unless you want to keep track of it as part of a cost center. Once you have allocated the item, it will remain as part of the journal entry.

| ← | to return to the Bedford main menubar |

- **Practice Exercise**

Enter two more items into the accounts **PAYABLE** module and allocate them as follows:

Vendor	Invoice #	Date	Account	Amount	Proj 1	Proj 2	Proj 3
2	956	Jan 31, 88	520	175.05	175.05		
4	957	Jan 31, 88	520	230.00	100.00	30.00	100.00

Displaying Jobcost Entries

To see how the items were allocated to the jobcost centers you can display the entries on your screen or print them out. Place your cursor over the word **JOBCOST** in the Bedford main menubar and press the following keys:

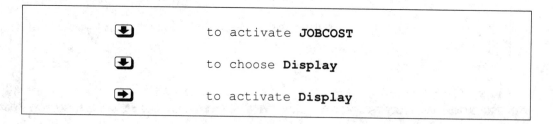

↓	to activate **JOBCOST**
↓	to choose **Display**
→	to activate **Display**

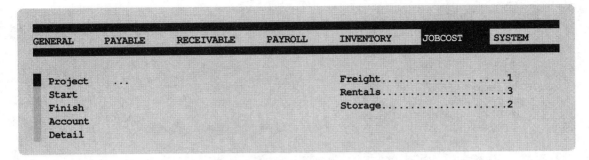

Figure 11.9 JOBCOST display screen activated

Your screen will now resemble Figure 11.9

3 [Ret]	to choose **Project** #3, Rentals, for display
013188	to enter the **Start** date of the display. This is the date of the first transaction that will be included in the display. The range must be between the **Start** date of the job and the present **Using** date that you entered when you started the Bedford Accounting System. The default date would be the first day of the current month.
013188	to enter the **Finish** date or the date of the last transaction to be included in the report. Again the range of dates is the start of the project and the current **Using** date. The default in this case is the **Using** date, assuming that you would want a report including the latest date.
[Shift] [Ret]	to accept the default account - all the accounts that have entries to this number.
Y	to display **Detail**

Your display will now appear on the screen as in Figure 11.10.

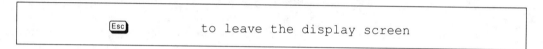

GENERAL	PAYABLE	RECEIVABLE	PAYROLL	INVENTORY	JOBCOST	SYSTEM
Rentals				start: 01-31-88	amount	cumulative

```
EXPENSE
520 Freight Expense
   01-31-88 Acme Supply Company        999   J23         150.00      150.00
   01-31-88 Williams Stationery Inc.   957   J25         100.00      250.00
                                                        _____
                                                         250.00
```

Figure 11.10 Detail display of all revenue and expense items allocated to project: Rentals

The report will contain a listing of all revenue and expense items with a total for each column. In this way, we can compare whether the cost center is profitable or if it is within the limits of the departmental budget. When you have completed viewing the report, press

Esc   to leave the display screen

Printing Jobcost Reports

Printing of reports is similar to the displaying of reports. You are still in the **JOBCOST** submenu. To see a printout of how the items are allocated to the **JOBCOST** projects, press

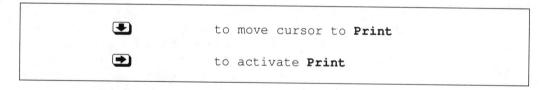

↓   to move cursor to **Print**

→   to activate **Print**

Now repeat the choices to generate the display above.

```
  3  [Ret]              to choose Project #3, Rental, for
                        printing

  013188               to enter the Start date of the display.

  013188               to enter the Finish date or the date
                        of the last transaction to be included
                        in the report

  [Shift] [Ret]        to accept the default — all the accounts
                        that have entries to this project number

  Y                    to print Detail

  [➡]                  to start printing
```

Be sure your printer is turned on and is online. Your report will now be printed out and look like the one shown in Figure 11.11.

Fast Delivery Inc. FOR INSTRUCTIONAL USE ONLY
Page 1
PROJECT: Rentals   START Jan 31,1988   FROM Jan 31,1988 TO Jan 31,1988

				amount	cumulative
EXPENSE					
520 Freight Expense	01-31-88 Acme Supply Company	999	J21	150.00	150.00
	01-31-88 Williams Stationery Inc.	957	J23	100.00	250.00
				250.00	
EXPENSE					250.00

Figure 11.11 Printed detail report of the allocation of freight expense to various projects

EXPORTING JOBCOST REPORTS

The Bedford Accounting System lets you export the **JOBCOST** reports created during the Print option, except that you can only export the summary information and not the detail. Furthermore, you can only export one project at a time. The file created by the exporting process is named PROJECT.EXT. The .EXT part of the file is based on the file format that you established as the default setting under the **SYSTEM** submenu (See Setting the Defaults in Chapter 5).

To export the report, choose **Export** from the **JOBCOST** submenu. Once you have exported the data you may manipulate the figures in a spreadsheet such as Lotus 1-2-3, Supercalc, or one of the spreadsheet clones. The export procedure was covered extensively in Chapter 6. Rather than go through it again, go to Chapter 6 and follow the procedure outlined there.

FINISHING THE SESSION

You have now completed the jobcost tutorial. You should finish this session to save your data to disk. After activating the **Finish** command you will be returned to the disk operating system.
To finish this session, press

⬅	to return to the Bedford main menubar
➡ or	
⬅	to move the cursor highlight on the Bedford main menubar to **SYSTEM**
⬇	to activate **SYSTEM**
⬇	to move to **Finish**
➡	to execute **Finish**

You have now completed the tutorials for the various Bedford modules. If you are also completing the Bedford practice set then continue with Part VI.

BACKING UP YOUR DATA FILES

You should always make a backup of the data files on your computer system to guard against loss of files or hardware failure. Follow the procedures outlined in Chapters 4 and 5 for making backups.

BEDFORD PRACTICE SET
AMERICANA HOME DECORATING AND SERVICE COMPANY

Part VI - Jobcost Module

OBJECTIVE

After completing this exercise for the JOBCOST module you should be able to:

1. Create DEPARTMENTS

2. Track daily transactions for revenue and expenses and itemize them by departments.

3. Print departmental statements.

INSTRUCTION: 1.   Set SYSTEM>Default>Module>Jobcost>: DEPARTMENT

INSTRUCTION: 2.   Insert the following five departments in the JOBCOST module:
Paint Department 1
Wallpaper Department 2
Fabric Department 3
Decorating Department 4
Delivery Department............5

INSTRUCTION: 3.   Enter the following transactions in the GENERAL, PAYABLE, RECEIVABLE, PAYROLL, INVENTORY and JOBCOST modules for December.

Track all departmental revenue and expense transactions that are specifically named to a department.

> Note: The departmental employees are:
> Gary Carter ....Paint Department
> Lou Gehrig ....Wallpaper Department
> Jackie Robinson................Fabric Department
> Babe Ruth ....Decorating Department
> George Washington ....Delivery Department

Dec.   1.   Received on account from Robert Redford, $10,365.29, in full payment of invoice S416. R159.

    1.   Received on account from Wayne Gretzky, $17,468.65, in full payment of invoice S418. R160.

    1.   Paid on account to Seattle Paint & Paper, $830.00, in full payment of invoice P247. Ch439.

1. Sold merchandise and services on account to Marilyn Monroe. S421.

Item	Quantity	Unit	Detail	Price	Amount
3	95	Gallon	Oil Base	$32.00	$ 3,040.00
7	85	Roll	Dimensional Living	10.00	850.00
15	105	Sq/Yd	Velvet	50.00	5,250.00
			Decorating Labor		4,587.56
			Freight		135.00
			SST @ 7%		639.80
					$14,502.36

1. Sold merchandise and services on account to Kay Wai. S422.

Item	Quantity	Unit	Detail	Price	Amount
4	105	Gallon	Satin Latex	$ 18.00	$ 1,890.00
7	125	Roll	Dimensional Living	10.00	1,250.00
12	230	Sq/Yd	Cotton/Polyester	30.00	6,900.00
			Decorating Labor		4,356.89
			Freight		155.00
			SST @ 7%		702.80
					$15,254.69

1. Sold merchandise and services on account to Guy Voyageur. S423.

Item	Quantity	Unit	Detail	Price	Amount
4	90	Gallon	Satin Latex	$ 18.00	$ 1,620.00
10	155	Roll	Waldec	16.00	2,480.00
11	165	Sq/Yd	Cotton	20.00	3,300.00
			Decorating Labor		3,456.78
			Freight		115.00
			SST @ 7%		518.00
					$11,489.78

1. Sold merchandise and services on account to Toby Tyler. S424.

Item	Quantity	Unit	Detail	Price	Amount
5	95	Gallon	Semi-Gloss Latex	$ 24.00	$ 2,280.00
8	45	Roll	Jack & Jill	12.00	540.00
13	125	Sq/Yd	Lace	40.00	5,000.00
			Decorating Service		3,456.76
			Freight		50.00
			SST @ 7%		547.40
					$11,874.16

5. Purchased merchandise on account from Sunnybrooke Paint & Paper. P252.

   Note: Display your stock order to screen and you will see that inventory item #13 is now below the minimum quantity on hand. An observant employee ordered immediately after the Dec. 1 sale and the order has been received today.

Item	Quantity	Unit	Detail	Cost Price	Amount
13	300	Sq/Yd	Lace	$ 20.00	$ 6,000.00
			Freight Expense		150.00
					$6,150.00

5. Purchased merchandise on account from Munforte Paint & Paper. P253.

   Note: Display your stock order to screen and you will see that inventory item #15 is now below the minimum quantity on hand. An observant employee ordered immediately after the Dec. 1 sale and the order has been received today.

Item	Quantity	Unit	Detail	Cost Price	Amount
15	300	Sq/Yd	Velvet	$ 25.00	$ 7,500.00
			Freight Expense		231.00
					$7,731.00

16. Record telephone expense as debt owing to vendor Bell Telephone, $134.78. P254.

16. Paid Bell Telephone for telephone expense, $134.78. Ch440.

16. Record fuel expense as debt owing to vendor Texaco Oil Co., $78.34. P255. Jobcost to department 5.

16. Paid Texaco Oil Co. for fuel expense, $78.34. Ch441.

16. Record the withholding taxes payable as debt owing to vendor Internal Revenue Service: Federal Income Tax, $2,431.22; Federal Insurance; $1,851.16, total $4,282.38. M133.

    Note: You must enter all liabilities as a purchase to a vendor account so you can then run check payments.

16. Paid withholding taxes to Internal Revenue Service, $4,282.38. Ch446.

16. Record State Income Tax payable, $944.03. M134.

    Note: You must record the debt owed to vendor State regulatory body so you can then process check using PAYABLE module.

16. Paid State of Oregon Regulatory Body for State Income Tax, $944.03. Ch447

16. Recorded company pension owed to vendor Merrill Lynch Co., $616.23. M135.

16. Paid Merrill Lynch Co. for company pension, $616.23. Ch448.

16. Record sales tax owed vendor State of Oregon, $2,013.20. M136.

16. Paid State of Oregon for sales tax, $2,013.20. Ch449.

16. Record medical plan owed to vendor Blue Cross, $270.00. M137.

16. Paid Blue Cross for medical plan, $270.00. Ch450.

16. Record bank transfer from General to Payroll account. $3,697.40. M138.

16. Paid middle of month advance to Gary Carter, $660.00. Ch451.

    Note: With Payroll integrated into the System you no longer have to make two entries like you did if the employee was entered as a vendor payable.

16. Paid middle of month advance to Lou Gehrig, $720.00. Ch452.

16. Paid middle of month advance to Jackie Robinson, $750.00. Ch453.

16. Paid middle of month advance to Babe Ruth, $690.00. Ch454.

16. Paid middle of month advance to George Washington, $877.40. Ch455.

31. Record bank transfer from General to Payroll account, $3,440.21. M139.

31. Paid month end payroll to Gary Carter, $573.02, covering: Salary Expense, $2,200.00 plus employer's FICA Expense $165.22; less deductions of Federal Income Tax, $471.35; State Income Tax, $170.41; Employee and Employer FICA Payable, $330.44; Company Pension, $110.00; Medical, $50.00; Advances Receivable, $660.00. Ch456.

Note: *The Bedford Program will generate the employer's payroll taxes internally to save you making a separate entry.*

31. Paid month end payroll to Lou Gehrig, $744.66, covering: Salary Expense, $2,400.00 plus employer's FICA Expense $180.24; less deductions of Federal Income Tax, $407.02; State Income Tax, $178.08; Employee and Employer FICA Payable, $360.48; Company Pension, $120.00; Medical, $50.00; Advances Receivable, $720.00. Ch457.

31. Paid month end payroll to Jackie Robinson, $578.93, covering: Salary Expense, $2,500.00 plus employer's FICA Expense $187.75; less deductions of Federal Income Tax, $597.16; State Income Tax, $201.16; Employee and Employer FICA Payable, $375.50; Company Pension, $125.00; Medical, $60.00; Advances Receivable, $750.00. Ch458.

31. Paid month end payroll to Babe Ruth, $696.42, covering: Salary Expense, $2,300.00 plus employer's FICA Expense $172.73; less deductions of Federal Income Tax, $401.77; State Income Tax, $169.08; Employee and Employer FICA Payable, $345.46; Company Pension, $115.00; Medical, $55.00; Advances Receivable, $690.00. Ch459.

31. Paid month end payroll to George Washington, $847.18, covering: Salary Expense, $2,924.67 plus employer's FICA Expense $219.64; less deductions of Federal Income Tax, $553.92; State Income Tax, $225.30; Employee and Employer FICA Payable, $439.28; Company Pension, $146.23; Medical, $55.00; Advances Receivable, $877.40. Ch460.

31. Recorded Bank Reconciliation adjustments: Short Term Loan Payment, $543.80; Mortgage Payment, $345.78; Interest Expense, $925.89; Bank Charges Expense, $42.34; Interest Income, $145.80; net total bank debit, $1,712.01. M140.

31. Recorded adjusting entry for insurance expense incurred, $400.00.

31. Recorded adjusting entry for office supplies expense incurred, $145.89.

31. Recorded adjusting entry for estimated depreciation expense incurred: Building, $1,750.00; Automotive, $185.00. Record automotive depreciation to Department 5.

31. Recorded ending inventory change from end of last period.

Item	Quantity	Unit	Detail	Cost Price	Amount
4	11-	Gallon	Satin Latex	$ 9.00	$ 99.00-
6	13-	Roll	Colorol	4.00	52.00-
14	35-	Sq/Yd	Sheer	5.00	175.00-
					$ 326.00-

Note: Since you have set the INVENTORY module to ready you must make your adjustments to inventory in that module. The program is integrated to the Inventory and Cost of Goods Sold accounts so just enter the figures and accept the defaults.

INSTRUCTION: 4.   Print a departmental report of revenue minus expense for all departments.
Print list of all stock showing: price; stock; minimum; cost; value; margin.
Print list of stock by department showing: price; stock; minimum; cost; value; margin.
Verify that the total stock by department agrees with the Inventory control accounts in the General Ledger.
Print individual employee's earnings records using Summary layout for current month and year to date.
Print payroll register of all employee's earnings records using Detail layout for current month and year to date.
Print Aging Schedule of Accounts Receivable in Summary and Detail form for all accounts.
Verify that the total of all customer's account balances agrees with the Accounts Receivable control account.
Print Aging Schedule of Accounts Payable in Summary and Detail form for all accounts.
Verify that the total of all vendor's account balances agrees with the Accounts Payable control account.
Print General Journal entries from 12-01-88 to 12-31-88.
Print Income Statement for 12-01-88 to 12-31-88.
Print Income Statement for 01-01-88 to 12-31-88.
Print Balance Sheet for 12-31-88.

This completes PART VI of a six part series that has taken you through all elements of the Bedford Integrated Accounting System. You should now realize that each module integrated into the system reduces the work load as the program takes over more and more becomes more involved with each transaction.

Chapter 12
CLOSING THE BOOKS
AND OTHER MATTERS

Chapter 12
CLOSING THE BOOKS AND OTHER MATTERS

PREVIEW

In Chapter 12 you will look at the accounting cycle and examine the procedures that you must go through at various times of the year. In addition you will learn about keeping backups, the storage limits of the Bedford Accounting System and why it is necessary to purge data, auditing considerations, and the setting of passwords.

OBJECTIVES

After reading this chapter you should be able to explain:

1. What you have to do at various stages of the yearly accounting cycle — at the end of a session, month, quarter, calendar year and fiscal year;

2. Why it is important to know about the storage limits of the Bedford Accounting Program, and why purging data is necessary;

3. Some major auditing considerations;

4. How to set passwords for various modules;

While the preceding chapters described the day to day use of the Bedford Accounting System, there are other features and functions that are used less commonly, but are nevertheless important to know. Some of these functions are required only once a year while others are required periodically throughout the year. This chapter will explain these features and functions. Before using the Bedford Accounting System for an actual company, you should read this chapter.

PERIOD END PROCESSING

The accounting cycle contains a number of significant periods. These are as follows:

1. End of a session
2. End of a month
3. End of a quarter
4. Calendar year end
5. Fiscal year end

It is important to record these periods accurately and follow proper procedures to maintain the integrity of the data. It is particularly important to maintain an audit trail that can be easily followed.

End of a Session

After you end each session, you should print out a listing of the journal entries made during the session. These entries should be checked for proper entry at that time to ensure that no errors were made. You will not likely review these entries again except under unusual circumstances.

To print out the report of journal entries made, activate the **GENERAL** module and choose the **Print** option. Then choose the **Journal** option, which allows you to print out any module, or all items entered during the session. It is best to choose the **Session** option since this will list all of the entries made.

Once you have finished with a session, make a backup copy of your data files. Put the date of the backup on the diskette. You should only keep this particular backup copy until the end of the next session at which time you can reuse it for a new backup.

End of a Month

Before changing the **Using** date to a new month, you should make sure that all entries for the present month are complete. Although it is possible to enter journal entries for a previous month, it is more convenient to finish completely with one month before going on to the next.

The monthly reports should be printed out. You should ensure that you have hard copies for the following each month:

     a. journal entries
     b. general ledger listing for all accounts for the month
     c. income statement
     d. balance sheet
     e. costing reports
     f. listings of all subledgers: inventory, payables, receivables, and payroll.

You should again backup all of the data files. Mark this copy as the archive file for the month that is being backed up. Keep this backup copy until the end of the fiscal year in case the data files are lost or destroyed during the year.

End of a Quarter

When the **Using** date is changed to a new quarter, the Bedford Accounting System resets quarter to date amounts. You should make sure that all entries for the quarter have been made before changing the Using date. You should print out the 941, 940 and SUTA reports for reporting to the IRS. The program will reset the quarter-to-date totals to zero and the reports will no longer be available. Once the **Using** date is updated to a new quarter, you will no longer be permitted to make journal entries having dates associated with the old quarter.

End of the Calendar Year

When a new **Using** date is entered that falls into a new year, the Bedford Accounting System will zero out calendar to date totals. This is especially important to remember if you are using the **PAYROLL** module. The payroll section keeps year-to-date totals for each employee. These amounts are needed for making up the employees W-2, Wage and Tax Statement information. These statements should therefore be run off before you enter a date in the new year.

When you do change that date, the program will warn you that you are about to zero these amounts. If you press the ENTER key, the program will go ahead and zero out the existing calendar year's cumulative payroll information so that you can start accumulating for the new year.

End of a Fiscal Year

Changing the **Using** date to a new fiscal year in the Bedford Accounting System will cause the program to reset all temporary accounts and balances to zero. Before changing to a new fiscal year, it is important to

1. Ensure that all adjusting entries for the year ended have been made.
2. Print out the current month's income statements.
3. Print out the yearly income statement and balance sheet.
4. Make an archive disk of the data. An archive disk is simply a backup of the files for the year which you will keep as an archival record of the transactions for the year. Unlike other backup copies, this one will be permanent. As you do not want to overwrite these files, place a write-protect tab over the square cutout at the side of the disk to ensure that it cannot be written to again.
5. Make a backup disk for the month.
6. Print out a general ledger summary of transactions for the entire year.

In order to proceed with a year end, you need only load the Bedford Accounting System and enter a **Using** date which is in a new fiscal or accounting year. The program will display the message shown in Figure 12.1.

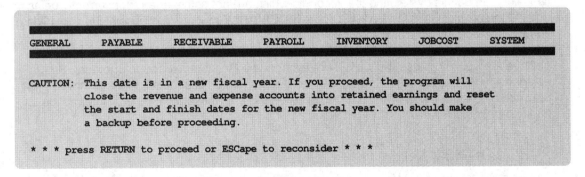

| GENERAL | PAYABLE | RECEIVABLE | PAYROLL | INVENTORY | JOBCOST | SYSTEM |

CAUTION: This date is in a new fiscal year. If you proceed, the program will
close the revenue and expense accounts into retained earnings and reset
the start and finish dates for the new fiscal year. You should make
a backup before proceeding.

* * * press RETURN to proceed or ESCape to reconsider * * *

Figure 12.1 Program message warning user of change to new fiscal year

If you press the RETURN or ENTER key, the closing journal entry will be made and the program will set itself up for a new fiscal year. The balances in the income statement will also be reset to zero for the new year. The **Start** date and **Finish** dates will be advanced by 12 months.

BACKING UP DATA FILES

Since we are talking about year end, this is the time to discuss backups. Backup copies of all transaction data will allow us to either restore the data if we lose it, or allow us to look at the accounting data from a previous period.

Backups should consist of three groups — daily backups, monthly backups and yearly backups.

Daily backups should be made after each session. These backups need not be kept more than one session; at the next session you can reuse the same disk for backing-up your new session. However, you may want to use a second session backup disk and alternate the use of each one.

Monthly backups should be made on a grandfather-father-son system as explained in Chapter 4.. You need three disks, alternating their use for backups at the end of each month. If you have limited memory in your computer and have to purge the data on a monthly basis, you will want to keep each monthly backup to retain the detail data.

Yearly backups, as indicated earlier in the chapter, should be made and archived for each year. These backups will not be used for restoring data but merely to allow the user to retrieve the detail for any fiscal year.

STORAGE LIMITS OF THE BEDFORD ACCOUNTING SYSTEM

The Bedford Accounting System has a limited storage capacity which could affect your data input. This could happen in the following ways:

1. the total financial records (excluding journal entry data) exceeds the capacity of RAM (Random Access Memory) in your computer, or

2. the total financial records (including journal data) exceeds the capacity of the storage disk.

In the first instance, it is possible to have so much data in the system in the form of ledger names that the information will not all fit into the RAM of your computer at one time. When this happens, you must either reduce the amount of information on the system or install more RAM into your computer. It is of course, much easier and less costly to reduce the amount of information. You can do this by deleting the accounts which are not active or are not currently being used. If the problem is in the **PAYABLE** or **RECEIVABLE** module, it is possible to consolidate some of the entries into a single carry forward entry.

In the second instance, it is necessary to decrease the size of the company files. The obvious answer is to purge the journal entries from the files to make room for others. Before doing this, you should backup the files. When you purge the files, detail will be removed and replaced by a single amount. By backing up the files, you will retain the detail information for audit purposes.

PURGING THE DATA

To make more room in RAM or on disk you must remove (purge) journal entries from the existing files. Before you do, make a backup of the disk.

To purge the data, place your cursor on the **SYSTEM** module and press

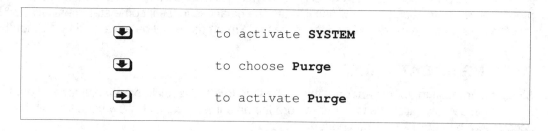

When you depress the right arrow, a message as shown in Figure 12.2 will appear. When you press RETURN or ENTER, the journal entries will be removed from the company files and replaced by a single balance as a carry forward figure. Since we don't want to do this now, press

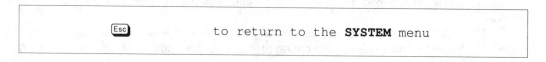

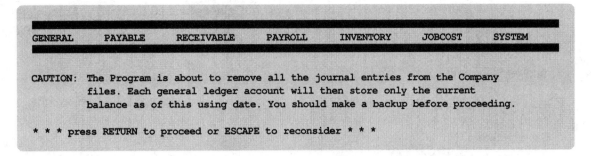

| GENERAL | PAYABLE | RECEIVABLE | PAYROLL | INVENTORY | JOBCOST | SYSTEM |

CAUTION: The Program is about to remove all the journal entries from the Company
files. Each general ledger account will then store only the current
balance as of this using date. You should make a backup before proceeding.

* * * press RETURN to proceed or ESCAPE to reconsider * * *

Figure 12.2 The message displayed by the program before the
journal entries are purged from the system

AUDITING CONSIDERATIONS

Journal entries that are recorded in any of the program's modules are stored in the program's general journal. Each journal entry recorded is automatically assigned a sequential number for referencing. Journal entry numbers are assigned from 00001 to 50,000: the counter resets itself when it reaches 50,000. Journal entries are recorded with the date assigned, usually the Using date.

All journal entries are stored with the comments that were entered as well as how the revenues or expenses were distributed to various projects in the **JOBCOST** module.

Check numbers are either generated and assigned by the program at the time the checks are printed or, if you are not using the computer generated checks, are assigned sequentially between 00001 and 50,000, again the counter resets itself when it reaches 50,000.

The journal entry reference numbers, the associated comments, and the invoice and cheque numbers, mean that your auditor has a complete audit trail. However, the reports must be printed and saved.

Figure 12.3 shows the reports generally required by your auditor.

Report	Month-end	Calendar Qtr End	Calendar Year-end	Accounting Year-end
Income Statement				
month-to-date	*			*
year-to-date	*			*
Balance Sheet	*			*
General Journal				
past month	*			*
Accounts Payable				
Purchase Journal-past month	*			*
Payment Journal-past month	*			*
Accounts Receivable				
Sale Journal past-month	*			*
Payment Journal past-month	*			*
Payroll Journal				
past month	*			*
Inventory				
Transfer Journal past-month	*			*
Adjustment Journal past-month	*			*
Ledger Reports (all accounts)				
past month	*			*
Chart of Accounts	*			*
Payroll Reports				
Employee Summary		*	*	
W-2			*	
941		*	*	
940		*	*	
SUTA		*	*	

Figure 12.3 Reports generally required by auditor

These reports should be printed as the data is entered and not generated from backups. If you lose the reports, it may be possible to recreate them using a monthly or yearly backup, but this should only be done in an emergency situation since the backups might have been altered, thereby making an audit trail useless. These reports should be kept in a safe place along with the backups.

SETTING UP PASSWORDS

In order to all the system to be used by various employees and yet protect some or all of the financial data from unauthorized access, the Bedford Accounting System allows us to put a password on each of the modules. The *password* is a code. Only those individuals who know the code to a particular module can access it. This allows you to have other people using the computer system without letting them have access to sensitive financial data. You can even set passwords for the various modules so that specific people only have access to specific modules. For example, you may have an employee who is responsible for accounts receivable, and who records the sales and cash receipts. You may not want this person to have access to financial data or to payroll information which may be the responsibility of another person.

To set the password, you must first activate the **SYSTEM** module from the Bedford main menubar. Then activate in turn **Default**, **Module** and **System**. The final data entry screen will be familiar since you accessed it in Chapter 5 (See Figure 12.4).

```
GENERAL     PAYABLE     RECEIVABLE     PAYROLL     INVENTORY     JOBCOST     SYSTEM


  Company     Fast Delivery Inc.
  Street      1251 Bel Del Road
  City        Bellevue
  State       Wa.
  Zip         98625
  Password    G000V000C000E000I000J000S000
  Label       6 lines
   Port       Lpt1
  Report      66 lines
   Port       Lpt1
  Date        mmddyy
```

Figure 12.4 Setting the Password through the SYSTEM module

The **Password** field is used for setting the password for each individual module. The initial display in the field is:

G000V000C000E000I000J000S000

If you look closer you will see seven capital letters, with each letter followed by three zeros. These letters represent the various Bedford modules — **G**eneral, **V**endor, **C**ustomer, **E**mployee, **I**nventory, **J**obcost, and **S**ystem. Each module can be accessed by a three letter password. If the password for the module is set to 000, anybody can enter the module without requiring a password. If you enter any three letter or number combination following the module letter, thereafter only a person with that password can enter the module. The **SYSTEM** module is always accessible; however, once a module's password has been changed, the password field will no longer be visible.

Any change to a password requires that you enter the **SYSTEM** module's password first, followed by a space and the new password you wish to enter for any module. For example, if you want to change the **SYSTEM** password to 222, you would press

```
    ⬇                  to move cursor to Password

    ➡                  to activate Password

S000 S222 [Ret]        to change the SYSTEM password
                       from 000 to 222.
```

You will now see that the password has changed to

G000V000C000E000I000J000S222

If you subsequently decided to restrict access to the payroll module by setting a new password "123", you do it as follows. Press

```
    ➡                activate Password

S222 E123            to change the payroll password to 123
```

The password shown on your screen now looks as follows:

G000V000C000E123I000J000S222

To define passwords for any of the other modules, merely activate **Password** and enter the **SYSTEM** module password followed by a space and the new password. It does not matter in which order you specify the modules in the definition of new passwords. You could even specify more than one at a time such as:

S222 G123V456

Once the password has been changed, the modules will continue to be available without having to enter a password until you **Finish** the current session. Once you exit to DOS, however, you cannot reenter the system without entering the proper password on the command line <u>at the same time as you load the program</u>. If you don't do this you will not be able to access a particular module. A message disallowing access will appear.

For example, let's assume that you have changed the passwords of the various modules for your company to the following:

G123V456C000E123I789J000S222

You would load the program as follows, entering the password at the same time, assuming the program is loaded on a hard drive named C:.

<u>Entry</u>	<u>Modules that would become accessible</u>
C:>bedford	RECEIVABLE, JOBCOST (all with passwords of 000)
c:>bedford G123	GENERAL, RECEIVABLE, JOBCOST
c:>bedford G123V456	GENERAL, PAYABLE, RECEIVABLE, JOBCOST
c:>bedford G123V456E123I789	All modules

Note: If you need the word MONO to operate your system on a monochrome screen, you can enter the word MONO either before or after the password.

The **SYSTEM** module password does not need to be entered since it is always accessible. However, if you change the password of a module, you must ensure that you do not forget the **SYSTEM** module password, because without it you cannot redefine any of the module passwords. If this password is not entered correctly, then the system will prompt you with an error message and ask you to enter it properly. You will be unable to proceed until the correct **SYSTEM** password has been entered.

13. USING BEDFORD WITH OTHER SOFTWARE PACKAGES

Chapter 13
USING BEDFORD WITH OTHER SOFTWARE PACKAGES

PREVIEW

In this chapter we will discuss three software packages that you can use to access accounting data produced by the Bedford Accounting System to produce graphs and reports of various types. In the last part of this chapter you will get a list of the various error messages that you may encounter while using the program. There is also a short note about program updates, which is particularly important if you are using the **PAYROLL** module, since employee deductions and other figures change regularly each year.

OBJECTIVES

After reading this chapter you should be able to explain:

1. The function of the Bedford Integrated Tool Box to produce graphs and reports of available accounting data;

2. The need for software updates particularly when using the Bedford PAYROLL module.

The Bedford Accounting System is an easy to use yet powerful accounting package. Just as other software packages have had their usefulness extended through add-on products, the information produced by the Bedford system can be made more meaningful by using programs specifically designed to generate charts and various reports.

ENHANCING THE INFORMATION PRODUCED BY BEDFORD

A general ledger is actually a data base containing business transactions. We can therefore extract certain parts of this data base and manipulate it with other programs to produce outputs in a particular form — reports and graphs, that can provide a better overview of how the business is doing.

Spreadsheets

We have already discussed how most of the reports produced with the Bedford Accounting System can be exported to a spreadsheet, specifically to a Lotus 1-2-3 spreadsheet or Symphony, or to a spreadsheet that can use a compatible data file such as Supercalc. Exporting data into a spreadsheet can make it easy to quickly calculate a predefined set of operating ratios — working capital, current ratio, quick ratio, return on assets, and so on. We can also produce a variety of graphs for easier analysis of particular aspects of the business data. Finally we can include accounting information in reports produced by word processors.

Bedford's Integrated Toolbox

As an add-on product to the Bedford Accounting System, the Bedford company has developed a series of programs to make it easier to graph and prepare reports from the data produced by the Bedford Accounting System.

▪ *Graph*

Graph is designed for using the historical data collected by the accounting system in the preparation and display of various types of graphs including

> line
> bar
> area overlap
> scatter
> pie

The graph display allows you to compare two years' data for the same company or to display one year's data for two companies at a time. If you want to display graphs for more than one company, the data files must be in different paths or subdirectories.

In addition to graphing the data, Graph can print and export the financial data into a tabular format. The results can be displayed in year-to-date form or in the monthly change in accumulated balances. With this function of Graph it is easy to prepare a statement of changes in financial position or other subsidiary reports.

For each graph style, with the exception of pie graphs, you can select up to three accounts or account groupings into Data Sets that can be used for comparison. You can use these groupings to compare one account to another, or to produce operating ratios. If you choose the pie chart option you can graph up to eight account groupings.

Using Graph is very simple for the Bedford user since the key strokes are similar to those used in Bedford. The use of special keys, pull down menus and input fields are identical in their operation to those of the Bedford Accounting System. This helps you to use the package quickly.

Although Graph will work on most monitors, it has been specifically designed for high resolution monitors in either monochrome or EGA color when using a color monitor and color graphics card.

The Graph program allows for exporting graph information to Symphony or Lotus 1-2-3 or to a spreadsheet that uses the Lotus 1-2-3 file format such as Supercalc.

▪ *Report*

Report is designed to provide greater flexibility in the presentation of financial statements, using the information provided by the accounting system. Financial reports such as comparative income statements or classified balance sheets in report form, (two page) can easily be produced. Report provides the user with a variety of formats, allowing the summarization of financial information by grouping accounts. These can then be displayed, printed or exported in the same manner as the reports that are now produced by Bedford.

The Report module can also output financial information arranged as a number of comparative periods. For example, you can produce reports for two periods within a single fiscal year for one company, two periods with two fiscal years for the same company, or one fiscal year for two companies.

Report will also allow you to use the **JOBCOST** function to report a jobcost over the entire life of the project, even if it spans more than one fiscal year. Without Report, the jobcost totals are reset to zero when the you change the **Using** date to a new fiscal year. The only way to report the total cost for the project is to manually add the total costs incurred in the various years together. With Report this task is done automatically, avoiding a cumbersome manual task.

Report produces the following report types for balance sheets and income statements:

1. Plain
2. Percentage of section
3. Comparative plain
4. Comparative percentage of section
5. Comparative percentage difference
6. Comparative dollar change
7. Comparative dollar addition

Report allows you to format as many types of reports as required. The various reports are stored in files with the extension (.EXT) of .MAP and can be reproduced as required.

Wordsheet

Wordsheet is an add-on software package not produced by Bedford. It is also designed for the generation of reports using the Bedford accounting files. When using Wordsheet you can create reports on the screen and see what they will actually look like. What appears on the screen is what you will get from the printer.

Wordsheet allows you to manipulate the data while reporting it. During the creation of the report you create spreadsheet like cells anywhere within the document. These cells can be used to manipulate the data by applying a formula to the data to report percentages, comparisons and differences. These cells may then be moved around and placed anywhere in the report without having to recreate the formula in the new position.

The major feature of Wordsheet is that it accesses the current data in your Bedford Accounting System in the form of a chart of accounts with the current year to date and the previous period closing balances. This information is loaded into memory when Wordsheet is executed. In addition to these balances, the user may specify two optional period ranges from which accounting information may be extracted and used for reporting purposes. The result is an on-line database that may be used for cell referencing anytime. Thus, when a template is created, the account number, rather than the actual balance, is stored in the report. When the report is called up, the current contents of that field are placed into the report. This method ensures that the information in the report is always current.

Another advantage of this method of generating reports is that the report template produced can be used for any business using a similar chart of account numbering system. Since the Bedford Accounting System encourages companies to conform to a default numbering system in its chart of accounts when first set up, reports generated with Wordsheet will in all likelihood only have to be created once.

BEDFORD ACCOUNTING SYSTEM SOFTWARE UPDATES

Because the Bedford Accounting System has a **PAYROLL** module it is necessary to have program updates each year, especially whenever the tax rates or withholding rates (UIC and CPP) change. These changes are usually available early in the new year. If you do not receive your notification of update, you should contact the Bedford company office listed in your manual. You should not run a payroll unless you have the updated program. Although it is possible to make subsequent changes to the data files, such manipulation can easily introduce errors into the data files.

The Bedford software company also provides continuing updates to its accounting program to make it easier to use and more powerful. As a registered user you will be automatically notified by the company of updates to the program.